W9-DGL-845

BREAKING THE LINKS

Development Theory and Practice in Southern Africa

BREAKING THE LINKS

Development Theory and Practice in Southern Africa

A Festschrift for Ann W. Seidman

Edited by
ROBERT E. MAZUR

Africa World Press, Inc.

P.O. Box 1892
Trenton, New Jersey 08607

Africa World Press, Inc.
P.O. Box 1892
Trenton, New Jersey 08607

Copyright © 1990 Africa World Press, Inc.
First Printing 1990

Chapter 4 reprinted with permission from William G Martin
and Immanuel Wallerstein, copyright © 1990

Cover Design by Ife Nii Owoo

Book design and electronic typesetting from author's disk
by Malcolm Litchfield
This book is composed in ITC New Baskerville

Library of Congress Catalog Card Number: 90-81572

ISBN: 0-86543-178-7   Cloth
           0-86543-179-5   Paper

to Ramahlasoana, Moipolai, and the generations of dispossession, to Semakaleng and the generations of resistance, and to Tsôlo, Neo and the generations of a free South Africa

CONTENTS

**PART THREE: *Popular Participation in the Struggle
for Peace and Development***

FOREWORD

Carol B. Thompson

his collection of essays from scholars in several disciplines
and across three continents is an appropriate tribute to Ann
Seidman. Accomplished as an economist, she is more than
an economist, for she demands that economic theory and statistics
serve the social and political goals of the people concerned. Her
outstanding and continuing contribution to economic theory is
made possible by her comprehension of sociological and legal
theories, as well as by her appreciation of the importance of
historical conjunctures. Seidman's work also spans the continents,
from analyses of expanding career options for American women
to proposals for economic development in Africa to investigation
of economic options in the People's Republic of China. Always a
comparativist, she asks seemingly impossible questions to those
with lees vision about the lessons of southern Africa for China or
the relation between the changing international division of labor
in the southeastern United States and South Africa.

As a foremost American critic of neoclassical economic
theory, Ann Seidman does much more than show that the numbers have limited significance. She critiques the fundamental
assumptions of mainstream theory, the choice of concepts and
their definition. She seeks to develop a democratic theory of
economics, one which aims not for a mere increase of profitability,

but for a higher living standard and expanded opportunities for productive employment for the majority of the population. Accepting the responsibility of a scholar to consider the policy implications of theory, she has suggested various alternatives for specific African economies, from how to block the overseas drain of investible resources to the need for restructuring banking systems.

Even the choice of research topics reveals the political commitment of Ann Seidman. Although her more than fifteen books focus on national and regional economic issues in Africa, she also consciously chose to investigate the American role in perpetrating the poverty of African peoples. As an American, she acknowledged her responsibility to investigate how transnational corporations from the center set up the "outposts of monopoly capitalism" to exploit southern Africa. She probed to the "roots of crisis" and found not only drought and war in southern Africa, but economic dominance by foreign corporations. And she brings the analysis home to investigate the related exploitation of American workers.

Seidman provides a valid alternative to the policies of the World Bank and the International Monetary Fund (IMF). Not often quoted in the sacred halls of international misdevelopment, when agencies do seek her advice, she has been known to turn them down. For example, from 1977 to 1979, the U.S. Agency for International Development (USAID) spent over $1 million on a massive nine-country study with eleven sector reports for southern Africa. Except for the Namibian Institute, none of the liberation forces in southern Africa was consulted about the studies which centered on development plans for the region. The U.S. government simply proposed plans for such crucial sectors as transportation, repatriation of refugees, and health care without consulting the people they were studying. When Seidman and a few other American scholars were asked to participate, they declined, suggesting that southern Africans be consulted instead. USAID refused.

Exactly because of her incisive analysis, she is sought out by African leadership and has worked as a consultant for African governments and taught for several years each in the universities of Ghana, Tanzania, Zambia, and Zimbabwe. Her work reflects insights that are gained only through such sustained interaction with African colleagues.

The perspicacity and commitment of Ann Seidman has more than once put her "in trouble." Even though two all-university committees ruled in her favor, Brown University denied her a professorial chair because she is not only female and feminist, but a critic of mainstream theories. Some African governments have taken umbrage at her criticism of economic policies which were entrenching the privileged and which failed to fulfill the promises of independence. Such are the times, however, when every scholar should be "in trouble." In almost any field, as scholars we uncover exploitation, corruption and cruelty, and we should use our competence to expose them to the best of our ability. The clarity and integrity of Seidman's inquiries have won her much esteem and respect from her colleagues.

Analyzing, but not working for, the "commanding heights" of economies, Seidman has chosen instead to work with nongovernmental organizations and grassroots development projects. Most ardent and challenged when she engages in lively debates, she thrives on interaction with other scholars or with local development leaders. Suspicious of all theories that are handed down from on high, be it from the left or right, she was the catalyst for a very innovative process of evaluating aid programs in Zambia, Tanzania, and Zimbabwe. Almost everyone criticizes the common practice of employing highly paid evaluators who breeze through in two weeks and leave. Seidman, however, had a different approach. She worked to find alternative processes, best expressed by two Zimbabwean participants: "You only get really self-reliant development when the people themselves raise questions and examine the causes of the difficulties they face and look for new answers."

The lesson from Ann Seidman for the rest of us is a challenge: as students of Africa and of the world's majority population in developing countries, we cannot be content to merely understand. We cannot be content to outline the policy relevance of our theories. We must share the visions and engage in critical dialogue about them. Economic, political, and social analyses are useless unless they come from the people's experience and answer their needs.

Seidman's praxis follows her theory at another level. She is an example to all professors in fulfilling the responsibility of engaging students in relevant research. Not tolerating cursory overviews, she demands that her students conduct detailed and in-depth research: they cannot simply criticize the dominance of the South African banking system over much of southern Africa. They must go out and collect data on the size of Barclays or Standard Chartered; they must interview banking officials and government partners. In the United States, this deep concern for teaching relevant research skills is exemplified in the Southern African Summer Program which she initiated and continues to direct. The program brings together southern Africa students who want to learn how to make their research germane to their own countries.

For example, Seidman has rescued more than one African graduate student studying in Southern California from the fate of making yet another analysis of Los Angeles' urban sprawl; instead, they learned how to investigate the problems of the townships in South Africa or Zimbabwe or Zambia.

As president of the African Studies Association, 1989-90, Seidman has led the community of African and American scholars in collective work on the crises of African economies. Initiating the project on a "Sustainable Strategy for African Economic Development," she once again motivated the collective talents of scholars to address seemingly intractable problems.

Accomplished scholar and teacher, Seidman has not relinquished a personal agenda. Establishing her career at a time when few women could intrude in the economics profession, she chose to take time to raise five children—fostering in them her own socially responsible values. Among female scholars, she has touched us most by helping us to find our way. She seeks out African female scholars and encourages them to find their own voices, even in such powerful male enclaves as African and American universities. In the United States, she also takes time to assist those junior to her, patiently answering theoretical questions or giving tips about survival in academe. What is most disarming to female scholars is that Seidman treats us as equals. She badgers, criticizes, and cares immensely that we think through our theories and find our own answers.

The diversity of theories and extensive analyses of the essays in this collection herald the work of Ann Seidman. Provocative, they continue the debates about development, transition to socialism, regional cooperation, constitutional transformation, and workers' control. We can all join the tribute to Ann Seidman's work by engaging in the debates and advancing the analyses.

Carol B. Thompson
University of Southern California
Editor, *African Studies Review*

ACKNOWLEDGEMENTS

MY DEBT in the completion of this book originates with Ann Seidman, whose untiring scholarship and commitment inspired this project, though she was totally unaware of it until it was in print. One of Ann's gifts is always to nurture relationships that are only possible among genuine colleagues, regardless of one's specialization or the stage of one's career. The authors who so eagerly contributed their work for the chapters in this book dedicated to Ann are the clearest testimony to that gift. Their excellent, committed scholarship made the task of compiling and editing the manuscripts easier than is usual in an edited volume. Particular thanks are expressed to Neva Seidman Makgetla, who translated Samir Amin's manuscript unhesitantly, skillfully and artfully. The enthusiastic manner with which Brad Shepherd assisted in the seemingly endless details of coordinating and editing this book was matched only by his dedication to completing the task with the highest standards and sooner than anyone, even I, could expect.

Robert E. Mazur

Introduction

CHALLENGES OF DEVELOPMENT THEORY AND TRANSFORMATION IN SOUTHERN AFRICA

Robert E. Mazur

ENTERING the 1990s, southern Africa represents both the vertex and the vortex of contemporary development dilemmas. At one level, southern Africa is inextricably linked to the world economy, constituting a "region" with elements of core, semi-periphery and periphery. Southern Africa is not a mere reflection or artifact of the world economy, but is an essential element in its emerging structure. Commensurately, the superpowers have been and remain deeply involved, regardless of their currently-feigned distance and disinterest. Their involvement ranges from social and cultural, economic and political, to military. Given the region's vast development potential, as well as its history, the interest of outside actors will continue to grow in the coming years and decades.

Lest obsession with global machinations prevail, fundamental to our understanding is recognition of the ongoing struggles at all levels. The struggles themselves concern, most succinctly, change and continuity. At each level, organized forces seeking change are in conflict with institutionalized forces clamoring to maintain continuity, to preserve privilege and process. In this regard, as well as with respect to integration in the world economy, the peasant farmer is integrated equally with the official in the "commanding heights," the shopfloor worker and the unemployed, the black no less so than the white, with capitalist society as interdependent as the "socialist."

How the 1980s measure up in terms of change and continuity rests, no doubt, with one's perspective. There is considerable merit in each viewpoint.

On the side of progressive change, most noteworthy are the creation of the Southern African Development Coordination Conference (SADCC) and Zimbabwe's independence in 1980, the formation of the United Democratic Front (UDF) in South Africa in 1983 and the Congress of South African Trade Unions (COSATU) in 1985, the South African township uprisings from 1984-86, the "defeat" of South African Defense Forces (SADF) in southeastern Angola in 1988, and the transition to formal independence in Namibia in 1989. None of these changes could have been definitively predicted; each represents a substantial improvement over the status quo and contains the potential for far-reaching changes in the intermediate future.

On the side of continuity, or even deterioration, must be noted the following: repeated South African police, commando and military raids into nearly all SADCC member states; the South African sponsored death, misery, destruction and refugee flight in Mozambique produced by the Mozambican National Resistance (MNR) and in Angola produced by the National Union for the Total Independence of Angola (UNITA); the resumption of more direct sponsorship of UNITA by the United States operating through southern Zaire; the economic recession and deterioration in nearly all countries in the region; the increased presence, mixed economic outcome and negative social impact of the International Monetary Fund's (IMF) "structural adjustment program" in Zambia, Zimbabwe, Tanzania, Mozambique and soon in Angola; South Africa's continued virtual total domination of Lesotho and Swaziland and its vociferous attempts to increase its relative control over all other countries in the region; the compromised nature of Namibia's "independence" that excludes the South West Africa Peoples Organization (SWAPO) from the "independence" negotiations and that permits continued South African control of Walvis Bay; as well as the internal failings of the SADCC countries in their development efforts that have been exacerbated by their uneasy coexistence with apartheid South Africa.

Such an overview serves to outline the overall dimensions of change and continuity throughout the 1980s. While current structures certainly will shape the course of events through the 1990s and beyond, they neither determine precisely those events nor do they preclude new initiatives and directions. It is in this realm that research is most instructive.

Indeed, the role of proper investigation is more paramount than ever if we are to understand the unfolding processes of change in southern Africa and elsewhere. Mere understanding is not, however, sufficient. The role of the committed scholar, exemplified in the life-long efforts and achievements of Ann Seidman to whom authors from various parts of the world have dedicated their present works, is to engage in active, critical dialogue with those shaping these processes of change. Thereby, the "reserved" nature of academic research is abandoned in favor of greater commitment to listen and observe, to focus on issues of greatest policy relevance, to reflect critically, and to provide stimulating ideas and alternatives for movements and leaders.

The people and states in southern Africa have before them a task significantly larger than that of mere "development." Because of the inheritance from the colonial era and present neocolonial relations, development necessarily entails transformation of both the structures and the relationships. Thus, issues of socialist transformation have been at the forefront of development policy and associated debates in Tanzania, Mozambique, Angola, Zimbabwe, Namibia and South Africa for several decades; while the specific issues have evolved over time, the basic nature of the debate remains.

Throughout the volume, the authors confront central issues in transformation and development. In Part One: Theories of Transformation, development in Africa is first assessed from the perspective of peace and of national and regional security, including a review of the southern African situation after a more broadly applicable analysis. This leads to discussions on the nature of socialism in theory and of key development theories from the point of view of problem solving and policymaking, with explicit consideration of a socialist approach.

Specific issues and policies of transformation are examined in Part Two: National Economies and Regional Development. Issues and prospects for peace and development are evaluated first from the world-system perspective. Then, a series of fundamental issues are considered: resource leakages associated with Lesotho's dependence on migrant labor to South Africa, realigning external trade structure in Botswana, experiences with state-owned enterprises in Tanzania and development banks in Zimbabwe.

In-depth analysis of Popular Participation in the Struggle for Peace and Development, Part Three, begins with the Horn of Africa and makes explicit comparisons to southern Africa. Then, trade unions and popular mobilization in South Africa are reviewed and assessed. Concluding insights concern institutions, laws and constitutional guidelines in Zimbabwe with implications for Namibia and South Africa.

Together, the essays in this book confront the central contemporary issues of conflict, peace and development. They do so in a manner that provides an integrated focus on the southern African region. Yet the implications of the challenges actively confronted and lessons learned are applicable, at least in part, to African societies more broadly and to classes, movements, leaders and peripheral and semiperipheral societies elsewhere. There are no pat "answers" that constitute easy solutions for apparently intractable problems. Yet the lessons learned provide some degree of cautious optimism that development, with peace, is not only possible but inevitable when and where the struggle continues.

In his essay on "Peace, National and Regional Security and Development: Some Reflections on the African Experience," Samir Amin examines the contradictions between national development of the periphery and international capitalism. He articulates an anti-reductionist view of the complex nature of the conflict between the logic of power and politics on the one hand, and the requirements of capitalist management on the other, in which only concrete analysis of each case is possible. In revealing traditional theories as incapable of formulating a strategy of change that could resolve contemporary crises in political economy, he elaborates the goal of socialism as not merely "socialist construction," but resolving the inequalities produced by the capitalist system based on the polarization of centers and peripheries. Using the examples of the Palestinian and South African situations, Amin examines the goals and hostility of imperialist and neocolonial forces toward national-popular movements, and cautions against the "enlightened paternalism" of the West (e.g., EEC under Lomé). In his view, post-capitalist societies will be "organized around a conflicting and dynamic compromise between three social tendencies: socialist, capitalist, and nationalist-etatist." He cautions against misplaced expectations of "anti-imperialist solidarity" when everywhere in the third world "it remains the work of the popular forces of the country in question to advance their own national liberation movement to the point where they can achieve a national-popular revolution." Finally, he outlines the parameters for national-popular disengagement to proceed.

The discussion of socialism becomes more explicit with Tamás Szentes' essay on "Socialism in Theory and Practice." He identifies the tasks of socialism: abolition of the private ownership and control of the means of production, social emancipation, repersonalization of human relations, establishment of universal rules in the distribution of income and social roles, and the unfolding of real democracy that extends over the economic sphere. He cautions against false signs of socialism, i.e., state ownership without appropriate changes in the content, direction and control of the state on the one hand, or employed workers becoming shareholders in "employee stock ownership programs" (ESOPs) or trade union representatives in the management of private firms on the other. Instead, socialism requires seizure of state power by the "working" class and breaking the rule of the bourgeoisie. He raises numerous questions that are key to socialist transformation. In identifying the inequalities of the capitalist system at both the national and international levels, he directs attention to appropriate units of analysis. Contradictions between national and international development in global capitalism represent additional problems that socialism must confront, particularly in a world economy still dominated by capitalism. He discusses with sensitivity the difficulties of inclusion versus isolation, particularly in the context of heavy international trade dependence under unfavorable world market conditions. He cautions against expectations of oversimplified, linear progress and of any "model" that can be applied to post-colonial societies. He argues extensively for the "possibility of reconciling socialist development with the existence of a capitalist world economy and the limits of this opportunity." He stresses that the struggle for socialism must involve those whose social emancipation is at stake. All of these central issues, and others, are taken up and further developed by the other authors in this volume.

Neva Seidman Makgetla embarks on "Using Development Theory to Solve Problems: An Application to South Africa." She examines development theories for their problem focus, methods of analysis, and relevance in providing solutions for real situations. The three development theories examined are the "supply side" theory, the "basic needs" approach, and the "socialist" strategy. In each case, the applicability to problem solving in the South African context is used as the criteria for assessing the relative merits of the theory. Strong contrasts between the solutions to South Africa's crises are implied among the theories: the supply-side theory mandates increased efficiency; the basic needs approach requires redistribution of income and productive assets by an increasingly democratic state; and the socialist strategy addresses the fundamental issue of powerlessness, manifest not only by poverty but by the position in the productive and political processes—it requires transformation of the political and economic decisionmaking structure.

In their assessment of "Southern Africa in the World-Economy, 1870-2000: Strategic Problems in World-Historical Perspective," William Martin and Immanuel Wallerstein highlight additional dilemmas faced by southern Africans from the beginning to the close of the tumultuous twentieth century. They identify three distinguishing features: the level of political and military conflict is exceptionally high for a region outside the direct orbit of East-West struggles; national struggles necessarily have a transnational character; and Western powers have acted from the premise that local conflicts place at risk their broader regional interests. They operationalize "development" as the struggle against the polarizing tendencies of the capitalist world economy, and "security" as the struggle between systemic and antisystemic forces within the world-system. Despite earlier characteristics of a classic peripheral area, class and national struggles have resulted in the southern African region developing its own core, semiperiphery and periphery, while still being inextricably involved in core-controlled capital accumulation. South Africa's development, in particular, has been predicated upon its ability to manage relationships between the core and periphery. In concluding that all players in the region have a stake in remaining a vital "region" of the world economy, they identify the priority of the progressive movements in the region as being sufficiently cohesive, now and in the post-apartheid era, to struggle for economic transformation instead of succumbing to the constraints imposed by the inherited structures.

The political economy framework is also employed by Sibusiso Nkomo in his examination of "Confrontation and the Challenge for Independent Development: The Case of Lesotho." The mechanism of dependence and pressure is South Africa's incorporation of Lesotho as a migrant labor reserve principally for its mines. Nkomo assesses the implications of South Africa's economic hegemony and Lesotho's dependence on the migrant labor system. His findings document the "leakage" of development resources from Lesotho that include the following: human-power utilization and development, surplus labor value, expenditures, venture capital, and distortions in sociodemographic and family structures. Genuine national development in Lesotho would involve internal integration which covers sectoral integration (i.e., between agriculture and industry), balanced rural/urban spatial development, and congruence between the needs of the people and what is being produced. In conclusion, he poses questions about Lesotho's prospects for development in SADCC and whether it can disengage itself and impose protective barriers from South African economic dominance.

Renosi Mokate considers "Realigning Botswana's Trade Structure: Constraints and Possibilities for SADCC." Botswana is a prime example of a country in which South African hegemony, manifest in the South African Customs Union (SACU), confronts an institution for which lessened dependence on South Africa and integrated national development are the principal goals (SADCC). With present trade (import and export) patterns heavily skewed in favor of South Africa, Botswana will have to bear heavy costs to withdraw from SACU and establish its own import-substitution (IS) industries. Moreover, South African retaliation and destabilization must be considered likely consequences. While the "optimal" solution presents itself as remaining in SACU while establishing IS industries within the rubric of SADCC, the contradiction of SACU perpetuating and even exacerbating the distortions in Botswana's economy warrants little optimism . In conclusion, Mokate outlines the complex process by which the regional goals set by SADCC can be achieved only with the concurrent internal structural transformation of the economies of the constituent member states.

Joseph Semboja and Lucian Msambichaka examine the implications of these ideas and implied policies by investigating "The Political Economy of State-Owned Enterprises in the Third World: The Case of Tanzania." The establishment of state-owned enterprises (SOEs) has been a logical response to several critical conditions: colonial governments had greatly shaped economic affairs; widespread desires to indigenize ownership of important economic activities; the state needed to establish the infrastructure and linkages for the indigenous private sector and to attract foreign investors; the state desired to control savings and investments; and many countries explicitly proclaimed an ideology of socialism and self-reliance. For various reasons, the international donor community supported state-owned enterprises. Yet the recently deteriorating economic situation has forced critical scrutiny of state-owned enterprises. Operating from a political economy perspective, Semboja and Msambichaka systematically assess the relative privileged position of SOEs, their contributions, performance and efficiency, and advance explanations concerning the evidence. Their analysis qualifies the successes and failures of SOEs and requires that any policies affecting the future of SOEs take into account the diversity of influences and experiences. They advance a model of symbiotic relations among the government, SOEs and the private sector, in which each mutually benefits from these relations but is, in turn, constrained by them. This condition of symbiosis is integrated into the discussion of the performance of SOEs and the debate over whether divestiture or reform and rehabilitation are in order. They conclude with an action agenda.

Complementing assessment of state-owned enterprises, Theresa Moyo examines the role of "Development Banks in the Era of 'Socialist Transition': Achievements, Problems and Prospects in Zimbabwe." Development banks have been viewed as a logical response to conditions of extensive foreign ownership of the economy, external trade dependency, and a shortage of skilled labor. More specifically, development banks in Zimbabwe have been expected to mobilize and make available financial resources to both local private investors, especially rural small-scale producers, and the state, for priority development projects and strategic sectors of the economy. Ultimate goals are employment creation, the development of small businesses, diversification of industry, and savings of foreign exchange earnings. These investments include establishing joint ventures with foreign partners. Moyo reviews the goals, experiences and constraints facing the four main development banks in Zimbabwe. A key to greater effectiveness and equity is decentralization of activities. She cautions against confusing criteria of short-term profit making with those of long-term economic development. While noting the roles of development banks in the transition to socialism, she discusses the problem of expecting development banks to advance socialism in the absence of a clear-cut industrial development strategy that would structure that process of change.

Basil Davidson considers the participatory nature of the struggle for self-determination in the Horn of Africa in "The Keys to Peace in African Regional Conflicts: Lessons from Eritrea and Ethiopia." The Eritrean People's Liberation Front (EPLF) has operated without slogans or external models of development. Based on the alliance of peasants and urban workers, it views people as resources. Rather than forming itself into a "party," it has consciously chosen to remain a front of common effort "within which the further processes of Eritrean self-identification and self-government may evolve." While recognizing the contradiction between mass participation and disciplined leadership required for a successful struggle, and that the full unfolding of democratic institutions must await the coming of peace, he documents the commitment to mass participation and local control over genuinely decentralized government structures. Specifically, he identifies the flexible structure of consultation, "reference back" to movement congresses, and mass organizations representing, for example, the interests of women and of peasants. One clear manifestation of this is the direct attack on the inequalities of status and employment of Eritrean women. Full realization of this potential, however, is predicated upon peace.

Working-class and popular movements' power in South Africa are directly addressed in Gay Seidman's chapter on "From Trade Union to Working Class Mobilization: The Politicization of South Africa's Nonracial Labor Unions." This detailed account of the evolving relationship between nonracial labor unions and the popular political movement in South Africa includes both historical and contemporary perspectives. The author produces a sensitive account of the changing context (particularly the international economy and state repression) and the implications this has had for the strategic options available. Her analysis reveals the dynamics behind the increasing class character of the popular political movement. Particularly in the 1980s, the trade unions and the popular political movement have needed each other to advance their respective causes, and have increasingly identified with the goals of the other and their respective constituencies. At key points in the essay, the author draws parallels between the underlying conditions in South Africa and the Newly Industrializing Countries (NICs). These parallels include, first, imported capital-intensive technology and semiskilled, low-paid workers; she suggests that it may be possible for workers in NICs to "normalize" labor relations in ways similar to those South African workers used in the 1970s. Second, rapid urbanization has created huge working-class and poor communities, few of whom have received the benefits promised by trickle-down theories; there is increasing evidence that urban social movements arising around housing, transport and educational issues have a distinct class character as they struggle against authoritarian states, and may develop a more explicitly political agenda. Finally, international recessions affecting NICs may make them equally incapable of carrying out reforms that require redistribution of social services to working-class communities.

Post-independence Zimbabwe is also the focus of Robert Seidman's investigation on "What Constitutional Lessons Does Zimbabwe's Experience Teach?" Like Namibia now and South Africa in the future, Zimbabwe has had to address six major issues that Seidman identifies: eradicating apartheid; transforming the economy to alleviate poverty; preventing reaction from exacerbating ethnic differences; ensuring popular participation in governmental decisionmaking; guaranteeing legality by government officials; and keeping the machine going even while effecting fundamental transformation.   He discusses the governmental structures required to address these issues. Socialism, to Seidman, involves not mere extension of welfare benefits to the masses and state intervention, but a fundamental shift in class forces and power.   In elaborating the relationship between change in the relevant institutions and the legal order, he formulates three broadly applicable tendencies, or propositions, which concern the "reproduction of institutions," the "transformation of the bourgeois state," and the "growth of the bureaucratic bourgeoisie."   In assessing Zimbabwe's progress in its self-proclaimed "transition to socialism," Seidman notes that the popular masses remain without access to economic resources and state decision-making. In conclusion, the author outlines and explains in detail key constitutionally-defined institutions that are fundamental for the type of development sought.

The lessons learned from these essays are too numerous to summarize. Indeed, the rich historical and contemporary detail revealed in them speaks as eloquently as the theoretical issues examined.   The very process of research among committed scholars demands praxis, synthesizing theory with analysis of empirical evidence; "getting one's hands dirty" with the empirical world fosters *critical* theory essential for planning and policy-making.

The contemporary development dilemmas facing southern Africans can be resolved only through fundamental transformation of existing institutions and structures.   But this transformation must be based on careful, critical analysis of recent experiences and on realistic planning.   Throughout Africa in the past three decades, the "African socialism" that independent leaders readily assumed would re-emerge when the colonial era was terminated has failed to materialize.   Aside from the obvious problems involved in creating viable political institutions in the post-colonial era, this "failure" in large part is attributable to arrogance concerning the ability to devise effective policies for transformation without prior analysis, inadequacies in the research process itself, and the unwillingness of policymakers to seriously incorporate critical research results into their primary tasks.

Without succumbing to undue optimism, southern Africa is characterized by societies and leaders who have developed more self-critical approaches than in much of the contemporary third world. Individually and collectively, there is a demonstrated willingness to learn from their own and others' experiences. Despite the considerable constraints imposed by the world economy in the 1990s and its major actors and institutions, development is occurring and will be greatly enhanced when peace characterizes fully the region and its peoples. It is hoped that these essays contribute to that development process.

PART ONE

Theories of
Transformation

Chapter 1

PEACE, NATIONAL AND REGIONAL SECURITY AND DEVELOPMENT: SOME REFLECTIONS ON THE AFRICAN EXPERIENCE

Samir Amin[*]

"**W**AR IS the pursuit of politics by other means," Clausewitz says. To study conflict, then, is to study a chapter in politics. From the start, however, we must admit that our analytical tools in this area are particularly weak.

Considered as a whole, social reality presents itself in three dimensions—economic, political and cultural. The economy probably constitutes the best-known dimension of this reality. In this area, bourgeois economics has forged tools for specific analysis and, with more or less success, for managing capitalist society. Historical materialism has penetrated further and deeper. Often with success, it explains the nature and extent of the social struggles inherent in economic choices.

---

[*]Translated by Neva Seidman Makgetla.

The area of power and of politics is considerably less well understood and the eclecticism of the associated theories reflects poor scientific mastery of reality.   American functionalist politology, like its older or newer components—geopolitics, systems analysis, etc.—sometimes proves effective in immediate action. But it is grounded in an extreme conceptual poverty that forbids it the status of critical theory.   Here, too, historical materialism proposes an hypothesis about the organic congruence of the material base with the political and ideological superstructure.   When not interpreted in a vulgar manner, this proposition has proven fertile.   Still, Marxism has not developed a conceptualization of the question of power and politics (modes of domination) as it has for the economy (modes of production).   Propositions made in this sense, for instance by the Freudian Marxists, while calling attention to neglected aspects of the question, have still not produced a fruitful conceptual system.   In short, the field of politics lies almost fallow.

It is no accident that Marx called the first chapter of Volume I of *Capital*, "Commodity Fetishism."   In effect, he proposed to reveal the secret of capitalist society.   That secret lets capitalism appear as a dictate of economics, which occupies the foreground of the social scene.   The character of the economic instance determines the other social dimensions that, it seems, must adjust to its exigencies.   Economic alienation thus defines the essence of capitalist ideology.   By contrast, pre-capitalist class societies are governed by the political, which occupies the foreground and to whose constraints the other aspects of social reality—among others, economic life—seem forced to submit. A work elaborating the theory of the tributary mode would require the title of *Power*, rather than *Capital*, with "Power Fetishism," instead of "Commodity Fetishism," as the name of its first chapter.

But no work has been written that provides anything analogous to the precise analysis—resembling a clockwork mechanism—with which Marx describes the economic functioning of capitalism.   Marxism has not produced a political theory for pre-capitalist society (and on that basis a general political theory) like it provided for the capitalist economy.   At best, we have some concrete analyses of how the political/economic congruence functions in this or that capitalist society—in the political writings of Marx, particularly dedicated to the vicissitudes of France. These studies highlight the degree of autonomy of political relationships in these conditions and, notably, the conflict that can result between the logic of power and the requirements of capitalist management.

As for the cultural dimension, it remains even more mysteriously unknown. To this day, no more than intuitive attempts have arisen out of empirical observation of phenomena found in this field of reality, for instance religions. In consequence, the treatment of the cultural dimensions of history remains permeated with culturalism. (This means a tendency in each author's theory about the social dynamic to treat cultural characteristics as transhistorical invariants.) Theorists who focus on researching that which is common to the dynamic of social evolution for all peoples put the accent on the analogous and shared characteristics of apparently diverse cultures. Those who renounce that approach direct attention, instead, to the particular and specific.

It follows that, except for *a posteriori* elaboration or excessively general abstractions (such as the affirmation that "in the last instance" the material basis is determinant), the dynamics of the mode of articulation of the three dimensions of global social reality remain almost unknown. Moreover, in the absence of important progress in this area, discussion remains encumbered by emotional reactions and romantic visions.

In this brief introduction to the debate, I cannot propose a general theory of politics or go beyond some critical observations concerning the theories—often more implicit than explicit—that underlie various authors' concrete analyses of past and present wars.

Lenin proposed that "politics is condensed economics." This suggestion has considerable merit, but its limits must be defined. These are twofold.

First, the proposition only makes sense for the capitalist epoch of history. That is, as a mode of social organization, capitalism is characterized by the domination of the economic instance. By contrast, in pre-capitalist societies, the political-ideological instance predominates. (And what shapes the post-capitalist societies called socialist? This question, which proves more complex than one might initially anticipate, will be addressed later.)

Second, analysis of the relationship between the economy and politics in capitalism obviously requires a valid theory about the economic base in question.

To simplify, it is useful to note that two schools of thought can both claim to derive from Marxism. For one school, the essence of capitalism is the fundamental class contradiction between bourgeoisie and proletariat, which is the social face of the contradiction between capital and labor that defines the capitalist mode of production. In that case, all political phenomena, including the wars of the capitalist epoch, must ultimately derive from this fundamental conflict and the means used to resolve it, however temporarily, by mitigating its acuteness. Moreover, political attitudes must be judged according to some "position of the proletarian class." For the second school, "real existing" capitalism, which opposes but complements the abstract capitalist mode of production, generates a further contradiction, the moving force behind real history. This contradiction opposes the peoples of the periphery (note the reference to peoples, that is to say a nonhomogeneous ensemble of popular classes, and never nations, states or proletariat) to the dominant internationalized capital. Politics and wars then result largely from the regulation of this contradiction.

As another step toward concrete analysis, one can seek to define how the "dominant capital" in question functions. Here, I suggest the hypothesis that the key is to discover how and when a correspondence emerges between a national bourgeoisie (as the dominant class in a given social formation), the constitution of its state and the crystallization of capitalist interests.

According to my theses on this subject, until now such a correspondence existed. The formation of nation-states in England, France, Germany, the United States and Japan corresponded to the emergence of a national bourgeoisie (English, French, etc.) and a national capital (English, French, etc.) The dominant capital is then conjugated in the plural, and politics (and wars) have been determined largely by the conflicting competition of these national capitals, notably to acquire domination over peripheral zones subject to the logic of their expansion. In this sense, as suggested by Oliver Cox, Herb Addo and in a general manner the "world-systems" school, imperialism and the conflict of imperialisms is a permanent characteristic of capitalism and not a relatively recent phenomenon or, in Lenin's words, the "highest stage of capitalism."

But is that inevitable?   The long crisis of contemporary capitalism, initiated by the American decline from the end of the 1960s, has brought an internationalization of capital that seems to have qualitatively new characteristics. This evolution arose out of the development of "transnationals" during the post-war boom period of 1945-1970.   The economic interests of the "transnationals" may conflict with those of the national capital that bore them.   For this reason, their strategy may collide with that of the national state to the extent that it expresses the collective interests of national capital.

In the 1960s, however, two factors restricted the extent of these contradictions. First, transnationals deserved the name only in terms of their operations;   their capital always remained national.   In the end, they stayed American, English, German or Japanese transnationals. Second, United States hegemony imposed on the transnationals as on other capitalist states.

Fifteen years later, what do we see? As Andre Gunder Frank has shown, from the end of the 1960s, recessions have succeeded each other in an accelerated rhythm, every three or four years. Moreover, in terms of the real economy (productive investments, growth and employment), each recession proved deeper than its predecessor and led to an increasingly fragile and weak recovery. Thus, the situation tends toward a long crisis with no obvious conclusion. The succession of unfavorable situations has initiated a flight toward the fore in finance and speculation. Its manifestations are the external indebtedness of the third world and the double indebtedness, internal and external, of the United States. The financial sphere of activities has taken on the proportions of a malignancy detached from the material basis of the economy.

In this financial and speculative escape, a new form of international finance capital, detached from any national base, seems to have developed. Moreover, interests with diverse national origins have fused to form new capitalist interests in industry and non-financial services: "European" capitals, American-Japanese capitals, international capitals. The oligopolies that, until now, had a determinant national territorial base from which they deployed their "multinational" antennae are progressively becoming multinational oligopolies in the full sense of the term. For example, until recently Japanese capital had a systematic policy of reinvesting its profits in the industrial stronghold of the Japanese islands. Today, as with Honda, it has begun to move its productive activities to the United States. Some people think this transfer may grow so large that, if we judge the oligopoly by the locale of its principal activities and nationality of control over its capital, we must consider it, no longer Japanese, but a new American-Japanese oligopoly.

I am not persuaded of the legitimacy of extrapolating these tendencies to define the future in terms of an internationalization of capital away from national bases. But the hypothesis that this evolution could reach the point of no return no longer seems absurd and impossible. From this standpoint, the correspondence between state and capital that has characterized capitalism to date has disappeared, leaving in place a new contradiction between the multiplicity of states and the internationalization of capital. I submit that, for the foreseeable future, the construction of a politically unified American-European-Japanese state is not on the order of the day.

This new contradiction compels us to reassess politics and wars that one could analyze previously in terms of the conflicting competition of national imperialist capitalisms. To date, the relatively brief hegemonies exercised by national states—England from 1815 to 1890, the United States from 1945 to 1970—fostered the technological and financial advance of capital from these nations and the progress of their state in military matters (British naval supremacy, American atomic quasimonopoly until the start of the 1960s and politico-military capacity for intervention until the defeat in Vietnam in 1975). Yet the norm was rather the conflict of imperialisms: between France and England through the eighteenth century; between the five powers—Britain, the United States, Germany, France and Japan—from 1880 to 1945; culminating as Germany and the United States fought a "thirty years war" between 1914 and 1945 to succeed Britain (the image is borrowed from Giovanni Arrighi). Phases of hegemony furthered the unity of the world-system—in the nineteenth century by British "free trade" and, following World War II, by American "free enterprise." In phases marked by war, however, the system tended to dissolve into rival zones, crystallized in colonial empires and zones of influence, notably between 1880 and 1914 and then again in the 1930s.

The internationalization of capital rules out repetition of the dissolution model. At the same time, in the absence of a new American- European-Japanese state, it makes the re-establishment of hegemony by a gendarme state entirely impossible. For some, this impossibility revives the hegemony of the United States, essentially by default. In that case, however, a fatal gap emerges between the interests of international capital and American politics, which necessarily reflects the exigencies of the dominant social alliance in the United States. It can only generate such chaos that no rationality can triumph.

The national political-economic dialectic operates in the framework of this theoretical model for analyzing politics and international conflicts. The stability of the national bourgeois state requires an internal social alliance, which defines the room for political maneuver. To illustrate: in the nineteenth century the French bourgeois state rested on the alliance of capital with the minor classes of the era—the still numerous peasantry, artisan producers, etc. This alliance isolated the working class, excluding it from power and the social contract. From the end of the nineteenth century, by contrast, the social contract progressively integrated the working class on the basis of Fordism and the welfare state, which emerged first in the United States and then throughout the West. Today, the discussion of "consensus politics" based on the right-left slants that underlie the democratic electoral game everywhere in the West reflects this novel dimension in politics.

Returning to Lenin's phrase on the relationship between economics and politics, I would argue that ignoring nuances of the sort I have presented leads to a fatally reductionist discourse. For instance, Juarès provides the brilliant formulation, "capitalism carries war in itself like the thunderclouds the storm." No: whether capitalism carries in itself war or peace depends on the circumstances. It only carries war when, in the course of expansion, it confronts contradictions (whose nature our theoretical framework indicates) that cannot be surmounted in any other way. After all, these wars principally represent conflicts between national bourgeois states: the emergence of new states and their denial by older ones, as in the 1970s; interimperialist conflicts such as the two World Wars; wars between expanding imperialist states and peripheralized peoples;   and, when no hegemonic bourgeois social alliance can succeed, internal conflicts of the civil war type.

The other school of thought on conflict, the bourgeois school, finds its factual basis in the nature of these wars, which include true class conflicts only in a minor place.   Bourgeois political starts by abandoning economic theory in the sense of an analysis of the system commanded by the laws and requirements of the reproduction and expansion of capital.   In consequence, it retains only isolated fragments of economic reality.   For the sake of realism, it may take into account questions of access to natural resources, the opening up of markets or the protection of profits. But it does so only on an *ad hoc* basis, without accepting a general theory of capitalism.   It centers its research on the grounds for potential conflicts, proceeding from the simple sociological hypothesis that states are always potential competitors, aiming, more or less spontaneously, to ensure their "domination."

In this, contemporary politology remains the follower of Hobbes, Machiavelli and the political thought of the absolute state and mercantilism, without having truly surpassed them. From the nineteenth century, it supplemented their hypotheses with views on the nationalisms of peoples, which it sees as seeking to constitute homogenous national states. As such, these states must also prove competitors and thus potential opponents. Later, the colonial conquest and the ethnology it inspired transferred the spontaneous collective aggression attributed to nation-states to other, pre-national types of community (ethnicities, tribes, religious groups).

Taken to extremes, this view holds that war results from traits inherent to humans and their organization in gregarious communities, whatever their particular form of social organization. A good example of this simplistic, absolutist psychologism appears in the solemn declaration that inaugurated UNESCO, in which the

Anglo-Saxon ideologues of the epoch affirmed that "war is born in men's spirit..."

The scientific tenuousness of this thesis requires no comment. Yet it seems to find justification in the frequency of violent conflicts between states, nations and communities, more than the relatively peaceful course of class conflict in the true sense of the term. The political man of action may be content, in effect, with concrete analyses of the conflict-ridden contradictions that appear on the immediate level, without worrying about their roots. The realpolitik that inspired analyses in this vein (written by political men such as Henry Kissinger) effectively derive from politics, not political science. Its geopolitical argumentation may prove effective for action within the system, but it is not designed to understand the system's nature.

Deplorably, many politologists in the third world, shaped by the American school, reproduce its clichés in an uncritical spirit. Thus, the Persians are presented as the inevitable foes of the Arabs, the Ethiopians of the Somalis, Christians of Muslims, etc., just as yesterday the French, British and Germans saw themselves as "hereditary enemies." This approach neglects the nature of the social system and the contradictions that characterize it, as well as the social forces and ideologies that move within these contradictions, in favor of a general, abstract and empty principle. As a result, it cannot formulate a strategy of change that could reconcile Persians and Arabs or Ethiopians and Somalis. It remains imbued with the ideological discourse both of the external opponents of liberation for the peoples in question, and of the local powers buffeted by a situation they do not control.

The nominally "realistic" acceptance of the "fact" of human aggressiveness originated with the laity at the start of the European Renaissance. Increasingly, however, it has assumed another ideological tendency: the humanist idealism of the religions, including Christianity and Islam. As a basic principle, this humanist idealism proclaims the need to overcome aggressiveness and build a peaceful world. The socialist movement of the nineteenth century had to propose a synthesis between this aspiration and its discoveries about the social mechanism. Socialism, and particularly Marxism, agreed that violence has its roots in the heart of the social system of exploiting the working classes, and in our modern era of capital's exploitation of labor. It follows that the conflict of states, nations or other communities merely expresses this more fundamental latent conflict. This analytical thesis demands, as a necessary corollary, a principle of action: that the abolition of the exploitation of labor—that is, in our era, the abolition of capitalism—must lead to peace in human relationships. The disappearance of the state, conceived primarily as an expression of the exigencies of class exploitation, as well as of nations and internal communities, arises from the liberation of the world's humanity. In turn, that liberation springs from this dual vision of social reality and its possible and hoped-for evolution.

Today, it is no longer possible to accept this programmatic discourse. Since the 1970s, a number of states have claimed Marxist socialism. That has not prevented Sino-Soviet antagonism from reaching the brink of war, Vietnam from invading Kampuchea, or the resurgence of dissatisfied nationalism in the Baltic, Central Asia, Tibet and Yugoslavia, among the Hungarian minority in Romania or the Turks in Bulgaria. From this arises much of the renewed glory of the bourgeois school: the facts seem to prove that nations transcend class, that even in the absence of classes, nations express themselves through states—which do not disappear—and the states still act on their hopes for domination. The ideological discourse of the socialist powers in question incorporate arbitrary and changeable justifications, and can only reinforce the convictions of those attracted to realpolitik.

It is time to smash this double specter, which involves social analysis in a dual impasse. That task requires a better understanding of the post-capitalist transition, and in consequence of the contradictions that constrain the nominally socialist societies born of the revolution. I have elsewhere (1988a) proposed an analytical framework derived from the thesis that capitalist expansion has a fundamentally unequal character. It follows that the post-capitalist transition cannot be reduced to "socialist construction." Rather, given its national-popular nature, its real function must be to resolve the inequality that unavoidably shapes "real existing" capitalism, which is a system based on the polarization of centers and peripheries. For this reason, I suggested analyzing post-capitalist societies as organized around a conflicting and dynamic compromise between three social tendencies: socialist, capitalist, and nationalist-étatist. From this standpoint, nominally socialist revolutions and national liberation movements participate in the same grand historical movement of laying to rest the capitalist system. They differ only in the intensity of their realization.

The societies and states of "real socialism" are torn by new and specific contradictions, different from those that characterize capitalism. To understand the reasons for their conflicts, we must understand these contradictions, which fall into two families.

The West views the socialist societies and states as adversaries—which they are to the extent that the national-popular construction they espouse escapes submission to the needs of international capitalist expansion. Conscious of their weaknesses, these states nonetheless aspire to "peaceful coexistence," to use their own term. But the West sees in their weaknesses only an additional reason to exert pressure on them in order to destroy the vision of successful national-popular construction. Depending on time and circumstances, these pressures may amount to a cold or even hot war, or an arms race, even though an occasional balance of "détente" may dilute them. Here, ideological discourse and wooden language change sides: the harsh leitmotifs (such as the satanic "autocracies" of the East, their total lack of principles, etc.) appear in the Western media, evidently in order to mobilize a Western "antisocialist consensus."

The permanent hostility toward the societies and states of "real socialism" duplicates the West's hostility toward national liberation, which participates in the same historical movement of laying to rest "real existing" capitalism. Antagonism to the third world provides an ideological expression of this hostility. In these circumstances, the states of the East, as well as the states of the third world in periods when their national liberation struggles become radicalized, confront the need to actively resist attempts to reintegrate them with the West. Their potential alliances, assistance and interventions must be seen more or less in this context.

Are there general principles to guide us in analyzing this maze of possible situations? Bourgeois politology researches them with its stock instruments, today doubtless favoring the givens of geopolitics and geostrategy imposed by the military equipment of our times. This type of analysis may provide some useful analytical elements. Nonetheless, it misses the key principle for understanding the global strategy of the Eastern countries, especially the Soviet Union and China: that the interventions of the two socialist powers outside their borders (especially in alliance with the forces of national liberation in sharpened conflicts with the West) remain means of "counterpressure" designed to compel the West to reduce its pressure on them. A reduction in the West's pressure on the East may then decrease these counterpressures.

The liberation movements of the capitalist third world are poorly equipped to understand the logic behind the strategy of the East. They have not reached the stage of strong national-popular crystallization that characterizes the nominally socialist societies. Engaged in an unequal struggle against capitalist imperialism, constrained by their own weaknesses to modest dreams, often liable to retreat, they are tempted to blame their own limitations on the hesitations and maneuvering of their outside allies. But it remains the work of the popular forces of the country in question to advance their own national liberation movement to the point where they achieve a national-popular revolution. "Anti-imperialist solidarity" can never compensate for fundamental inadequacies at this level.

The "external" contradiction between "socialist" societies and states (and states of radical national liberation) and world capitalism obviously does not operate in isolation from "internal" contradictions—the second family of contradictions—inherent in national-popular societies. The entanglement of these two groups of contradictions—internal and external—makes it almost impossible to distinguish the general principles governing their development. Only concrete analysis of each case seems possible. Nonetheless, let me note, perhaps as a warning, one dangerous simplification: the view that socialist forces operate in the ideological mode, on the basis of anti-imperialist solidarity, where the forces of national capitalism and étatism appear more pragmatic by temperament and interest and thus more easily tempted by compromise and the cynicism of realpolitik.

Africa and the Middle East are the theater for the most numerous and almost permanent conflicts. But the diversity of these phenomena and the apparent impossibility of finding solutions discourages many analysts, even the relevant national and foreign politicians. Some relinquish the search to understand and content themselves with analogies to a misunderstood feudal Europe. In this view, African societies, victimized by their backwardness, are the contested terrain of various "tribes," peoples and communities. As such, they provide room for the race to power of autocratic potentates, who may use unprincipled alliances with any great powers that agree to enter the destructive game, whether to maintain their "presence" in economic and "cultural" terms or to further their global geostrategy. The metaphor is facile; the vision, which won ground as the illusions of the 1960s dissipated, remains false. Every case has its own peculiarities, which must not be ignored. In this sense, concrete analyses remain irreplaceable. Almost every one of these innumerable cases combine in a unique manner four sources of conflict: first, the suppressed conflict between the requirements of popular national liberation and submission to capitalist expansion imposed by imperialism; second, internal conflicts arising out of the fragility of national society, its popular forces and governing classes; third, the East-West conflict, whose own logic drives its projections on the continent; and fourth, the commercial competition of those capitalist powers with interests in the region.

The order of presentation corresponds to a hierarchy of importance. It reflects, on the one hand, the degree of potential violence attached to each cause of the conflict, and on the other the consequent impact of a solution to the conflict.

Today, it seems, good manners demand that we accept that political independence ended the epoch of national liberation. It follows that later developments result principally from the dynamic of "internal causes" within the societies and states of the third world. Yet the initial proposition ignores the fact that the states of the capitalist third world obtained their independence in conditions that ruled out their "disengagement." On the contrary, their unequal inclusion in the capitalist world-system generally deepened. In contrast, for good or evil, societies that pursued a "socialist revolution" achieved disengagement in the sense we have given this term. As a result, the capitalist third world remains far from the goal of national liberation, a prerequisite for taking the path toward eradicating the legacy of unequal development. In varying degrees, local bourgeoisies controlled the national liberation movements that won independence. They directed the movements' development thereafter toward perspectives that did not threaten the expansion of world capitalism. Thus, responsibility for national liberation returns to the popular classes, who are victimized by the new stage of peripheral capitalist development.

By corollary, the invariably and increasingly unfavorable external factor continues largely to condition the evolution of internal factors. In the same measure, the conflict between imperialism and the national-popular movement must become more violent. Are not the most violent wars of the third world, as a rule, precisely those where this direct confrontation occupies center stage, as in Nicaragua, the permanent Israeli-Arab conflict, and the struggle initiated by the people of Southern Africa with their fight against the apartheid regime?

In analyzing the Palestinian and South African conflicts, I have developed some relevant propositions (Amin 1986a, 1987, 1988b). Here, I only summarize some of my conclusions.

The Palestinian conflict does not result exclusively from the collision between two nationalisms—in this case, Arab and Israeli—whose legitimacy, for those who consider nationalism legitimate as such, remains equal. In fact, Israel is an instrument in the service of world capitalist expansion, designed to thwart the Arab national-popular revolution.

Naturally, the defeat of the national-popular revolution in the Arab countries has not resulted exclusively from the external aggression of the West. We have never failed to insist on the partial responsibility of the historic limits of the Egyptian and Arab liberation movements, from Mohamed Ali at the start of the nineteenth century through Gamal Abdel Nasser, via the endeavors of the liberal bourgeoisie from the 1920s to the 1940s. Nonetheless, to date external aggression has effectively prevented the Arab peoples' movement from overcoming its internal limitations. It has even inflicted serious reversals, as today.

While external aggression has taken Israel for its favored instrument during the past forty years, it is no recent phenomenon. The Middle East occupies peculiar position in geostrategy and history. Thus, Egypt was sited yesterday on the route to India, and today is on the route to oil; and Europe explicitly fears the reconstitution—in an initiative of which only Egypt seems capable—of a unified, modern Arab state on its southern flank. Doubtless for these reasons, Europe has bitterly and systematically opposed all efforts toward modernization in Egypt.

As early as 1839, forty years before the first appearance of Zionism, when Mohamed Ali's armies made him Sultan of the Ottoman, British diplomacy invented the Israel project. The London *Globe* reported at the time that Britain imagined organizing Jewish emigration to Palestine so as to create a "European" state in order to keep an eye on Egypt and cut it off from the Arab Mashreq, the eastern part of the Arab world. Unfortunately, this primary function of the Zionist project remains largely hidden by anti-Semitic blackmail, which its proponents exploit expertly.

Stalemate in these conditions leads to retreat, which again places in center stage the internal conflicts that result from the fragility of peripheralized Arab societies, which both cause and reflect the historical limits mentioned above. Religious and sectarian disintegration and the passive return to a comprador system dominated by the United States with the active complicity of the oil regimes of the Gulf do not constitute primary realities, whose progress inevitably proves determinant. Rather, they dissipate during moments of national-popular upheaval, and reappear in moments of popular passivity.

The Palestinian conflict also demonstrates the limits of the alliance between national liberation and the Soviet Union. The Soviet Union remains interested in supporting anti-imperialist struggles only to the extent its permanent global strategy of peaceful coexistence dictates. This principle, while not in itself necessarily evil, must not be ignored.

Rather than hiding it behind ideological discourse or burying it in excessive diplomatic secrecy, its consequences in each situation should be made explicit.

Finally, the Palestinian conflict illuminates the real-world position—which is entirely minor—of contradictions within the West. Despite the economic competition between the United States and Europe, which many emphasize, the West appears united and aligned behind the United States against the Arab national-popular revolution. Certainly, at one point General Charles de Gaulle sought, through France, a margin of autonomy for Europe. It was premised, however, precisely on his attempt to establish an Arab-oriented politics freed from Zionist dictates, a whimsy, ultimately, with no important consequences.

The South African conflict only achieved an important place in Western public opinion after the South African people forced it into a new, decisive phase. That phase represents a potential threat to imperialist interests in the region after the inevitable liquidation of apartheid.

For a century, the imperialist system of domination in the Southern African region was built on the linkage of the "white" regime in South Africa and the old direct colonialisms of England and Portugal. The collapse of the latter in Angola and Mozambique in 1975 and Zimbabwe in 1980 did not immediately eliminate the role of South Africa. On the contrary, South Africa's attacks, designed to destabilize the states established at independence, complemented the many pressures the West exerted on the frontline states in an effort to prevent potentially irreversible advances in a national-popular direction.

In other words, the abolition of apartheid opens the door to evolution in two contradictory directions. One, the strategic objective of the West, would stop with the realization of "majority rule," which implies a black government in South Africa disposed to play the game of integration in the capitalist world-system. *Mutatis mutandis*, it would repeat Zimbabwe's experience after achieving independence under the Lancaster House agreement. The alternative prospect involves advancing beyond neocolonialism. South Africa's material basis, which has no equal on the continent, reinforces this possibility. Obviously, this kind of progress threatens neocolonialism at least throughout southern Africa.

In these conditions, Western strategy has a dual objective which, despite appearances, is not at all contradictory. On the one hand, it seeks to use negotiations and pressure to eliminate apartheid before the struggle becomes so radicalized that it adopts another social perspective. On the other hand, it aims to accelerate the neocolonial reconquest of the fragile states in the region—Angola, Mozambique, and to a lesser extent Zimbabwe, Madagascar and Mauritius. The destabilization of these states, in collusion with apartheid South Africa, fits logically with the strategy of the West against the national popular struggle.

As in Palestine, the South African conflict illuminates the limits of Soviet involvement. It also reveals the West's common front against national-popular liberation. Doubtless, at the level of the media, the "antiracist" dimension sets ideological limits. Moreover, the existence of an Afro-American population with which American liberals want to show solidarity often provides, oddly enough, for a less retrograde discussion on South Africa in the United States than in Europe, although neither approach fails to condemn the "pro-Soviet" governments of Angola and Mozambique.

In both regions, internal quarrels between ethnicities, the bureaucratic responses of the local powers and their tendency to ignore these realities, not to speak of the notorious inadequacies of their economic and social policies—all these are undeniable. They reflect the insufficient maturity of the liberation movements, which cannot be considered national-popular movements in the necessary sense of the term. The West does not stress these realities in innocence, however. It aims, not to help these peoples overcome their inadequacies, but to exploit them by imposing a return to neocolonial subordination.

Obviously, the Middle East and South Africa do not exhaust the fields of conflict between national-popular aspirations and Western imperialism. Without fear of exaggeration, one can say that the African continent as a whole constitutes the permanent and major theater of this conflict. In the course of the last three decades, at various times half the African states have gone beyond neocolonialism—in Egypt, Algeria, the Sudan, Libya, Mali, Guinea, Guinea Bissau, Burkina Faso, Cape Verde, Ghana, Benin, the Congo, Zaire, Ethiopia, Somalia, Tanzania, Uganda, Zambia, Zimbabwe, Angola, Mozambique, Madagascar, Mauritius and the Seychelles. In various degrees, their efforts all met with the hostility of the West, in forms ranging from economic and financial pressure to subversion and even military invasion.

Certainly, the national aspirations of the various governments did not permit a uniform degree of radicalization. Often they lacked sufficient popular power, sometimes because the governments themselves did not want the popular movement to acquire dynamic autonomy. Moreover, these attempts seemed, at least, inherently weak, and they reverted to the rut of neocolonialism. Some could not surmount the ethnic and other contradictions among their own people. But the economic and political apparatus established by Europe on the eve of independence was designed not to support popular forces, but to maintain the neocolonial order that they confront. There is little reason for surprise, then, that so many "rapid interventions" by paratroopers have reinstalled dictators totally devoted to Western interests. Hypocrisy reigns when the West laments the state of Africa and its peoples without mentioning its illegitimate but united support for the most retrograde and corrupt local forces against the most honest, whose errors and inadequacies it complacently underlines.

The association of Africa with the European Economic Community (EEC) under the Lomé Accords must be understood in the framework of the perpetuation of the neocolonial relationship. Some Europeans advance the argument that the weakness of Africa's popular forces make it too immature for anything else. Others observe that even if the association benefits neocolonial interests, its documents and institutions authorize a margin for maneuver that neither the national-popular forces in Africa nor the forces of the left in Europe (which could push their governments and the EEC) adequately exploit. This argument is tenable even if, like us, one believes that choosing the worst evil rarely proves the most effective tactic in seeking to modify the strategic balance of forces. But it should not inspire misgivings about the prospects for national-popular disengagement. Africa will not develop through an "enlightened paternalism," which remains as utopian as that "enlightened colonialism" of yesteryear to which some forces on the European left appealed, perhaps even sincerely. The African peoples cannot escape the general law: rule or submit.

We do not mean to imply that the wars of Africa appear only in an anti-imperialist dimension. The list of inter-ethnic conflicts, for instance, is as long as that of conflicts between African nationalism and the West: Zaire, Uganda, Ethiopia, the Sudan, Rwanda and Burundi, Angola, Mozambique, Nigeria, and Chad have been or remain theaters of violent conflict, sometimes even civil war. In other countries the conflict remains latent, contained only by means of continued repression. No less significant is the list of wars between states over boundaries and open or hidden territorial ambitions: to name a few, Ethiopia/Somalia/Sudan; Algeria/Morocco (and the Western Sahara); and Mali/Burkina Faso. None of these conflicts has been fabricated by agents foreign to Africa. The pronouncements of local governments to that effect seem dubious even when, as is often the case, various external forces exploit the occasion, often cynically, by supporting some forces and opposing others to achieve their own strategic or tactical objectives.

Are these conflicts, then, the inevitable result of some hostility inherent in all human "communities," as superficial political proposes? I have suggested an alternative analysis (Amin 1986b). Briefly, let me summarize my major conclusions.

First, the coincidence of state and nation during the formation of central capitalism produced a unique history in Western Europe, which the bourgeois ideology of the nation reflects. Even in Europe, its results prove debatable east of the Elbe and south of the Alps. Elsewhere in the world, they seem still more dubious. In large measure, the ideology of ethnicity is a byproduct of the ideologization of the nation, and so provides only a deformed, sometimes mythical, picture of reality.

In these conditions, we propose the hypothesis that "communal" conflicts result fundamentally from the struggles between fractions of the ruling class. The most obvious shared characteristic of the ruling classes is their fragility. Some are comprador classes constrained to act within the narrow limits set by world capital. These may be merely comprador bureaucracies—the apparatus of a comprador state. Others constitute a comprador bourgeoisie, which at least has economic interests, however inferior its position in world capitalism. A third type comprises groups with nationalist aspirations that have not managed to become the "intelligentsia" of an alliance of truly popular forces. In all these cases, the various segments of each class face a strong temptation to develop power by mobilizing fractions of the people behind "symbols" that leave them in control. Either ethnic or religious symbols are often well adapted to this kind of competition for power.

Thus, it is not ethnocentric atavism which compels people to misapprehend realities other than those of the communities to which they belong. Nor does some other kind of autocratic atavism constrain the rulers to manipulate "ethnic satans" as the "causes" of such conflicts. Rather, we must look to the weakness of peripheral society as a whole, and particularly its ruling classes.

The national-popular perspective here requires a strategy at once democratic and unitary. That is, it must work toward maintaining, even creating, large territories and thus states powerful enough to undertake the defiance that national-popular disengagement demands. At the same time, it must respect the diversity that permits large territories. In this political perspective, the right of peoples to rule themselves must be realized.

The global conflict of the superpowers does not imply some necessary symmetry between the objectives of the actors. The United States assumes the lead among the capitalist forces that adopt the conservative objective of perpetuating the neocolonial integration of Africa in the global system. The forces of national-popular liberation cannot avoid confronting it. Neither the Soviet Union nor, by extension, China, has the ambition—or the option—of armed support for the progressive transformation of the continent. At worst, if the prospect of a serious and durable dètente emerged, the "socialist" superpowers might accept a retreat from Africa, abandoning its peoples to solitary confrontation with their internal and external enemies. More probably, they will find some "presence" in Africa useful in two ways. First, it could provide a means to compel their adversary to dètente. Alternatively, if—as is always possible—armed conflict should emerge, Africa could provide bases for action in the Mediterranean, the North and South Atlantic and the Indian Ocean. Specialists in military questions argue that such geostrategic preoccupations become irrelevant in an era of intercontinental missiles, much less "Star Wars." Can they disappear entirely, however, if the risk of conflagration has not been reduced to all or nothing, but includes intermediary options that require regional initiatives?

Finally, diplomacy retains its rights. That is, even the Soviet and Chinese states tend to take into account only what exists, which means those authorities in power. It would be naive to believe or even hope that their preoccupation with the longer term (hopefully "socialism"), however sincere, goes beyond the ideological level. In the future as in the past, diplomacy provides for approaches that must seem opportunist to anyone who considers national-popular goals an uncontestable requirement of progress. These approaches appear whenever an alliance between a "socialist" state and a more or less nationalist local power (and thus one in conflict, to some degree, with the West) fails to facilitate or even prevents the evolution of the local power toward an irreversible national-popular crystallization.

Finally, the last point involves the competition between Europe and the United States. It is easy to be brief here, since this competition has not led to a political competition in either Africa or the Middle East. On the contrary, the resources of the United States and those of Europe have here been mobilized in complementary fashion. In this region, Europe is perfectly aligned.

Chapter 2

SOCIALISM IN THEORY AND PRACTICE

Tamás Szentes

Socialism in Theory

THE IDEA of socialism originated in the centuries-old dream of humanist philosophers, political thinkers and social scientists about a just social order with equal rights, equal opportunities and social welfare for all members of society and a collective decision making. Its rise was also due to the frustration caused by the post-revolutionary new, bourgeois order of society, born under the aegis of freedom, equality and fraternity. This new, bourgeois order of society has, in reality, replaced the feudal order of the openly admitted and declared social inequalities only by a formal equality of the individuals being in substantially unequal social (class) position. Thus, socialism has appeared as the true heir, politically, of the radical movements of the bourgeois-democratic revolutions, particularly of the 1789 French one, and behind that, intellectually, of the European Enlightenment.

Owing to the stress on the spirit of collectivism and on a collectivist reorganization of society to achieve social justice and equality, as opposed to the selfish individualism of the capitalist entrepreneurs, socialism has often been associated or identified with communism. It has also been misinterpreted as the suppression of individual ambitions and interests.

Since the nineteenth century socialism has manifold, varying meanings reflecting widely different, often opposite political views, interests and movements.

Scientific socialism, identified with Marxism, has been primarily distinguished from "utopian socialism" which marks the views and practical efforts of those early socialists who, like Owen, Saint-Simon, Fourier and others, had a normative rather than realistic concept of socialism. Utopian socialists believed that the given, capitalist society can be transformed into the desired idealistic society merely by convincing all people, including the capitalists, to share their wealth with the poor. The other alternative, they believed, was to establish first a new, just order in small communities, on micro-level, and thereby exert an educational effect on the macro-society.

This utopian concept and also those idealist views of socialism such as "Christian socialism," according to Marxists, all neglect or underestimate the importance of the actual power relations of society which are rooted in the "economic base." Neglected also are the impact of "social existence" on "social consciousness," i.e. the influence of the objective conditions on the subjective behavior and the way individuals think. Scientific socialism, on the other hand, has been based, by Marx, Engels and their followers, on the political-economical analysis of the objective conditions, laws of motion, historical tendencies and social (class) forces of human societies, particularly of capitalism. It has also been linked organically with the labor movement.

The Marxian concept of social transformation relies on a historical assessment of the role of capitalism in human progress and on the political economy of capital accumulation reproducing capitalist property. It also relies on the perception of the dialectical contradictions of society as motive forces of its development. This concept contrasts with those ahistorically moralizing and romantic (e.g., Proudhon's) views which attack property itself as a "theft" without investigating its source and content. The Marxian concept differs, too, with those views that suggest a return to precapitalistic socio-economic conditions or a mere reform of capitalism by eliminating only its "evil aspects" and contradictory nature.

Since the works of Marx and Engels, the theory of scientific socialism has developed further and has also undergone a great many modifications in details and reinterpretations. Such modifications reflect the new phases of development of capitalism and its world-system, the beginnings of the socialist transformation of the world, the lessons of the first socialist revolutions and also the social-democratic policies, the success or failure of the local efforts to put the socialist ideas into practice and the controversial experiences of the first socialist regimes. These modifications also depict the problems of developing a socialist society in single and less-developed countries (such as in Tanzania), in former colonies or semi-periphery, economically dependent countries under the conditions of a capitalist world economy and international conflicts, the national or regional specificities and the subsequent phases, occasional crises and self-correcting changes of socialist development in various parts of the world.

Some conceive of Marxism, or wish it to appear, as a kind of religion with a set of eternal dogmas and a Messianistic prophecy. For such people, all modifications in the theory of scientific socialism and all divergences in its practical implementation are viewed either as the consequences of heresies and distortions or as the result of the incompatibility of Marxist principles with national endeavors. Many modern Marxists such as Gramsci, Lukács and others, however, have stressed that Marxism contains a scientific method, a certain approach to social reality, besides its committed politics to serve the cause of the working masses and all exploited, oppressed people. Further, if Marx has succeeded "only" in revealing the most general laws of motion of capitalism as it was working in his own time and in the most developed countries, then, of course, the application of this "method" to new realities and different circumstances necessarily implies (as it did in the case of Lenin's work) further elaboration and corrections in the theory of scientific socialism.

The founders of scientific socialism were both unable and unwilling to provide "recipes" for the future process of socialist development; they were also obviously unable to foresee the actual picture of the future capitalism for which, or under the presence of which, socialist transformation would start. This picture was rendered even more unpredictable by the impact of the labor movement—for which the Marxian theory had been elaborated—on both the subsequent development of capitalism and on the conditions of socialist transformation. What's more, the operation of capitalism and of the first socialist systems have been mutually affecting each other today.

Despite the divergence of theorists' views, changes in theory and practice and the rise of new problems and questions, unexpected or unanswered by the founders of scientific socialism, there are some basic assumptions, theses and principles. These stem from the Marxian approach and analysis and have proved to be the lasting components both of the theory of scientific socialism, and of the practical guidance of socialist development.

One enduring thesis is that of the historical inevitability of the transformation of capitalism into socialism, leading to a world communist society. It follows from the Marxian concept of historical development of human society in general and from the Marxian analysis of the antagonistic contradictions and inherent tendencies of capitalism, in particular. The former is known as historical materialism which defines social formations as the dialectical unit of an "economic base" and a more or less corresponding institutional, legal, political, cultural, moral, "superstructure." This explains the historical necessity of changeovers from one social formation to the next, a necessity mandated by the increasing objective contradiction, manifested in the sharpening struggle of classes with their subjective consciousness, between the ever-developing productive forces of society and the given set of social relations of production.

Accordingly, the decisive motive force of social progress is the development of productive forces, i.e. human labor power and its means of production, i.e. social relations of ownership, division of labor and income distribution. Each class society, with its basic and characteristic production relations, gives an impetus to the development of productive forces in its early, rising stage, but increasingly hinders the latter in its late, declining phase. The basic classes of society, distinguished by their opposite position in respect to the ownership over the main means of production, by their different roles in the social division of labor and by differences in their source and level of income, are conflicting each other.

By their struggle against the ruling class the oppressed and exploited classes undermine the stability of the given social order and by means of revolutionary ideologies, organizations and actions pave the way for a new social system to arise from the womb of the latter.

The Marxian perception of the historical progress of human society is often misrepresented, depending on which aspects of their dialectical interactions between the objective processes of socio-economic development and the subjective actions of the socio-political struggle are overstressed. It is misinterpreted either as a theory of "economic determinism" underestimating the role of the human factor and its free, conscious activity, or as a "conflict theory," as the doctrine of a permanent class struggle justifying all revolutionary actions, violence and political voluntarism. In both cases the fundamentally humanitarian substance of the Marxian idea is neglected, namely the very aim of social transformation, the liberation of humanity, the humanizing of social relations and the elimination of the roots of violence. It is also forgotten that Marx applied a dialectical approach and that in his views the economic base of society does involve the human factor since the social relations of production are, indeed, human relations. It was also his belief that the primary force of production, the "engine" of economic development, is human labor, the only source of all values.

The Marxian analysis of the antagonistic contradictions of capitalism points, first of all, to the antagonism between the increasing socialization of production and the private appropriation of the social product. Secondly, it points to the subordination of live labor to appropriated and accumulated "dead labor" (i.e. capital). Thirdly, it points to the characteristic process of social alienation, i.e., to the appearance of human relations and human values in the dress of relations to "things" and commodities.

According to Marx, capitalism (where fully developed), by eliminating slavery and feudal serfdom and making free the laborers as individuals, has given a great impetus to the development of the social productive forces and also to the rise of formal political democracy. At the same time, it has also set fundamental obstacles to a full and socially useful development of productive forces and to the unfolding of a real and overall democracy. This was accomplished by making the workers "free" while depriving them of the means of production, and by letting a small minority of capitalist owners to command, directly or indirectly, via their paid representatives, the operation of the increasingly socialized production process.

In Marx's view capitalism has replaced the former systems of exploitation based upon open, personal coercion by a new one based upon economic coercion and market mechanism. Its inherent tendency of capital concentration and centralization leads to monopolization, which besides increasing the economic power in fewer and fewer hands, sharpens the contradictions between the increasingly social character of production and the private nature of appropriation and management.

Capitalism as a social system, in general, has introduced the method of surplus appropriation by economic coercion and tends to substitute it for the thousand-year-old methods of noneconomic violence. The capitalist system is based on a monopolistic private ownership (originally established by noneconomic force and excluding the working majority from property rights) over the main means of production. It appropriates the surplus of the expanded reproduction, i.e. the product of the labor (as the only value-creator) performed in the past and accumulates it as capital, i.e. as an accumulated past-labor already appropriated. Thus, it ensures and reproduces the conditions of the economic appropriation of the surplus product of the live labor to be performed in the coming cycle of reproduction as well.

This mechanism is the very ground of the antagonism between labor and capital, i.e., between live labor of the present and "dead" labor, appropriated in the past, which can by no means be reduced to an "income gap" between capitalist owners and nonowner workers. It also explains why the rules of the allocation of social roles and the rules of income distribution are not identical and universal but rather dualistic. For the owners it is basically, if not exclusively, capital-ownership which determines the social position, the functional role in the social division of labor and its reward, and the way and level of income earning. On the other hand, for the nonowners it is basically their own labor, sold in the market and performed in employment, under conditions governed by capital, that determines socio-economic status.

Individual freedom of the laborer, free mobility and marketing of labor are the great achievements of the capitalist society as compared to pre-capitalistic ones. But economic coercion, capital-dominated conditions of freedom and economically determined social inequalities are the historical price of these achievements.

The freedom of individuals implies the freedom of laborers to sell their only "commodity," their labor power as a capacity to work for the capitalists, and also the freedom of the latter to exploit the laborers, to live and enrich themselves from the labor of other people who seem to be only less fortunate or less talented and ambitious. Democracy in politics can develop, but as without the democratization of the economy, only in a formal way, i.e., preserving the real power in the hands of the capitalist minority. Exploitation relations appear as merely exchange relations and human labor is degraded to a marketable commodity priced according to the supply and demand conditions of the market. Commodification extends over nonmaterial products, services and values, including moral and cultural ones. Human relations, in general, become increasingly indirect, impersonal and mediated by the process of exchange, and thus appear as relations to "things" rather than to other people. This gives birth to the fetish of commodity and money.

It follows from the above Marxian concept of capitalism that the task of socialism is to dissolve the antagonistic contradictions by abolishing the private ownership of the means of production and to liberate human live labor from the domination of capital as "dead labor." Its task is also to personalize again human relations by depriving them of the false appearance, to take the nonmaterial values out of the command of the market and to apply to all able-bodied members of society identical and universal rules in the distribution of income and social rules, namely according to their own labor. Socialism would thereby not only ensure the further development of the forces of production by establishing new, adequate relations of production, but also lead to the unfolding of a new, real and overall democracy extending over the economy, too. Thus, socialism implies the process of social emancipation, the liberation of human live labor from the dominance of materialized "dead" labor, and the liquidation of the dualism of the objective rules determining role allocation and income distribution within society. This process necessarily involves, mostly as a departure point, the elimination, in one way or another, of private capital ownership, but also great many other changes in society, in its economic, political, institutional and cultural relations. The replacement of private ownership of capital by public (state) ownership does not mean socialization per se, without the appropriate changes in the content, direction and control of the public (state) sector. Nor does the joining of the employed workers to the company of capitalist shareholders bring about socialization of private ownership. The same applies to the participation of trade union representatives in the management of private firms.

The social, collective management of economy requires a socially controlled decisionmaking and implementation in the socially owned economy, which makes it necessary to introduce and develop new forms and effective machineries of political as well as economic democracy.

The enforcement of single, identical and universal rules of role and income distribution within society prescribes, over and beyond the changes in ownership relations, also objective guarantees for full employment, and for an access to appropriate job, one that corresponds with knowledge, skill and performance. It also dictates the elimination of all the major obstacles to social mobility, not only those set up by capital ownership, but also those stemming from educational monopolies. Free access to education and training as well as to re-education is, therefore, also a requisite.

A Marxian perception of history embodies the Hegelian dialectic of the "negation of the negation." The logic of history suggests a trend of social development from the ancient classless society of "primitive communism" to its full negation and then further to the negation of the negation. Under the point of departure in history known as "primitive communism," there are primitive productive forces, communistic ownership and distribution relations and a normal, directly personal appearance of human relations. Through various intermediary formations such as slavery, feudalism, the "Asiatic mode of production," and so forth, "primitive communism" is fully negated and gives way to a class-antagonistic society. This society, capitalism, is characterized by developed productive forces, private ownership and falsified indirect and impersonal forms of human relations. Finally, this negation is itself negated to become a classless society of advanced communism with once again normalized, directly personal human relations. In this logic socialism is only an intermediary formation before or at an early stage of communism.

Thus, in the Marxist theory of scientific socialism the thesis about the historical inevitability of socialism is complemented by the thesis about its transitional nature. This has often been neglected, however, by those adventurist political leaders (such as Pol Pot, to name only the most illustrative figure) wishing to introduce immediately a "communistic" order of society under immature conditions, contrary to the wish of the people and thus by violence, political voluntarism and intolerance. It has also been ignored by those doctrinaire Marxists who, having lost their former illusions about the societies of "existing socialism," compare the latter with the ideal of a communist society.

The transitional nature of socialism implies both the fact that for a while it necessarily bears many marks of the capitalist society, and the task that it has to prepare, indeed, the birth of a communist society. This task is to be accomplished by developing the productive forces, by increasing the social welfare and by changing the institutions, and also by modifying the pattern of social behavior, the way of thinking and lifestyle.

This preparatory role of socialism calls for a highly conscious and purposeful organizational activity which extends not only to the economy where planning and social control become necessary, but also to the sphere of education and culture. One of the most debated issues among Marxists is how, in which form, on what level and by whom these organizational activities have to be done, more concretely; what is the appropriate role of the state, the party and other social and political organizations? what is to be centralized or decentralized? and how centralism should be reconciled with democracy.

It is a generally accepted thesis that socialist transformation preconditions a qualitative change in the state power, its seizure by the working class led by its party, (whether by a proletarian revolution, a large-scale organized revolt, a "long march" of rural masses or in a parliamentary way), and thereby the breaking of the rule of the bourgeoisie.

The primary role of the new state power is to protect the new social order, to change the social relations of ownership by "appropriating the appropriators," i.e., by "nationalizing" or collectivizing the private properties of the main means of production (such as land, factories, mines, etc.), to eliminate thereby the capitalist exploitation relations and the socio-economic causes of unemployment. Its purpose as well is to introduce a social management, planning and control over the process of social reproduction and to thereby promote the development of productive forces. It has to implement a "revolution" in culture and education by providing the working masses and the new generations with educational and cultural facilities, access to schools and universities, theaters and museums, etc., by eliminating the privileges of the elite, and by supporting the development of humanistic and democratic culture and arts.

Socialism in Practice

In practice, however, a great many questions arise as to the necessary measure of nationalizations and the appropriate ways of the collectivization of agriculture, the implications of social management and the planning and control over the economy. Questions develop regarding the application of economic and/or moral incentives to increase productivity and effectiveness, the methods and measures of cultural and educational "revolution," and so on.

Even more debated problems arise in regard to the required progress towards a communistic society. Such a society should have no state power of a coercive nature, but instead a fully developed and overall system of social self-management, with the self-coordinated activities of various social organizations and local communities. Rather than operating without commodity production and exchange, money and market, it would be based on a direct contribution of the individuals ("each according to his/her abilities") to the common welfare and a direct share of each ("according to his/her needs") from the common products and services.

Though it is evident that socialism cannot do without a central state power and commodity production, in practice these questions remain open: which are the adequate ways of the "withering away of the state?"; what is the nature, and the appropriate role and scope of the market mechanism?; which are the preferred perspectives of the transformation of commodity production? Answers to such and similar questions have often differed not only from country to country but also from time to time in the practical process of socialist development. These differing answers point to the rather experimental nature of the latter, to the wide differences, among those countries developing socialism, in their endowment, conditions, development level and historical traditions. They point also to the merging of this process of socialist transformation with that of national emancipation, with the rise from a peripheral or semiperipheral position in the world economy to a more equal status.

The Marxian theory of scientific socialism, by deriving the inevitability of socialist transformation from the sharpening contradictions of capitalism, has indicated the birth of socialism at the highest stage of capitalist development. This may be interpreted either as referring to the most developed capitalist nations becoming mature for a socialist revolution, or as a reference to the development of capitalism on the global level, in the context of its world-system. Accordingly, socialist revolution was expected to erupt first in the most developed countries and spread as a chain reaction therefrom or take directly the form of a world revolution. Instead, it has taken place in single and less developed countries without the collapse of the capitalist world-system. This fact has not only put on the historical agenda the lasting coexistence of the two social formations but has also given a new context and dimension to the practical process of socialist transformation, namely by making it a process in single countries surrounded by the capitalist world-system and under the conditions of a single, capitalist world economy.

Marx himself perceived capitalism not merely as a national system, a national economy and society, which has given birth to a nation state, but as a system arising also on the world level, creating a world market for international capital. Many of his prominent followers such as Hilferding, Lenin, Hobson, Bucharin, Trotsky, Kautsky, Luxemburg and others have also revealed some laws of motion of the capitalist world-system, its imperialism and internationalization process, etc. Pragmatic Marxism, however, has been rather inclined to take the nations as the only or primary unit of analysis and unit of action.

As a matter of fact, the basic inequalities of the capitalist system manifest both within the national framework and on the international scene: (1) inequalities of the relations of ownership and control, (2) inequalities in the allocation and distribution of the roles, within national societies as well as in the international division of labor, and (3) an unequal income distribution system which is basically the consequence of the above, both within the national societies and within the world community.

Capitalism, whose emergence and operation have presupposed from the outset a wider scope and sphere of activity than its product, the national economies, was the first in history to bring about a world economy.

The capitalist world economy involves the relations of dominance and asymmetric dependence between its center and its periphery.

A natural concomitant of the operation of a capitalist world economy is unequal development. One of its manifestations is the modification of the hierarchy among the developed capitalist countries of the center and the shift of the leading role within it (in favor of the countries which succeed in developing their productive forces and technology, at least temporarily, at a rate faster than others). These changes take place in alternating directions. Another, cumulative variant of the manifestations of unequal development is the widening of the "development gap" between the center and the periphery, the reproduction of relative "underdevelopment." These two variants are interrelated in the sense that the exploitation of the periphery provides the possibility and at the same time the negative incentive—owing to protected markets—to develop the productive forces. They are also interrelated because the groups of countries of the center and the periphery are also connected by the marginal cases called the "semiperiphery" which, depending on the direction of their movements, are exposed simultaneously to the effect of both variants. These marginal cases do not refute the dichotomy, the bipolarity, of the system, but are exactly indicative of its movement, development and change.

While capitalism has created and developed national economies in the "central" or "core" countries, it has prevented the countries of the "periphery" from developing their own national economies. Since the very birth of capitalism a dialectical contradiction has appeared between national and international development. Capitalism is unable to resolve it.

The theory of capitalist world economy was not elaborated by Karl Marx, nor was there even a "chapter" on international trade. His general theory of political economy, however, has provided numerous pillars for it. His theses on the most general laws of motion of capitalism as a system, and his several concrete remarks on the worldwide actions of capitalism (such as on the "extra-national" side of the primitive accumulation process, the world-wide activity of merchant capital, the specific nonequivalence of international exchange, etc.) are relevant in this context. Equally relevant are his critical comments on the classical dogmas and illusions as well as his political views about a worldwide solidarity and united revolutionary action of the working classes of all countries as the motive force of the transformation of the world society from the capitalist system into an advanced collective system, a world communist society through the transitory stage of socialism.

Certain important analytical and methodological questions, however, were left open or ambiguous in the Marxian work. One example is the question of the actual unit of analysis of capitalism. On the one hand, his primary interest and merit were in analyzing and revealing the most general motions laws and inherent tendencies of the capitalist system in its pure form, as a highly abstracted model as compared to other socio-economic systems. On the other hand, he had the opportunity, at that time, of making such an analysis on the basis of the empirical data of the national economy of only a few European capitalist countries.

As a consequence, many of his followers in the past and at the present, take for granted the national economy as the appropriate unit of analysis. They conceive the world-economy processes merely as "external" relations between autonomous national units thereby forgetting about not only those notes of Marx which obviously contradict such an assumption, but also the "internationalization" process.   Others look upon capitalism primarily as a world-system and neglect the specificity of the internal processes within the national units.

In any case, capitalism both on the national and on the world level has further developed, in practice, into a new stage which could not be analyzed, in its full form, by Marx. This stage, called imperialism or monopoly capitalism by Lenin, has given an even greater significance to the question of the appropriate unit of analysis. It has also shown the importance and necessity of the empirical studies of the nonEuropean areas and of the relevant interpretation of the Marxist political economy.

Marxism was born in Europe and bears certain birth marks of the European culture including the philosophy of rationalism, Darwinism, the Hegelian dialectics, the French utopian socialism and the British classical economics. The illustrative examples, the concretely analyzed cases in the Marxian work were mainly, though not exclusively, European ones. This explains why its universal message and its applicability or adaptability in the nonEuropean and less developed parts of the world has often been questioned.

Lenin's theory of monopoly capitalist imperialism has given an implicit rather than explicit answer to the question of the unit of analysis by referring to the "chain of imperialism" with its stronger and weaker "links." His theory also implicitly answers the question of adaptability by his Marxist analysis and political conclusions on the less developed Russia and her Asian territories. These and other related questions, however, did not cease to be debated.   This is so not only because Lenin's views were not unanimously accepted by all Marxists that time, but also because the actual historical circumstances shed some new light on the practical problem of world transformation.

Lenin's theory of imperialism as monopoly capitalism obviously involves a world-system approach, without denying, however, the national framework of some basic socio-economic processes in the developed countries of capitalism. His five characteristics of imperialism are partly related to the development of capitalism on a national level and partly to its expansion on the world level. In the first case are the monopolization process stemming from the further accumulation and centralization of "national" capital, and the rise of a domestic finance oligarchy. In the second case are the distribution of the world to economic interest spheres among the monopolies and its division to politically and militarily controlled territories among the imperialist powers.

The third characteristic is the most central element, namely the "export of capital." The international mobility and activity of capital connects the national and world levels and can actually give the key to understanding the development of the capitalist world economy as an organic system. It can also resolve the one-sidedness of the question of the unit of analysis. The international separation of the ownership and the operation (the "function") of capital and thereby the "internationalization" of the labor-capital antagonism has often been misinterpreted or missed in Marxist literature. Perhaps this is due to the ambiguous wording of this very key factor. The internationalization of the contradiction is called an "export." "Export" also refers to an exporting nation, its transactions in a given year, and its financial capital (which includes loans). Lenin's theory has clearly pointed to the process of monopolization *cum* internationalization, and also to the center-periphery relations, both of which are related to the international separation of the ownership and operation of capital. Nevertheless, many Marxists overemphasize either monopolization or internationalization, and some of them question even the empirically proved fact of the periphery's economic dependence.

Since its birth capitalism undoubtedly has developed both as a national system, namely in the advanced part of the world, and as a world-system under the dominance of the latter, preventing national capitalism from developing in other parts. This resulted in contradictions between national integration and trans-nationalization and between the developed, dominant center (or "core" areas) and the "underdeveloped," dependent peripheries of the capitalist world economy. These contradictions explain why socialism cannot unfold directly on the world level and has to fulfill the task of liberating labor from the dominance of capital, i.e., the task of social emancipation. It must also face the consequence of uneven international development, the legacy of capitalism, and the task of national emancipation. Thus, in practice, the process of social emancipation may be interlinked and interacting with the process of national emancipation, making national and social (class) interests that largely interfere with, strengthen or weaken each other.

The first successful proletarian revolution in the industrially underdeveloped Russia in 1917 was explainable in terms of the Marxian theory of scientific socialism only by the uneven development of world capitalism and by Lenin's theory of imperialism referring to the "weakest link" of the chain of the worldwide system of imperialism. Afterwards, an unexpected historical dilemma emerged in practice. Namely: what to do with the proletarian power in a single (though large) country concerning the lack or delay of a world revolution, and the start of socialist transformation of the most advanced countries? Should it be used as a mere means for promoting the latter, by an "export of revolution," or should it be given up and used, instead, for developing industrial capitalism and bourgeois democracy in Russia?

The actual choice made by the leadership was an alternative to both. It was to start socialist transformation and, in a parallel manner, to modernize the country by developing an industrialized national economy. This meant proceeding both in social and national emancipation as far as possible under the conditions of an international environment influenced by politically and ideologically hostile, often militarily threatening and economically dominant capitalist powers. The implementation of this double task has been undertaken in the given international circumstances and on the soil of the local traditions, historical legacy and underdeveloped socio-economic structure. It has rendered some *specific* features to the pattern of development of the Soviet Union, without invalidating the common, universal principles of socialist transformation.

Doubtless achievements of this country were made, at the price of enormous efforts and sacrifice of its people, in industrialization, rural transformation, education and science, employment and public health, culture etc., in a few decades. These achievements induced, besides other effects and circumstances, the ideologists in the early phases of socialist development, particularly in the period from the mid-1930s to the mid-1950s, and first of all Stalin, to promote the idea and justify the practice of political voluntarism and personal cult. Identifying in all details the contemporary Soviet pattern of development with the universal "model" of socialism-building was another result.

In the dogmatic, vulgar-Marxist literature of that period the socialist transformation of the world was perceived as an increase in the number of countries having broken away and becoming isolated from the capitalist world-system. This involved copying in all details the example of the first socialist state and building up a socialist society within a national framework. Their interstate economic cooperation, whether on a bilateral or a multilateral basis such as the Council for Mutual Economic Assistance (CMEA), was supposed to make up a new, "second" world economy and market. This was to be fully independent of and insulated from the capitalist one, saved from the effects of the latter and would establish its own price and monetary system.

The idea of a "breakaway" of the socialist countries from the capitalist world economy was reflecting *ex post facto* what actually happened, rather than predicting and predetermining the practical policy. The motivations and considerations behind it were primarily of a political nature.

Economic isolation was imposed upon these countries rather than voluntarily chosen by themselves. The nationalization of foreign capital ownership was only a part of the process of the general socialization of the main sectors of economy and the means of production (land, factories, banks, etc.), motivated by the socio-political (class) aim to eliminate capitalist ownership, both foreign and national, in the economy. Moreover, in some of these countries, for economic reasons, certain exemptions were made in favor of foreign capital investments at the beginning when concessions were given to foreign companies in some areas of the economy. Apart from the measures to control foreign trade (under the trade monopoly of the state), and the efforts to change its pattern and to increase the trade and cooperation within the community of socialist countries (when such a community with its CMEA has already come into existence), there was no intention to cut or freeze the trade relations with the capitalist part of the world. Even the refusal of the Marshall Plan by the Eastern European countries under socialist transformation after the Second World War and their long, purposeful absence from some international institutions can be explained by political rather than economic considerations, namely by the fear of the political rather than economic dominance of the leading capitalist power.

Theoretically and primarily the "breakaway" concept implied merely the end of homogeneity of the capitalist world-system, the rise of an opposite system in certain parts of the world, without indicating the necessary changes in the nature of economic relations, if any, between the latter and the other parts of the world. Practically, it was the temporary economic isolation of the socialist countries whether following, as primarily, from the necessity imposed upon them by the capitalist powers or, as later, from their own policy of autarchy, and their increased cooperation among themselves, which rendered this concept a certain economic content as well.

It has, of course, always been obvious that a socialist-oriented transformation of society in any country cannot leave its relations with the capitalist world economy unchanged. Necessarily, some conflicts will arise also between the efforts to build a new type of economy according to socialist principles and the capitalist "rules of game" in the world economy.

The very conflict, however, between the socialist transformation in one or a few countries and the capitalist nature of the world economy is but the consequence of the historical paradoxon which manifests itself in the fact that the process of the building up of a new, post-capitalistic social formation, presumed to be a worldwide system of an internationalized society, had to start within a national framework. The answers to the problem of this conflict (and how to solve it) reflect, of course, the various interpretations of both socialism and the world economy.

If socialism is understood as a full antithesis of capitalism in which commodity production, market, "law of value," economic law and incentives, etc., cease to exist, then two possibilities follow. It may be that no economic links with the outside capitalist world are admissible, i.e. a complete isolation and also a radical elimination (such as in Kampuchea under the Pol Pot regime) of the domestic market, commodity production, etc., are needed for the socialism-building countries. Alternately, the world-system as a whole has to change at once, by a world revolution, to a truly socialist system with central planning, allocation and distribution.

If, however, we agree with Marx and interpret socialism as a historical process of transition into a communistic world society, then the actual problem of socialism-building in a single country or a few countries is *how* to reconcile the tasks of such a transition with the existence and effects of a still capitalist world economy. This is contrary to the Marxian expectation from the historical paradoxon mentioned above.

If the world economy is interpreted as a juxtaposition of the otherwise autonomous national economies or the aggregate of their "external economic relations" only, then it may seem possible to accomplish the transition into a communist society. It may have the potential to build up a fully unfolded socialism, or even to construct a communist society, and to reach its final, perfectly developed "stage" within a national framework. Besides the necessary measures of defense and security of the new regime against external military threat and internal political counterforces, that is, besides the strengthening of the state, a necessary condition for the building of socialism is protection and isolation of the domestic processes of the economy from the world market and the narrow limiting of the country's external trade relations.

An institutional isolation of the internal life of the economy (and society) from the outside world is, in a sense, similar to the function of the "ports of trade" in the archaic societies. It promised a solution to the conflict between the development, inside, of a socialist economy and the capitalist nature, outside, of the world economy. Most of the socialist countries institutionalized the separation of the foreign trade sector from the rest of the economy by means of the foreign trade monopoly of the state, specialized state trading corporations, centralized planning and control of export and import, severe foreign exchange regulations, double exchange rates, etc. They thereby prevented the external effects of the capitalist world market from exerting themselves directly on the micro-units of the economy.

Without such an institutional isolation, it undoubtedly would have been much more difficult, perhaps impossible, to carry out in such a short time radical changes in the structure of economy. This would first involve reorienting both investments toward import substitutive basic industries with low rates of return and consumption toward local products of low quality. It would then involve controlling the income distribution system adjusted to new social principles and to the required or planned changes in the production structure. As long as the world market conditions are relatively stable ,or improving, and as long as foreign trade plays a marginal role in the country's economy, this isolation of the internal processes and micro-units from the world economy does not lead to significant negative consequences. This is apart from the risk for the economic leadership to give a direction to the development of productive forces, science, technology and production structure which diverges from the general direction of the world, causing thereby a lag or future conflicts in structural readjustment. The more unfavorable the world market conditions become, however, and the greater the role of foreign trade in the economy (as in the case of the smaller countries and of the heavy import dependence of the technological reconstruction or the energy supply), the more the negative consequences of such an isolation appear. The price of protecting the micro-units (enterprises, cooperatives or even certain branches of the economy) versus the unfavorable world market effects are paid by the economy (and society) as a whole. At the same time, their activity may run and expand just contrary to the required reactions, owing to the negative incentives of protection.

As regards the required limitation of the external trade relations of the countries building socialism, it was, and is still often assumed that, in contrast with the "export-led economy" of capitalism for the socialist economies, the export is merely a necessary means of financing the "absolute" needs of import. Consequently, the external trade relations of the socialist countries with the capitalist world must be kept within the limits that correspond to those of the (individual or collective) self-sufficiency of their economy.

Following thus from the interpretation of the world economy as a juxtaposition of the individual national economies, the concept of socialist development within a national framework was largely associated with a Physiocratist concept of developing a more or less self-sufficient economy. This is an economy in which the export activities are directly subordinated to the import needs determined by the physical inability of the national economy. However, along with the development of productive forces in the socialist economies and the increasing complexity and diversity of their patterns of production, came an undesired excessive growth of an economic bureaucracy of the central planning and management machinery, induced by the latter, and the exhaustion of the internal resources for the "extensive stage of development." In addition there were the increasing difficulties of ensuring balanced sectoral proportions within the given economy, one which was specialized and which developed an organic division of labor, at least among the CMEA countries. All these have led, or are going to lead, to the reappraisal of the role of foreign trade and specialization, and point to the importance of the value relations in foreign trade. They also shed new light on the question of the East-West economic relations, even apart from the political considerations of detente.

The world economy is understood as an integrated system in which the exchange relations and a worldwide division of labor provide the (sufficient) basis of cohesion forces, integrity, and the exploitation by world capital of the dependent countries. If this is true then, of course, the socialist transformation itself can proceed and start only on the world level, or at best in countries which have no exchange relations at all with the capitalist world and do not participate in the international division of labor. This interpretation, again, suggests a total isolation and excludes *ab ovo* the socialist nature of those economies with any organic links to the capitalist part of the world.

The complex system of social relations of production is generally reduced to market relations or to only one important element of the former, namely the division of labor, and thereby fails to distinguish between "world market" and "world economy." This interpretation also neglects the objective tendency and progress of the transnationalization of the productive forces which make the policy of total isolation necessarily fail.

A world economy, as mentioned above, can also be seen as an organic system which is neither homogenous nor fully integrated. Such an economy involves international exchange relations; a division of labor and exploitative relations concerning income distribution among its parts; and social relations of capital ownership and the progressing internationalization or "transnationalization" of the productive forces. All of these characteristics exist without an adequate superstructure, that is, conditions of an institutional pattern based upon separate national states and with heterogeneous moral, cultural, religious, political and legal values, ideas and organizations. If the world economy is conceived of in this way, then the problem of conflict between the national framework of socialist transformation on the one hand and a predominantly still.capitalist world economy on the other is far more complex. This makes reconciliation more difficult and necessarily varying from country to country and from time to time than is assumed either by the "juxtaposition" concept of a homogenous world economy integrated by exchange relations. At the same time, since this conception leaves more room for maneuvers, reconciliation is relatively more feasible as well.

It follows that careful distinctions are to be made between the various forms of international economic relations, types of linkages, dependencies, terms of division of labor, etc., and also according to different phases both in the process of socialist transformation and of the worldwide internationalization of the productive forces. Those socio-political (class) and cultural or other relations crossing the national frontiers that may promote or hinder the socialist transformation within national framework and also in the world as a whole should not be neglected either. No single recipe, valid forever and everywhere, can therefore be elaborated. The only general conclusion which can be drawn is negative. This is that a full integration of the socialist or socialism-oriented countries in the capitalist world economy, under the unaltered, typical terms and conditions of the latter and in all the fields of social relations of production, is irreconcilable with the process of building socialism. Nor can the latter be completely autonomous and fully accomplished even in the case of total isolation.

Several countries in Eastern Europe (except Yugoslavia) began their socialist transformation after the Second World War and under the circumstances of the cold war and the protection of the Soviet Union. These countries attempted or were forced to copy the former practices of the Soviet Union, despite their different internal endowment and local conditions. This meant copying its over-centralized management system, accelerated industrialization and heavy-industry bias, its methods of collectiviza-tion, cultural policy, political machineries, institutions and also the personal cult. In these countries such a policy has resulted in the elimination of obsolete feudo-capitalist regimes and foreign capital domination as well as in profound changes in the structure of economy and society, promoting the process of both national and social emancipation. It has produced also an excessive, artificial acceleration of the latter by means of coercive methods, grave incongruencies between the local conditions and the applied policies, and growing socio-economic tensions, in some cases crises and revolts.

In the period of the cold war the complexity of the process of world transformation toward socialism and, in general, both international and national relations were to a great extent reduced to a simple formula. It was a formula of antagonism between the imperialist states with their local agents, on the one hand, and the socialist states with their natural or potential allies, the anticolonial liberation movements, on the other. This reduction, even if it followed from the historical conditions, did not help the analysis of the contradictory tendencies and mixed phenomena.

Since the cold war also prevented the economic relations between the capitalist "West" and the "communist East" to develop, the breakaway from the capitalist system appeared as an isolation from the capitalist world economy, as the autarchy of the individual national economies concerned or of their community. What followed from this was neglect of the substantial issue, characterizing a long historical period, of how to develop a socialist system in countries which do participate in the world economy, i.e. under the "normal" conditions of international economic relations. Ignored also was a certain over-emphasis on the purely economic performance (besides, and as a background to, the military power) of the group of socialist countries as taken alone, outside the capitalist world economy, and being in a "great competition" with the capitalist countries they tend to "catch up" and surpass economically. This and other circumstances contributed to the birth and temporary prevalence of an economistic and primarily quantitative approach to socialist development.

The famous Twentieth Congress of the Communist Party of the Soviet Union revealed the errors, mistakes and distortions of the former period and has opened a new era. Since Stalin's death the actual progress of socialist transformation has been reassessed more realistically in the Soviet Union and other socialist countries.

This reappraisal has pointed to the shortcomings, unsolved problems, contradictions, difficulties and the need for corrections or reforms, and refers to the still rather early stages of the long historical process of building socialism. The national specificities, historical traditions and local differences are also taken into due account. A great many changes have occurred in practice which follow both from the corrections of the former errors and a further stage of development. Besides the internal reforms and the transition from the stage of an "extensive" to that of an "intensive" development in the Eastern European countries, the experiences of a few nonEuropean countries such as China, Cuba, Vietnam, etc., have also contributed to a more realistic approach to the problem of socialist development in practice.

Besides détente and the more or less normalized economic relations between "East" and "West," the increasing participation of socialist countries in a worldwide division of labor and world market, etc., have made the contradictory interactions and the complexity of the world transformation problematics obvious enough to defeat the over-simplified, dogmatic visions. It has become obvious that socialist development within a national framework or a community of nations is by no means a linear process of economic growth following the elimination of the private ownership over the main means of production. Nor is it a ready-made "recipe" of socialist development that can be taken for granted by the example of the pioneering countries. It has also turned out that no "model" can be applied to the post-colonial development of the third world either, and that decolonization does not necessarily mean independence in making a choice.

The rise of socialist tendencies often originates in anti-colonial national liberation movements of such third world countries as Tanzania that have no national bourgeoisie nor even a sizable industrial working class and labor movement, and are burdened with an underdeveloped colonial economy, and large-scale precapitalist remnants of society. This ascendancy has increased not only the variety of the "roads" of or transitions to socialism, and of the views on them, but also the complexity of the problems to be faced in practice.

The reality of the last two decades has dispelled many of those early illusions and theoretical over-simplifications attached to the concept of "noncapitalist development" in the third world. In the literature of scientific socialism in the 1950s and 1960s, an easy and almost automatic transition from the struggle against colonialism to the struggle for socialism was assumed to be in accordance with the concept of the natural alliance between forces of national liberation and of socialism. The former views on socialism in single countries and on delinking from the capitalist world economy are combined with the anachronistic theses about the avoidance of capitalism in countries having been de facto organic parts of the capitalist world economy for a long time.

The historical experiences of the socialist countries and particularly the effects of the recent world economic crisis on their economy have demonstrated both the possibility of reconciling socialist development with the existence of a capitalist world economy and the limits of this opportunity.

There have been undeniable achievements in the structural transformation of their economy and society, in the fields of industrialization and rural transformation, national planning, educational revolution, science and technology, local research and development facilities. They have also accomplished social security and large-scale welfare services, eliminated pauperism and mass unemployment, reduced the income gap and traditional class differences, and attained a higher level of social mobility. The working masses suffered relatively less harmful consequences of the world economic crisis. These achievements are obvious proof of the relative advantages which may follow for a nation and its working class from a socialist path of development with a relative delinking and a partial isolation. They are also evidence of the actual feasibility of starting and bringing ahead socialist transformation and defending its basic results, within a national framework and under the conditions of a relative delinking.

Similarly undeniable difficulties and contradictions of socialist development in these countries are evident, however, particularly those associated with their recent steps of a certain relinking with the capitalist world economy. The subsequent economic crisis phenomena, sectoral imbalances, supply problems, structural and technological bottlenecks, disturbances in the planning and regulating mechanism, which cannot fully and simply be attributed to internal factors, errors and mistakes. These point to the price of even a relative and temporary delinking, to the limitations of an autonomous socialist development independent of the world economy, and to the need and consequences of a certain relinking with the latter.

The recent experiences of the Soviet Union, other Eastern European socialist countries and China have shed new light on the complexity of issues of socialist development in the context of a single world economy and the international power structure. This is primarily due to their relative relinking with the capitalist world economy, the uneven "normalization" of political relations with the capitalist West, and their increased cooperation with the third world, as well as the impact of the world economic crisis and the ongoing arms race on their development. Three problems arise. The first concerns the possible divergence between national and socialist interests, the possibility of conflicts between socialist states, and the limitations and specific contradictions of socialist development in single countries linked necessarily with the capitalist world economy. The second involves the consequences of the demonstration effect of Western "consumer society" lifestyles and technologies. The last is represented by the problems of specialization and competition in the world economy and the need for a new international economic order, coupled with the impact of the arms race and military burdens.

Along with the above issues, the trimming of state bureaucracy and reforms of the economic management and planning system, are ever-pressing issues. Moreover, the development of socialist democracy necessarily involves reconciliation of individual, group and community interests. At the international level, the need to play a more active role in a democratic reform of the international economic order and in solving the global problems of the world have also come to the fore in the practice of most of the socialist countries.

Summary

As a summary of the above we can say that socialism has to resolve all the contradictions inherent in capitalism. It has not only to develop science and technology further but also to put them under the control of community and make them serve social welfare, the satisfaction of the real human needs of the working masses. It has to liquidate the antagonistic contradiction between labor and capital by changing the social relations of production and by socializing ownership and control over production. It has to promote and carry out a real internationalization, by eliminating first the dominance of certain nations over others, the economic dependence of developing countries, and by ensuring equal opportunities of development and full sovereignty for all nations.

The fulfillment of such and similar tasks requires, of course, a long historical process which, as the transformation of the world, can be described as a liberation or emancipation process. Namely, it requires (a) the liberation of human beings from both the fatalistic domination of nature and the dominance of their own products: technology, wealth, power; (b) the liberation of society from group and class dominance, exploitation and alienation, i.e., social emancipation; (c) the liberation of nations from the dominance of others, i.e., national emancipation; (d) the liberation of the world from the dangers of wars, self-destruction and ecological deterioration.

The liberation of human beings and their societies from the dominance of nature requires an appropriate development and social management of science and technology. The liberation of human beings from their alienated products and of the society from class dominance and exploitation requires fundamental changes in ownership, control and power relations within the societies concerned. The liberation of nations from others' rule requires not only a formal political independence for them but also their economic sovereignty and cultural identity. The liberation of the world from the dangers of destruction requires not only a military power balance and some anti-pollution measures and a global ecological policy, but the elimination of the fundamental causes of international conflicts, of the war business as well as of the fundamental inequalities in the international relations.

It follows from the above that a socialist transformation of society is not an overnight action but a long historical process (with trials and errors, difficulties and roundabouts). It also follows that the process of socialist transformation involves conflicts, and cannot be started and pushed forward without the struggle of those whose social emancipation is on agenda. This explains why the organized labor movement is the basic social force of this transformation.

The process of social emancipation cannot start directly on a world level. This is because of the primarily national framework and internationally unequal pattern of the social class formation. It is also owing to the role of the nation state in the struggle of the socio-political forces—that is, its role in both the protection and elimination of the "status quo," the existing order of social relations.

Capitalism, however, has developed as a particular system of society with the labor-capital antagonism in the individual countries. It has also evolved as a world-system of economy with the dichotomy of a dominant center of economically developed and well-founded national societies and a dependent periphery of economically underdeveloped, disintegrated and unfounded (i.e., nonnational or quasinational) societies. As a result, the world transformation necessarily implies also the process of national emancipation.

On the one hand is the unfolding of capitalism in a national setting, its operation tied to the defense by the institutional system and ideology of the nation state, and the corresponding scene of the class struggle. Organically interrelated, on the other hand, are the exploitation of other nations, the international activity of capital and, consequently, the international scene of the class struggle. In other words, the dialectical contradiction between the antagonistic pair of *national* and *international* ("supranational") is the natural concomitant and law of movement of the worldwide development of capitalism. It manifests itself equally in economic, social, political and other processes.

The national emancipation (just like social emancipation) cannot be reduced to and achieved by the declaration of a formal equality, independence and political rights. Over and beyond a declared and respected (!) political sovereignty it must involve also the objective and subjective conditions, the economic and intellectual basis of a real sovereignty and equality, i.e. economic as well as cultural sovereignty and integrity. Without overcoming "underdevelopment," the developing nations, being in economically subordinated and culturally dominated positions, cannot be internationally emancipated.

The capitalist world economy has developed into an increasingly organic unit. Despite the worldwide interlinkages of the production process in a widening and deepening international division of labor and the growing "internationalization" of science and technology, this development cannot lead to the full absorption, by the world economy, of the national units. Nor can it lead to the disappearance of the national framework of certain economic, social and political processes. The full and real internationalization or "transnationalization" of capital, the transformation of the local production as a whole directly into world commodity production, and the transformation of all commodities into "world commodities" all come up against obstacles.

In addition, the process of the development of the capitalist world economy has hindered the unfolding of integrated national economies in a substantial number of countries in the periphery. Therefore, the local efforts (organized by and implemented with the help of the local "nation-state") to overcome dependent, peripheral capitalism are designed at the same time to create a real, integrated national economy and to gain relative economic independence. They thereby counteract "globalization" even within the capitalist world-system.

Thus, capitalism as a world-system does not mean the worldwide unity of the capitalist social formation. Such an entity would presuppose the complete internationalization of the economic basis, i.e., not only the integration of national markets into an international one and the coalescence of all national divisions of labor into a worldwide division of labor, but also the disappearance of the national affiliation of capital. It would further imply the globalization of the entire superstructure of legal, political and other institutions, of social consciousness, and the formation of a real "world state" designed to protect "world capital" and to ensure the safety of the global production relations of the world-system. Such a "globalization" appears only as a tendency which cannot be fully realized under capitalism.

Socialism is supposed to be a transition to a really worldwide and communal (communistic) society. Capitalism is unable to complete the internationalization, however. It is unable to produce a really transnational world-system, while, on the other hand, it has also prevented the rise or development of the world. It follows, then, that the emerging socialist systems have to face the task of the elimination of the social (class) inequalities and of the great many social, cultural and moral distortions inherited from capitalism. They must also come to grips with the problem of how to reconcile the process of internationalization with national development, the double task of developing the national economy (or even creating such where it cannot arise yet) and at the same time bring about further and more complete internationalization.

Owing to the unequal development of capitalism in the world and also to the multidimensional, complex character of social development, with contradictions between its various (technological, cultural, economic and political) elements, the process of the transformation of the system is also unequal. The transition to socialism in certain spheres may begin along with the further development of capitalism in others. The socialist system may arise, and it actually has in some parts of the world, while capitalism survives or tends merely to unfold in other parts. All these make the world society an increasingly mixed one in which capitalist and socialist elements are contradicting and also influencing each other.

In the process of the socialist transformation of the world, social and national emancipation must go hand in hand, which implies that both social and national forces are acting. They may either reinforce or weaken each other—depending on the actual phase of the transformation process, the interference of external and internal effects and the concrete issues on the agenda.

Chapter 3

USING DEVELOPMENT THEORY TO SOLVE PROBLEMS: AN APPLICATION TO SOUTH AFRICA

Neva Seidman Makgetla[1]

An Analytical Framework for Development Strategies

TRADITIONALLY, economists identify policy-oriented theories with normative approaches, in which they first select desirable social goals, then discuss ways to achieve them. That defines an end-means methodology: to achieve A, do B. It has two drawbacks: it excludes research from discussion of the policy agenda; and it discourages assessment of the analysis that led to particular policy proposals (Makgetla and Seidman, 1989).

By contrast, an analytical methodology rests on the belief that, at least implicitly, powerful theories parallel the procedures of practical policymaking. Each first selects a particular set of

---

[1]For a longer version of this article, see, Makgetla (1988).

social problems, suggests the principle causes, and finally proposes measures to modify or remove them. Frequently, these solutions ultimately reappear in normative guise, becoming the means to a desirable end rather than a solution to social problems. This problem-solving methodology effectively demands that, before adopting a strategy, policymakers explore whether it addresses an appropriate social problem and identifies important causal factors.

In effect, the analytical methodology sees normative goals as the negation of particular social problems. Thus, every economic theory promises higher living standards and freedom. We may interpret them equally, however, as addressing particular technical and social restrictions on consumption and choice. Reformulating these restrictions as problems defines two implicit propositions— that they both affect an important social group and can be alleviated—whose validity depends on both facts and values.

Determining the social problems incorporated in each theory demonstrates the improbability of a durable national consensus around any strategy. Abstract goals may seem beyond reproach: who would quarrel with freedom and prosperity? But virtually every constraint on choice or consumption affects different social groups differently. In South Africa, for instance, different groups suffer from popular unrest, delays in debt-service payments abroad, low profits or rising taxes, widespread poverty and a lack of economic and political rights. In the short term, no government could solve all these difficulties simultaneously, and so must please some at the cost of others.

Generally, normative arguments present the analytical foundation of a strategy solely to justify particular policy proposals. As a result, the analysis remains disjointed and largely implicit, and relies heavily on a restatement of general theory, with little attempt to assess its relevance to the case under consideration. Research aims merely to determine the most effective measures to carry out the strategy. Thus, researchers may discuss ways to eliminate state intervention in the economy or, alternatively, to establish state control of industry, without first exploring whether particular types of state intervention or private ownership actually caused the posited difficulties. If the theory neglects important causes of the difficulties addressed, however, the policy will fail.

In large part, uncritical acceptance of a development strategy follows from the economist's tendency to treat general theory as a compendium of abstract truths. In that case, the main criteria in assessing a theory become its internal consistency and ability to generate sound predictions. Carried to its logical conclusion, this approach permits policymakers to reject a theory only after it gives rise to ineffective measures (Friedman, 1953).[2] By contrast, the methodology proposed here treats general theories as a source, not of general truths, but of tentative explanations for widespread social difficulties.

In short, recasting general theories to discover their problem focus and analysis encourages more systematic evaluation of their relevance in particular situations. The next section therefore considers the problem, explanation and solutions proposed by the three schools studied, in general and in the South African case.

Development Theories in a Problem-Solving Framework

In presenting general theories, this short article must ignore debates within each approach and neglect important caveats. Even in this condensed form, all three schools generate powerful and (usually) falsifiable hypotheses to explain underdevelopment in particular countries. In South Africa, various authorities have presented these propositions in whole or in part. While many do not identify consciously, politically or fully with a particular school, their arguments suggest the impact of the general paradigms.

The Supply Approach[3]
Supply-side theory rests on the fundamental models of neoclassical economics, which claim to apply in all economies. It

---

[2]As McCloskey (1985, p. 8 ff.) points out, and inspection of most introductory economics texts confirms, despite the reluctance of modern economists officially to adopt them, Friedman's views have remained influential.

[3]On supply-side theory in general, see Thomas Swartz et al., 1983. For applications to the Third World, see IMF, 1985; IBRD, 1987, especially Chapter 4; and Berg, 1982.

essentially holds that economic stagnation results from the disempowerment of entrepreneurs to benefit government bureaucrats, workers and the poor. In this view, economic policy becomes a battleground between the imperatives of the market and those social groups dissatisfied with the market outcome. By extension, in South Africa inefficiency resulted from government coercion of entrepreneurial choice, in an attempt to protect and promote the interests of the white minority.

Supply-side Theories in the Third World

For supply-side theory in general, low productivity, which combines with rising demand to generate inflation, forms the central social evil. In the third world, the theory's adherents—many of whom were associated with the International Monetary Fund (IMF) in the 1980s—argue that low productivity appears in stagnant national production per capita and balance-of-payments difficulties.

Supply-side theorists argue that in the long term low productivity affects everyone because it forms the main cause of poverty. In the short term, income inequalities may aggravate the position of the poor, but they represent a necessary reward for efficiency and growth, which will ultimately ensure higher living standards for all. These arguments lead supply-side theorists to reject pressure to equalize incomes. Instead, they endorse "austerity" measures designed to finance investment by reducing living standards for the majority.

To explain low productivity, supply-side theory points to inefficient resource allocation, which results primarily from inappropriate government action. It defines inefficiency in neoclassical terms as a situation where enterprises produce at relatively high cost and/or market supply does not equal market demand—that is, when shortages, oversupply or high prices by international standards prevail. Supply-side theory then argues that, at least in the absence of monopolies, to maximize their profits entrepreneurs must seek to cut costs and meet market demand. In effect, it maintains that, in the absence of government action, virtually all free markets in the real world approach perfect competition sufficiently to ensure efficiency. Inefficiency must therefore result from government interference in entrepreneurial decisionmaking, whether to control resources directly or to constrain individual choice.

In this view, first, when governments divert resources from enterprises they cut into productive investment, both by directing funds toward consumption and by maintaining high wage levels. In the process, they spend extravagantly on social infrastructure, administration and the military, as well as transfers to the poor, funded either by taxation or borrowing. For supply-side adherents, these expenditures do not represent necessary inputs for economic expansion. Governments further undermine investment by maintaining high wages through support for trade unions, minimum-wage laws and high civil-service salaries, which pull up wage rates throughout the economy. The higher wages squeeze profits, and in supply-side eyes only profits can finance investment.

Second, supply-side theory holds that governments cause inefficiency by distorting market signals. In this view, long-run free-market prices must equal the cost of production, including the normal rate of profit required to attract investors. Consumers will then buy a good only when their desire meets or exceeds the social cost of producing it. Consequently, when entrepreneurs produce to meet market demand, they will both cut costs and equilibrate the costs of production with social utility. Third world governments interfere with this balancing act principally through price controls, subsidies and taxes, leading to excessive investment in some sectors, inadequate growth in others. In the name of nonmarket goals such as higher employment or defense, they may also use their power to compel investment in sectors where current market demand and profits remain low.

If the free market will bring about higher productivity, and that will benefit everyone, government intervention in entrepreneurial choice ultimately proves irrational and selfish. In supply-side theory, it reflects the lobbying power of special interests. In particular, the IMF held that third world governments tended to favor urban workers over peasant and informal-sector entrepreneurs.

To support these propositions, supply-side adherents had to demonstrate that interventionist policies caused inefficiency. But many merely demonstrated that the presumed causes co-existed with the predicted result, then argued that their general theory "proved" a causal relationship must exist in every case. For instance, in Zambia the IMF discovered that market shortages coincided with price controls, and argued that low prices discouraged production. In effect, it assumed significant elasticity of supply, an assumption contradicted by statistical analysis (Hassan, 1986).

The supply-side analysis concludes, logically, that third world governments should expand entrepreneurial control of resources by diminishing the power of state agencies. For instance, governments should cut real wages by eliminating price controls and ending support for trade unions. In the short term, supply-side theorists agreed that these policies might aggravate income inequalities and poverty. But over the long term, they argued, by empowering entrepreneurs—the only social group able to raise productivity— supply-side policies would ensure the increase in national output needed to improve living standards for all.

An Application to South Africa

In South Africa in the early 1980s, supply-side theory would underline the coincidence of stagnant productivity and massive government intervention in the market. In this view, apartheid laws and vigorous industrialization policies gave the white minority benefits the free market would disallow. Higher productivity required the elimination of openly racial laws and interventionist measures. But a massive redistribution of wealth would frustrate the market mechanism. To prevent such policies, a weaker central government appeared appropriate.

"Put in a nutshell, the main problem with the South African economy today is that it does not produce enough goods and services" (Truu, 1986:346). Between 1920 and 1975, South Africa's per capita national income grew, on average, some 2 percent a year. In consequence, most neoclassical theorists acclaimed the country's "sustained economic progress" (Kantor and Rees, 1982a:5).[4] After 1976, however, South Africa's economic expansion faltered. Between 1980-85, real GDP per capita fell,

---

[4]O'Dowd (1974) argues that since South Africa's growth rate equalled or exceeded that of most other countries, apartheid could not be labelled inefficient.

on average, 1.5 percent a year (calculated from EIU, 1987:29) and inflation climbed to over 15 percent. A persistent balance-of-payments deficit emerged. Between 1970-85, in dollar terms, foreign debt multiplied six times (Stadler et al., 1986, Figure 1).

Supply-side economists would agree that, "There is still much poverty in South Africa, especially among the African, colored and Asian groups; but if the past rate of growth can be maintained this can be eliminated" (Houghton, 1980:44). It follows that government policy must focus on expanding productivity rather than on alleviating poverty, which is "one of the nasty, brutal facts of life and a problem that can only be overcome by the slow process of economic growth, and ameliorated by welfare benefits and other income transfers" (Kantor and Rees, 1982b:48-9).

In South Africa, supply-side theory would blame low productivity on "the racially institutionalized arrangements and all that flowed from them in terms of wasted resources and an interventionist mentality in major areas of the economy," which led to "rising wages, stagnant productivity, the growing use of scarce capital relative to labor and a deteriorating balance of payments" (Dickman, 1986:59). These policies took the form of apartheid and vigorous support for white-owned industry and agriculture. From this perspective, as usual, these misguided policies arise from workers' efforts to circumvent the dictates of the market.

The apartheid system interfered with entrepreneurial control in two ways. On the one hand, it required heavy government spending on the security forces and bureaucracies to oversee different ethnic groups (Lipton, 1985:247; Leatt et al., 1986:37; BI, 1982:48). To finance its growing deficit, the government held down interest rates and compelled financial institutions to invest in government securities. In the process, it discouraged productive private savings and investment (Kantor, 1982:104-5; Stadler et al., 1986). Furthermore, the regime subsidized housing, transportation, healthcare and some basic foodstuffs for the black population, which in this paradigm "distorts the pricing system" (EIU, 1987:21).

On the other hand, by restricting skilled jobs to whites, apartheid created an artificial shortage and thus higher wages for artisans. The government limited black advancement through discriminatory education, (Kantor and Rees, 1982b:49; BI,

1982:99) restraints on the mobility of black labor and support for white unions (Horwitz, 1967:183; Bromberger, 1974:62; Rupert, 1981:39). In 1980, people of color, who constituted four-fifths of the population, occupied merely a third of managerial, professional and technical positions (calculated from Lipton, 1985, Table 6:382,235-8). A "wages spiral" for skilled (white) workers resulted (BI, 1982:44) which leading businessmen termed "catastrophic" for economic growth (BI, 1982:96-7).

Finally, the civil unrest spawned by apartheid generated economic costs and risks, with an attendant capital flight. Worse still, the future threatened international sanctions and possibly a revolution, which might install a government hostile to private enterprise (Lipton, 1985:253). In the supply-side paradigm, neither would prove conducive to freedom and higher productivity.

Supply-side theorists would consider South Africa's industrialization strategy the other side of its interventionist regime. As in many third world countries, the strategy combined trade and price controls with state financing for basic industry. In supply-side eyes, it aimed above all to protect or create jobs for a privileged urban class—in South Africa's case, for the white minority. To that end, the state channelled resources into activities that displayed low productivity by international standards, and so operated "usually to the detriment of the private sector, [although] occasionally to the advantage of individual companies" (BI, 1982:82).

Regulation of foreign trade and payments sought to channel resources into industry by limiting capital outflows and consumer-goods imports. Import restrictions and tariffs permitted domestic firms to charge as much as 50 percent over the international price (BI, 1982:88). Furthermore, supply-side theorists expect government control to overvalue the local currency compared to the presumed free market rate, thus raising export costs and cutting import prices. Unfortunately, in the mid-1980s analysts disagreed on whether the rand was overvalued (compare Holden, 1985 with Stadler et al., 1986). Finally, the state prevented foreigners from capital export and local borrowing, which much discourage foreign investment according to supply-side theory (BI, 1982:93-4). When the IMF lent the South African regime over a billion dollars in 1982, the only published condition was that the regime relax these measures.

The state also managed industry and white agriculture directly. By the mid-1980s, parastatals (state-owned companies) produced most local armaments, three-fourths of the steel, and much of South Africa's basic chemicals; held shares in many light industries; and ran the utilities and railroads. Their assets climbed from 6 percent of total investment in 1961 to 21 percent in 1981 (BI, 1982:83, 87; Horwitz, 1967:196, 251). In supply-side terms, their dependence on a variety of direct and indirect subsidies, including government credit guarantees, demonstrated their inefficiency (see Horwitz's discussion of ISCOR:252-3). Similarly, for supply-side economics, the direct and indirect subsidies granted white farmers through the inflated prices paid by government marketing boards, credit, low-cost inputs, and extension services permitted inefficiency.

Lastly, through the early 1980s the South African regime controlled the prices of various industrial inputs, transport and basic foods. Supply-side theory indicates that by squeezing profits, price controls ultimately reduced investment in these sectors. For instance, Sentrachem shelved a R630-million ammonia plant because price controls on fertilizers limited its potential profits (BI, 1982:87).

In sum, for supply-side economics, South Africa's economic crisis derives from the limits on the free market. As always, government interventions "appear as if they are wilfully imposed by the prejudiced and selfish behaviour" of a powerful minority (Bromberger, 1974:63)—in this case, whites in general, Afrikaners in particular, and white workers above all. Historically, in this view, these groups used their political strength to create and protect well-paid jobs.[5] Authors in this tradition point to the Rand Revolt, white workers' rebellion against mineowners' attempts to promote black labor (Horwitz, 1967:8; Lipton, 1985:113-6; Nattrass, 1981:73-5).

In the mid-1980s, a number of authors argued that even without racist legislation, white workers would retain high wages

---

[5]Supply-side adherents usually only imply that members of interest groups pressing for unfair advantages must be more or less lazy and dishonorable. Horwitz (1967) expresses the position more openly in his discussion of poor whites, (p. 31 ff.)

because of their near-monopoly on skills. The survival of apartheid then reflects, not immediate economic interests, but the white polity's anxieties about black administrative ability and possible vindictiveness (Lipton, 1985:294).[6]

In short, for supply-side theory the causes of low productivity in South Africa would be clear. In the current situation, in order to benefit white workers, racial laws and interventionist industrialization policies disempower entrepreneurs. Necessarily, inefficiency and poverty ensue.

The supply-side solution for South Africa follows logically. To establish "the sort of socio-economic environment that would best provide the conditions for optimal investment and growth" requires "the complete elimination of segregation at the economic and social level" (Dickman, 1986:58). On the other hand, a massive redistribution of incomes through taxation, social services, stronger trade unions and other measures would raise consumption at the cost of investment, and ultimately impoverish the country (Dickman, 1986:62). In effect, this approach assumes that every rand diverted from the entrepreneur would otherwise finance socially desirable investments (Simkins, 1986:19-20). Redistribution should occur only to head off unrest that would affect economic expansion (van Zyl, 1986; Dickman, 1986; Lipton, 1985:246).

> In another fundamental sense, white supremacy has been good for economic growth . . . . If poor Blacks had a larger influence on government spending and taxing decisions, taxes would be higher and economic growth inhibited . . . . More redistribution would undoubtedly mean lower growth. (Kantor and Kenney, 1982:34)

Supply-side tenets suggest special caution on measures to raise black wages. Any differentials between ethnic groups that lingered after the abolition of racial laws must reflect white workers' monopoly on skills. The state could alleviate them efficiently only by gradually improving black education (Kantor

---

[6]Hill (1974, p. 352) argues that liberals have a "temperamental reluctance" to accept the risks of revolution.

and Rees, 1982b:47; Moore and Smit, 1986:93). At the same time, to limit state expenditures and discourage excessive consumption, it should support social services through measures that would "call forth a corresponding private effort" (Simkins, 1986:19-20; Lombard, 1979:11). For instance, it should let schools set fees, and provide building sites for the poorest rather than housing for all (Simkins, 1986:15-7).

Happily, as the free market equalized incomes, a "broader acceptance of a substantially market-orientated [*sic*] type of economic system" should result (van Zyl, 1986:67). For supply-side theorists, this modest proposal would have the additional attraction of obviating the dangers, coercion and economic risks of revolution (Lipton, 1985:12). They could hope that black South Africans, who "have experienced an unusual degree of governmental coercion" will not "be opposed in principle to the concept of a limited government" (Rees, 1982:36). A federal solution with local authorities to represent different ethnic groups would fit the bill. It would "remove constraints on Black advancement while eliminating or reducing the possibility of the wholesale redistribution of wealth and future wealth that Whites fear most" (Rees, 1982:38; Lombard, 1979:13).

In the early 1980s, as supply-side theory recommends, the South African regime reduced its control of resource allocation in a variety of ways (EIU, 1987:21-2). In the supply-side view, only the halfheartedness of the regime's efforts then explained the continued recession (Dickman, 1986:60).

In short, supply-side solutions follow necessarily from its analysis. If we assume the free market promotes efficiency, apartheid and interventionist industrial policies cause inefficiency. Remedies should only eliminate explicit state intervention in entrepreneurial choice. Redistribution of income or wealth would buy, at best, only a fleeting improvement in living standards; the cost would be falling productivity and national impoverishment.

Basic-Needs Strategies for Development[7]

---

[7]Generally, see Meier, 1984; Leipziger, 1981; papers published by the Carnegie Commission into Poverty in South Africa, 1984.

The basic-needs approach explicitly rejects the supply-side emphasis on inefficiency, focusing instead on poverty. Its adherents normally agree that private entrepreneurship provides the motor for economic growth, but argue that only small, local producers can achieve broadly based expansion. It follows that the disempowerment of small-scale entrepreneurs ultimately causes underdevelopment. By extension, poverty in South Africa results from the manifold oppression of African entrepreneurs, particularly peasants in the bantustans and squatters in the cities.

The Tenets of the Basic-Needs Approach

The basic-needs strategy contends that economic policy in the third world must remedy the inability of the "poorest of the poor"—perhaps 40 percent of the population—to satisfy basic human needs for food, shelter, healthcare and education. That target group comprises poor peasants, informal-sector entrepreneurs and the unemployed, constituting what will be termed here the peripheral sector. In effect, then, basic-needs adherents focus on the poverty of actual or potential small-scale producers.

Basic-needs theorists provide two responses to the supply-side argument that governments should ameliorate poverty solely by encouraging higher productivity. First, given massive income inequalities, higher productivity may benefit the majority little if at all. Second, where, as in the third world, the rich prove inefficient or reluctant to invest in production, redistribution to more dynamic entrepreneurs should enhance efficiency. In this view, the prosperity of the third world's elites arose less out of managerial virtue than out of state support at the cost of the poor.

Basic-needs theory explains the third world's poverty as a function of economic dualism. On the one hand, the modern sector swallows the bulk of investment, but remains capital intensive and import dependent, and fails to provide essentials for production or consumption by the poor. As a result, its expansion generates only a limited domestic multiplier effect, barely stimulating employment. Meanwhile, the small-scale producers of the peripheral sector stagnate for lack of capital. Yet their reliance on domestic inputs and markets, as well as labor-intensive technologies, could ensure integrated and egalitarian growth.

Basic-needs theories ultimately blame this pattern of investment on the profound divergence of third world economies from perfect competition. In contrast to supply-side adherents, they note not only inappropriate government intervention, but also massive income inequalities, high levels of monopolization, factor immobility and the lack of information on investment opportunities in the peripheral sector (Makgetla and Seidman, forthcoming).

Capital intensity and import dependency in the modern sector reflect the excessive prices of labor and local products. This situation arises in large part as modern-sector workers use their disproportionate political and economic clout to secure their jobs and relatively luxurious living standards. To that end, they demand high wages, low fixed prices on agricultural goods, the lion's share of government spending on services and, through the overvalued exchange rate, cheap imports. Moreover, to encourage investment, governments often cut the cost of capital, typically through depreciation allowances.

Furthermore, the dominant private (largely foreign) and parastatal companies and banks enjoy monopoly profits, which reduces the need to risk innovative investment, sales or lending in the periphery. They may even use the government to restrict competition from smaller producers, for instance through licensing laws.

These market imperfections foster two vicious cycles. First, small-scale producers depend on simple, unproductive technologies with profits well below the modern-sector norm. As a result, given the risk-aversion of the modern sector, they can neither generate nor attract the investment needed to introduce more profitable technologies. Second, the huge income inequalities created under colonialism distort market demand. Foreigners and the tiny minority of prosperous urban consumers, who account for the bulk of consumption, reject the simple goods produced in the peripheral sector. In consequence, peripheral producers cannot profitably expand output.

This analysis suggests that to break the vicious cycle of poverty, governments must alleviate market imperfections, if necessary by intervening in entrepreneurial decision-making. Above all, they must eliminate restrictions on peripheral producers and funnel resources to them from the modern sector. On the supply side, this strategy would ensure broader employment and rising productivity. On the demand side, more equal incomes would expand the market for simple local goods. At least initially, however, it would divert resources from the politically powerful businesses and workers of the modern sector. In consequence, while most third world states adopted it in name, in practice they merely support local modern-sector businessmen against foreigners and provided a little credit and market for the peasantry.

An Application to South Africa

In South Africa, the basic-needs approach explains the extreme poverty of the majority as the consequence, above all, of the past and present oppression of black producers. If these entrepreneurs had equal access to productive assets, they would raise productivity and employment while improving living standards for the very poor.

Despite fairly high productivity, poverty ground on in South Africa. In 1985, only forty-nine countries reported higher per capita output, but seventy-two boasted lower infant mortality rates, and eighty-one had longer life expectancies (calculated from IBRD, 1987:203, 258). Falling black incomes (Keenan and Sarak, 1987:108-9) and rising unemployment (Bromberger, 1984:3-4) affected living conditions disastrously, although "basic needs deficiencies are probably far greater among some groups than others" (Tollman, 1984:11). In 1980, life expectancy for Africans came to around fifty-five years, compared to seventy years for whites (EIU, 1987:10). In the mid-1980s in Soweto, half the children studied showed signs of stunted growth because of malnutrition; a fifth displayed wasting. Tuberculosis caused 6 percent of African deaths (Keenan and Sarak, 1987:114-117; Ndaba, 1984).

Basic-needs theories look for the lowest living standards in the rural areas (Tollman, 1984:6). In the early 1980s, about half of bantustan households earned incomes below the minimum needed for health (Keenan and Sarak, 1987:110; Ndaba, 1984:8). In 1970, when the country was divided into 275 administrative districts, per capita income in the richest thirty districts surpassed R1000, over ten times that in the poorest thirty (Nattrass, 1981: 182). On a smaller scale, the gap between urban and rural Africans parallelled that between whites and blacks. Africans in the cities earned, on average, eight times as much as those in the countryside (Nattrass, 1981:288). Similarly, between 1960 and 1975, while the average annual wages of African farmworkers rose almost 10 percent a year to reach something under R300, income for subsistence farmers grew not at all (Nattrass, 1981:125).

In terms of the basic-needs approach, in South Africa, an "inescapable fact about rural distress and deprivation is that it is, at bottom, an outcome of urban-rural conflict" (Nassim, 1984:30). The state supported large-scale, capital-intensive growth in the modern sector, which whites dominated, at the cost of small-scale black producers.   Meanwhile, giant local and foreign firms discriminated against smaller entrepreneurs, preferring import-dependent, capital-intensive production processes (Nattrass, 1981:31).

For basic-needs adherents, South Africa presented a classic dual economy, with modern activities in the white areas and primitive technologies and living standards in those territories left to Africans—the bantustans, townships and squatter compounds. As a result, in the countryside, moving from a white to a black area was "almost like stepping through a time warp" (Nattrass, 1981:99). The dominant urban areas around the Witwatersrand, Durban and the Cape absorbed three quarters of all manufacturing plant and bank deposits. Meanwhile, the bantustans, which officially housed two-thirds of the population, accounted for under a twentieth of national output (Nattrass, 1981:29).

As a result of the rising capital intensity (Bell and Padayachee, 1984:12, Table 2; Nattrass, 1981:167) and continued import dependence of the modern sector, (Black and Stanwix, 1986:5,22) its rapid expansion in investment and production excluded many South Africans. By contrast, black entrepreneurs employed mostly local inputs and labor-intensive technologies, but their output stagnated.   Between 1936 and 1975, the cereal production of the bantustans remained virtually unchanged, although their population trebled. By the 1970s, they had become net importers of food (Nattrass, 1981:112-3).

In basic-needs eyes, small-scale business did not stagnate because of some inherent inefficiency. Rather, urged on by a white electorate, the state intervened to protect the modern sector from competition and maintain its supplies of cheap labor. To that end, it suppressed black farmers and urban entrepreneurs.

Limiting African agriculture to the bantustans, which comprised less than a seventh of the national territory, efficiently prevented its expansion. Moreover, black farmers faced discrimination by credit, marketing and extension services, both public and private (Leatt et al., 1986:27). In these conditions, enterprising blacks preferred to work for white employers in the urban areas, further reducing agricultural productivity. By 1970, over a quarter of the black labor force worked as migrants in the urban areas. Since their families continued some subsistence farming in the countryside, modern-sector employers could pay lower wages. Thus, the impoverished rural areas "actually subsidized the labor costs in the growing urban areas" (Nattrass, 1981:66).

The apartheid system generated a classic poverty cycle, since "rural family incomes are too small . . . to finance investment" (Nattrass, 1981:116). In KwaZulu, between 1936 and 1970, investment in cultivators rose 2.5 percent a year; in ploughs, under 1 percent a year; in cattle, not at all. Meanwhile, investment in education, seen as the route to good urban jobs, climbed 6 percent a year (Nattrass, 1981:117). Moreover, the lack of social and economic infrastructure in black areas "makes it virtually impossible for private [modern-sector] enterprise to locate any new investment profitably in these areas" (Nattrass, 1981:96).

To prevent black entrepreneurs from competing with established modern-sector producers in the towns, the state barred their operations from city centers and most industrial sites. It also imposed strict licensing regulations on a number of activities, notably retail trade and brewing, and restricted black access to education (Leatt et al., 1986:28).

Finally, the South African regime aggravated the position of the poor by neglecting to provide adequate services to the black population. Even during the economic boom after World War II, the proportionate contribution of services to personal income fell (Simkins, 1984:30). In the bantustans, the regime left services to local authorities that were usually corrupt and invariably underfinanced. In the mid-1980s, health services in most bantustan regions "collapsed" (Keenan and Sarak, 1987:114). Moreover, the state provided virtually no infrastructure for urban squatters, perhaps a tenth of the African population.

These measures combined to skew the pattern of demand in South Africa, reinforcing the imbalance in production structure.

The high-income white group demanded comparative luxuries that required imported inputs and capital-intensive technologies. The low-income black population used simpler goods; but their incomes remained artificially depressed, unable to generate significant market demand (Black and Stanwix, 1986:20-1,56-7).

Turning to the modern sector, the basic-needs analysis suggests that both workers and employers benefited from the persistence of inappropriate production structures. On the one hand, the modern sector remained subject to huge local and transnational corporations and banks, whose monopoly position permitted them to discriminate against black entrepreneurs (Nattrass, 1981:187). They favored technologies developed abroad, where labor proves expensive relative to capital, (Nattrass, 1981:86) and lobbied for measures to reduce the price of capital relative to labor (Black and Stanwix, 1986:22-4). From the 1970s, faced with rising black unrest, they sought purposefully to replace black workers with machines (Black and Stanwix, 1986; Nattrass, 1981:109). On the other hand, white workers used their political power to encourage the development of capital-intensive sectors, where higher productivity permitted higher wages. By 1975, unambiguously capital-intensive industries employed almost two-fifths of white workers in manufacturing; labor-intensive sectors, a mere seventh. State support for projects that employed whites thus fostered capital-intensive industries (Levy, 1981:14-5).

Basic-needs adherents would add that the privileges of the modern sector extend to its black employees, who enjoy comparatively greater skills, incomes and trade union rights. As a result, their interests may clash with those of the rural majority. In these conditions, the analysis suggests, black unions themselves may become "an agent fostering the division between the urban and rural areas of South Africa" (Nattrass, 1981:291-2).

In sum, the basic-needs approach suggests that poverty and unemployment in South Africa resulted from the unequal distribution of wealth between the modern (white-dominated) sector and its periphery of urban squatters and bantustan peasants. In turn, these disparities reflected, above all, the deliberate impoverishment of black entrepreneurs. In short, "if the social and political system had not possessed discriminatory features, a far larger group of prosperous black capitalists would have emerged" (Leatt et al., 1986:28), and brought about more egalitarian growth.

Since basic-needs theories blame both poverty and slow growth primarily on the skewed distribution of income and wealth, the principal solution becomes enhanced economic equality. In this view, "some measure of redistribution...will be a prerequisite for the creation of an equal opportunity society in South Africa" (Nattrass, 1981:303; Black and Stanwix, 1986:44-5). Redistribution could restructure demand so as to "provide new avenues for expansion that are less demanding in terms of imports and capital than existing strategies" (Black and Stanwix, 1986:57). Moreover, only greater equality can "induce black South Africans to desire the perpetuation of a 'free-enterprise' economic system" (McGrath, 1982:59).

On the other hand, the basic-needs approach would seek to eliminate, not the market itself, but rather market imperfections.

> As experience all over the world has shown, the "market process" is essential for the proper and effective functioning of a sophisticated economy. This, however, does not imply unbridled market freedom or the lack of state intervention. (Thomas, 1986a:104)

In sum, the preferred option for South Africa, in basic-needs eyes, would be "reform capitalism (which may initially be introduced in the guise of either capitalism or socialism)," that would seek "to plot a course . . . between the Scylla of dictatorship and the Charybdis of revolution" (Nattrass, 1981:307-8).

To carry out redistribution, the state should improve social services, infrastructure, marketing and credit in historically black areas, both through its own agencies and by putting pressure on private institutions. In particular, "only a massive effort to develop black rural areas and extend their resource base could generate higher real income for the poorest among the Southern [sic] African population" (Levy, 1981:17). Rural development policies could relieve the pressure on squatter areas by encouraging (if unavoidable, perhaps compelling) the urban unemployed to return to self-supporting farming. While this strategy requires some kind of land reform, most basic-needs adherents would favor expropriating only underutilized white-owned land.

In addition, some basic-needs adherents call for reforms of modern-sector enterprise, to ensure that it takes a "community-oriented view," rather than looking solely toward "the generation of short-term profit" (Nattrass, 1987:189-90). To that end, the state might encourage greater worker and community participation in management committees, decentralize parastatal decision-making and regulate transnational corporate investment (Nattrass, 1987:189-90; Thomas, 1986a:104).

In 1979, moved by arguments in the basic-needs tradition, the Rembrandt group and the Volkskas bank established the Small Business Development Corporation to assist small-scale entrepreneurs "in all population groups" (Rupert, 1981:99). In its first year, it granted R250 million to twenty-five small-scale businesses and assisted "in legalizing the informal business sector in Soweto" (Rupert, 1981:100). After 1979, the regime helped raise the corporation's capital to R1000 million. Nonetheless, most basic-needs theorists hold that only a more democratic state structure could compel a significant redistribution of wealth (Black and Stanwix, 1986:45).

In sum, where supply-side theory would argue that active equalization of income and wealth must harm investment, basic-needs theorists suggest that South Africa's inequities cause both hardship and stagnation. In this view, restructuring economic control to empower small-scale entrepreneurs will permit the market system to bring about balanced, equitable growth. But only a more democratic state could support such policies.

The Socialist Analysis[8]

Since socialist theories arose to explain the difficulties facing industrialized capitalist countries, deriving useful propositions for the third world evoked modification and debate. In contrast to basic-needs and supply-side paradigms, the theory focused on a problem—the disempowerment of the majority of the population—that had noneconomic aspects. It identified as root causes, not impairment of an ideal market, but rather ability of a tiny

---

[8]See, generally, Marx, 1967, 1978a and 1978b. On socialist development theory, see, among others, Baran, 1957; Seidman, 1985, 1980 and 1974; Szentes, 1971.

minority, whose power flowed largely from the nature of management, the market and the state, to control social resources in their own interests.   In South Africa, then, socialists explained the economic and political oppression of the majority by examining the range of social institutions that gave tremendous power to a minority of capitalists in the state and private sector.

For Marx, alienation, in the sense of individual powerlessness and isolation, constituted the central social evil.   In capitalist economies, he argued it affected wage workers through low wages, inability to control working conditions, and the lack of political power.   In the third world, most socialists stress the poverty and political powerlessness of the majority.   Peasant and informal producers enjoy greater control than wage workers over what and how they produce, but remain subject to the vagaries of climate and the market.   And even where democracy exists formally, neither workers nor peasants really shape government decisions.

By focusing on the poorest of the poor, basic-needs adherents imply that, to some extent, everyone in the modern sector benefits from the *status quo*.   By contrast, socialists argue that compared to the rich ruling class, wage workers suffer an unacceptable living standard.   Thus, even if profits prove low and urbanites more prosperous than peasants, socialists consider wages inadequate.

Marx explains alienation as the result of the control—not legal ownership alone—that a minority of the population, whether private managers or government bureaucrats, exercises over the bulk of productive resources.   This minority constitutes the capitalist class.   In the enterprise, management dictates the product, conditions of work and employment of surpluses. At the national level, resource allocation accords with the interests of the wealthy, not with social needs.   Finally, as profit becomes the principal motive for economic activity, workers and employers, consumers and producers lose all human empathy for each other, and deep social conflicts emerge.

Socialists conclude that the market does not protect freedom; rather, it reduces the power of society to allocate resources rationally and collectively. Above all, it imposes a ceiling on wages. Where workers organize and insist on higher pay, employers go bankrupt or replace workers with capital or cheaper labor, often from abroad. Furthermore, where supply-side and basic-needs adherents suggest the state can establish flexible, competitive markets, the socialist paradigm assumes monopolized, rigid and speculative markets, where shifts in supply or demand cause large-scale unemployment.

For Marx, various related factors explain the persistence of minority control over resources. First and foremost, the state protects managerial control, notably through property laws. Furthermore, capitalists decide which technological advances to pursue. They encourage production methods that permit, indeed require, centralized control by a few skilled managers and technicians. Finally, the market's apparent implacability combines with conservative ideologies cultivated by the ruling class to blind most people to the possibility of more rational and humane economic systems.

In the third world, most socialists focus on the structure, rather than the process, of production. Like the basic-needs school, they blame poverty on the disarticulation and dependency of third world economies. But they suggest that the colonial state disrupted precolonial societies less to suppress competition than to generate cheap labor. In this view, by devastating peripheral incomes, colonial regimes enhanced the attractions of producing cheap cash crops for foreign trading firms or working at low wages for foreign-owned enterprise.

Socialists hold that given the small size of most third world economies, a handful of interlinked private and state-owned firms necessarily controls industry and finance. Except in rare revolutionary situations, that economic power ensures political dominance. To hold down wages, the top companies influence the state to suppress both workers' organizations and development in the peripheral sector. As a rule, they remain closely associated with foreign interests, which foster external dependency and extract capital through profit repatriation and, increasingly, payments on loans.

For socialists, monopoly power in the modern sector rules out investment in peasant or informal-sector enterprise. Thus, they contradict the basic-needs view that small-scale production is inherently profitable and dynamic. In their view, large-scale enterprises cannot control small-scale producers technologically, and so avoid them. Furthermore, many socialists assume that modern technologies require fairly large-scale operations. In that case, injecting capital into the periphery would merely enable a few producers to expand and join the modern sector. The majority would lose their land or markets, and become still more impoverished.

The only solution becomes the transformation of economic and political institutions to permit national or community control. As a first step, state institutions must be transformed to empower the majority. (That, of course, is easier said than done.) The newly democratic state can then guide investment to provide essential productive inputs and basic consumer goods, and markets for smaller producers. While these projects may not themselves return great profits in the short term, they should stimulate productivity and employment, and raise living standards and investment on the national level.

Given their limited skills and funding, however, third world states can attain operational control of only a few industries. They should therefore concentrate on those sectors, sometimes called "commanding heights," that help define the overall structure of production and investment: finance, domestic and international wholesale trade, and basic industries. In other sectors, for instance primary-goods exporters, the state may encourage workers' ownership or retain private management, demanding only a larger share of profits. In the peripheral sector, producer cooperatives could adopt modern technologies without aggravating inequality.

These policies require that a significant group of people act to transform society because of ideals, not personal profit. In effect, socialists expect a politically motivated cadre to play the dynamizing role that basic-needs and supply-side adherents assign private entrepreneurs.

An Application to South Africa

In South Africa, socialists argue, poverty and powerlessness afflict the black majority. They trace these evils to the way in which a minority in the state and private sectors controls the bulk of the country's resources. The ruling class maintains its power by fostering unity among whites and disunity among the working majority, and exercising force on a large scale. Effective solutions, then, must not only redistribute wealth, but also transform both

political and economic institutions to ensure democratic control
of major social decisions.

For South African socialists, poverty reflected the failure to
earn what the Congress of South African Trade Unions (COSATU)
termed a "living wage" of about R850 a month—enough to
"provide for certain comforts and amenities of life, not mere
survival" (LRS, 1987b:124; Jack, 1987).[9] Most South Africans
suffered not only poverty, but also severe restrictions on where and
how they could live, work, go to school or relax, and on political
and social associations. These restrictions gave birth to the
migrant-labor system, the most vivid example of employers' use of
political and economic force to control workers (Motlatsi,
1987:44). According to COSATU's Executive Committee,

> The problems facing us at work and in our communi-
> ties are the same. Nowhere do we have control over
> the decisions that affect our lives: the rent we are
> forced to pay; high transport costs; terrible conditions
> in the townships. These are issues directly related to
> the starvation wages workers are paid (1987:52).

South African socialists stressed the interaction between unemployment, rural poverty and low wages. Since the employed
had to support unemployed family members in the cities and rural
areas, rising urban unemployment and falling real wages slashed
living standards for all (Keenan and Sarak, 1987:110). Thus,
where basic-needs theorists typically saw a potential conflict
between urban workers and the rural poor, socialists pointed up
their shared interests (COSATU Executive, 1987:53).

Socialists note, with COSATU's executive, that women in
South Africa "carry the heaviest load of all." COSATU (1987:53)
adds, "If our liberation does not succeed in creating free people,
equal to each other in every way, then we would not be liberated."

Socialist theory suggests that given South Africa's colonial
background, the state's responses to the needs of capital created
the apartheid system and basic industry. On this foundation, a

---

[9]The Labour Research Service (1987b) cites Lloyd George, writing
in *The Beehive* in 1874, to argue that workers should earn "not a miserable
allowance to starve on, but living wages."

partnership of local private and state capital and transnational corporations and banks arose to dominate the economy. To protect its economic and political power, it effectively bought the support of most whites and a fraction of blacks, and used outright violence.

South African socialists take issue with the supply-side hypothesis that the economy produced too little to provide acceptable living standards for all (Motlatsi, 1987:41; COSATU Executive, 1987:82). Rather, the nation's riches were misallocated to produce comparative luxuries for well-off whites and for export, and to finance capital outflows and apartheid. In 1987, when over half of South Africa's population belonged to households earning under R100 a week, the average salaries for directors of Anglo-American, the country's leading conglomerate, averaged R6410 a week (LRS, 1987a).

Socialists hold that state intervention in the economy ultimately benefited most capitalists by enhancing their profits and protecting their control over production (Naidoo, 1987:33). Thus, while the "institution of migrant labor and compounds was a pattern of labor relations which neither the mineowners nor the workers chose," it functioned to enhance the power and profits of employers at the cost of workers (Turrell, 1982:67-8). Moreover, interventionist industrialization policies ultimately benefited— indeed, to a large extent created—modern South African capital. While those policies reduced the profits of some investors in the short term, they permitted growth and prosperity for local white entrepreneurs. Ultimately, too, foreign investors profited enormously in South Africa, where they located the lion's share of their investments in sub-Saharan Africa.

Socialists contend that the small size of South Africa's markets permitted only a handful of firms to survive in each sector. In contrast to supply-side and basic-needs perceptions, then, they suggest that in South Africa the market inevitably concentrated economic power, ensuring highly unequal incomes and power relationships as well as inappropriate investment patterns. In the early 1980s, a coalition of local conglomerates, foreign investors and parastatal management controlled the bulk of productive assets in South Africa. Six conglomerates controlled almost three-fourths of the assets of all listed companies, and the single most important, Anglo-American, also owned one of the country's three largest banks. According to James Motlatsi, the president of the National Union of Mineworkers (NUM),

> Put simply, monopoly capitalism . . . has put the owner-ship and control of the wealth of this country in the hands of a few giant companies. It is this class, which controls the resources, that refuses to invest the mil-lions they have made in profit so that jobs can be created, and [to] improve the quality of life (NUM, 1987:41-2).

The main threat to freedom for the majority thus became, not the intrusive state, but economic power exercised on the shop floor, on the market and in politics. The state threatened the freedom of the majority, not only when it denied them the vote, but also when it protected entrepreneurial power, shutting workers out of crucial economic decisions (Motlatsi, 1987:42). The regime's moves toward privatization appear "as nothing more than the legalization of even greater exploitation of the poor . . ." (Adler, 1986:86).

Finally, socialist theory suggests that to maintain a system so inimical to the well-being of the majority required their political disempowerment. Repressive measures rested on three pillars: the unity of the white population, the comparative disunity of the black and working class population, and the regime's access to modern military equipment.

For decades, to maintain cohesion among whites, the state and employers subsidized their living standards and isolated them from blacks. By the same token, they did all they could to split up the black population on the basis of ethnic differences. These conditions made possible the disenfranchisement of the black majority. From this standpoint, the Rand Revolt no longer appears as evidence that white workers imposed apartheid. Rather, it reflects the way the mining houses structured the choices facing labor, both black and white. The remediable causes of black oppression become, not white workers' inhumane reaction to the capitalist system, but that conflict-ridden and dehumanizing system itself (Simons, 1983: Chapter 10). In this view, whatever the immediate motives of the actors, the revolt fostered a compromise crucial to the maintenance of apartheid:

capitalists paid white workers higher wages, and white workers provided the political and military force needed to counter black aspirations (Marks and Rathbone, 1982:6).

As black militance grew, despite the regime's best efforts, explicit repression went hand in hand with moves to divide the black population. On the one hand, by the 1970s, "an immense and all-pervading security system" became "an essential part and necessary buttress" of apartheid (Muad, 1974:322). But only the coherence of the white community and the sophisticated transport, telecommunications and other equipment provided by Western transnational corporations ensured the state's military might. On the other hand, moves to strengthen the bantustan administration and small-scale entrepreneurs reflected the hopes of "government and big business" for a "black middle class which will see capitalism as the best solution for South Africa" (Hofmeyr and Nicol, 1987:84).

With growing black resistance, white unity came under strain. But socialist theory suggests that unless an increasingly united and militant black resistance imposes greater costs on whites, various factors foster continued white coherence. First, important sectors—mining, agriculture, and small-scale trade and manu-facturing—needed cheap labor to turn a normal profit. Further-more, racism permeated all aspects of society, preventing many whites from accepting change (Muad, 1974:297-8; Welsh, 1974:273 ff.). Finally, as the harsh treatment of unions in the mid-1980s showed, the dominant capital groups' advocacy of reforms to stave off revolution remained halfhearted. After all, they benefited im-mediately from low wages, while any convincing reform would have involved the great expense of establishing a significant black bour-geoisie. Besides, South African capitalists knew that by raising expectations, reforms might have precipitated, not frustrated, a revolution.[10]

The socialist perspective implies that only the eradication of control over the economy by a limited group of large-scale capitalists, whether in the private or state sector, can eliminate all the ill-effects of apartheid and dualism. Motlatsi asserts his "firm

---

[10]This becomes clear from examination of country risk reports by major American banks; and from Brand (1986) and Dickman (1986).

belief" that when "the South African working class take control of their lives at all levels, we will be able to solve the problems facing this country of ours" (Motlatsi, 1987:39). But the socialist analysis also suggests that in key industries, small-scale production cannot provide the democratic alternative. To run large-scale enterprises, then, their solution becomes the establishment of democratic political, planning and managerial systems.

As a first step, socialists call for black and working-class unity. The NUM asserts that "The unity of mineworkers in particular and workers in general as part of the working class is of paramount importance" (NUM Congress, 1987:47-8; COSATU Executive, 1987:79 ff.) Popular unity should permit the extension of community control over political and economic processes in defiance of repressive laws, and ultimately the overthrow of the minority regime. COSATU and the UDF called for the formation of street committees in the black townships to fight for "control over every aspect of our lives through our own democratic organization under the leadership of organized workers" (COSATU Executive, 1987:52). Similarly, the NUM called for workers committees to run the mines hostels and defense committees to protect union members. According to Motlatsi,

> . . . we wish to control our lives on every front. To start
> this process is to lay the foundations of a new order. It
> is a task we cannot postpone. Because the kind of
> society we want to build, we must build today and not
> tomorrow or on liberation day. As one great teacher of
> the struggle put it: "The birth of a new society must be
> laid in the womb of the old" (Motlatsi, 1987:44).

In addition, as a basis for establishing democratic institutions, socialists argue the need to study and discuss how the existing structures of economic and political control disempower the majority. COSATU aimed "to understand how the economy of the country affects workers and to formulate clear policies as to how the economy would be restructured in the interests of the working class" (COSATU Executive, 1987:79). [11]

---

[11]The COSATU Executive (1987) also resolved to "fight to open the books of every organised company so that workers can see exactly how the

In the long term, to redirect investment to overcome dualism and external dependence, socialists call for democratic state control of modern financial institutions and industries. Only the transformation of management could ensure that national goals, not profitability, guide investment; merely transferring legal title to black entrepreneurs or even the government would not suffice. Thus, true social control requires, first, central planning of resource allocation according to social need and, second, "transformations in the organization of management and labor processes which permit direct producers to assume increasing control over decisions at enterprise level . . ." (Davies, 1987:94). The present scale of modern industry, however, rules out a perfectly egalitarian society. In particular, a tension arises between the push for worker control of management and the need for centralized investment decisions to initiate structural change (Davies, 1987:94).

Despite the economic and social risks, in view of the present suffering of the majority, socialists urge radical change.

> Under capitalism we will never find a solution to our problems. It is only with a democratic socialist South Africa that the working class and all the oppressed people will have the wealth which they produce under their control (Motlatsi, 1987:47).

Conclusion

Reframing development strategies in terms of a problem-solving methodology provides insight into their perspective, and opens the door for research to test their applicability and viability for particular countries. The theories disagree fundamentally about what problems policymakers should address, and what social relationships they can change.

---

wealth they have produced is being wasted and misused by the employers' profit system, and on that basis can demand their full share of the wealth they have produced. Should the wealth not be there, then it will only prove the inefficiency of employer management and strengthen the case for worker control and management of production." (p. 82)

In South Africa, what strategies appear appropriate to eliminate apartheid depend largely on which group's difficulties form the focus of analysis. Given the concern of supply-side economics with efficiency, apartheid represents only one cause of economic problems; and a revolution might prove even more debilitating. In terms of the basic-needs approach, the poverty of the bantustans and shantytowns calls for resolution through redistribution of income and productive assets by a more democratic state. An evolutionary procedure remains conceivable, however; and once the state established greater equity, it should let the free market rule the economy. Finally, socialists concentrate on the powerlessness of the majority, not only in the sense of poverty but also in terms of their position in production and political processes. That approach requires substantial changes in both political and economic decisionmaking structures.

Even where they agree about specific facts, then, these three schools arrive at very different analyses. In consequence, each would eliminate apartheid through a unique reallocation of social and economic power. In every other African country, they would similarly point to very different problems and explanatory propositions, and so propose widely divergent policies.

PART TWO

National Economies and Regional Development

Chapter 4

SOUTHERN AFRICA IN THE WORLD-ECONOMY, 1870-2000: STRATEGIC PROBLEMS IN WORLD-HISTORICAL PERSPECTIVE

William G. Martin and Immanuel Wallerstein

THERE can be little question of the importance of strategic issues for the peoples of southern Africa. Over the last twenty-five years the area has been racked by war. From the very moment when the southward sweep of African liberation reached the advance bastion of southern Africa, Katanga, in the Congo in July 1960, one or another part of the area has been embroiled in military struggles engaging local and extracontinental forces. Even the decolonization of Angola and Mozambique in 1975 and of Zimbabwe in 1980 failed to usher in a period of peace. Indeed, as the struggle for majority rule in South Africa escalated, and the halls of power in Pretoria became more encircled, Pretoria has organized ever-intensifying campaigns against neighboring states. The result was that interstate conflict came to be at its highest pitch ever, forestalling in the process hopes for economic improvements.

If we examine the battle for southern Africa in the post-1945 period, three distinguishing features emerge. First, the level of military and political conflict is exceptional for areas located outside the direct orbit of East-West struggles. Secondly, conflict has increasingly exhibited a transnational character, with national struggles being embedded within, or quickly engaging, regional forces and actors. Finally, as demonstrated by the forces arrayed against colonialism in the near past and majority rule in the present, Western powers have acted from the premise that local conflicts placed at risk broader regional interests. Any one of these three elements would by itself be notable. Together they offer us a composite that raises serious questions about the underlying, structural foundations of conflict in southern Africa. Why should the struggle for national liberation be so long and intense? Why have nationally contained conflicts turned out to embroil regional and world powers? And in the context of the present and near future, what are the options for different actors, given these historical patterns?

Detailed analyses of contemporary events and actors alone cannot answer these questions. We need to grasp in addition the structural conditions that underpin strategic actions, both those features that are of a long-term or enduring nature and those that are subject to change over the short- or medium-term. This leads, in turn, to a recasting of the commonplace notions of "security" and "development." If these latter concepts are to be useful, they need to be placed within the historical construction and operation of the capitalist world-economy, wherein true "development" may be defined as a struggle against the polarizing tendencies of the world-economy and the issues of "security" refer to the continuous struggle between systemic and antisystemic forces in the world-system. In order to analyze the full import of this it is necessary to grasp clearly the changing position of southern Africa within the capitalist world-economy. It is therefore useful to look at the impact of the emergence of southern Africa as a "region" has had on the trajectory of conflict and then the role of changes in the balance of forces at the level of the interstate system, including the role of antisystemic movements heretofore and their possibilities in the near future.

The stakes in the current struggle for southern Africa are high. This in itself is nothing new. From at least the turn of the century, when Britain committed a half million troops in its effort to control the area, southern Africa has engaged the attention of a worldwide cast of actors. The reasons adduced for such attention at the turn of the century match those most often proposed today, namely the value of the area's strategic resources and the existence of settler political power. With both these elements coalescing in South Africa, we are told, it is hardly surprising the level and forces currently at contest are of such depth and intensity.

While factually correct, such explanations actually tell us very little more than that the South African regime is powerful and controls considerable resources. This does not necessarily explain, for example, why struggles in the economically marginal regions far beyond South Africa's boundaries necessarily engage South Africa, independent African states, and world powers. Clearly part of the answer rests on the ability of South Africa to extend its military and economic might throughout the region. One still must ask why this so readily occurs. And even more important is the origins of this pattern: its construction, its enduring and changeable features, and its present and future trajectory.

In the opening decades of the twentieth century, there was little doubt as to the role of southern Africa in the capitalist world-economy's axial division of labor and interstate system. Incorporated into the world-economy under the aegis of British hegemony, the area as a whole rapidly became a classic peripheral area, specializing in the export of minerals and agricultural products. Processes of class and state formation moved in concert with this trend; even the creation of settler polities in South Africa and Zimbabwe was designed so as to ensure the unimpeded, transterritorial flow of labor, commodities, and capital befitting full and open participation in the global division of labor. If South Africa was the richest prize in this network, it was nevertheless clear that the possibilities of capital accumulation in South Africa, as in neighboring territories, rested upon ever-deepening linkages with core areas of the world-economy.

Local political struggles and transformations in the world-economy as a whole in the interwar period shook up this pattern and began to alter southern Africa's role in the world-economy. The motor of these alterations was the class and national struggles that broke out in South Africa during and immediately after the First World War. Afrikaner nationalists seized the chance, and by using the nascent powers of South African state, inaugurated a process by means of which South African production processes were to be inserted in a new position in the commodity chains of the global division of labor. This process entailed a series of measures designed to alter the relational networks, binding South African economic activity to core areas, ranging from the first protectionist tariff (1925) through the promotion of core-like production (as in the establishment of one of the very first modern steel plants outside Europe and North America) to the diversification of technological sourcing among competing core suppliers. At the same time, and largely unnoticed, South African capital and the state sought to demarcate local processes of accumulation from those of surrounding peripheral areas. Imports of competing raw materials and other inputs were restricted (e.g., cattle from Botswana; Rhodesian tobacco; Mozambican sugar, cement, and labor), even while the new products of South Africa's emerging industrial sector retained access to surrounding markets.

As is readily apparent, this was not a program of autarky, but rather one of the selective management of relations with both core and peripheral zones of the world-economy, leading to a considerable enhancement of the power of the South African state. Overall, the whole process took place amidst two decisive, facilitating conditions, namely, the final decline of British hegemony and the Great Depression between the two World Wars. It was in this setting that the South African state's program became possible and successful. For southern Africa as a whole, these conditions stimulated parallel if later tendencies of disaggregation, as Portugal established the policies of the Estado Novo in the 1930s while Rhodesian settlers (stung by South African moves and advances) similarly began their own program of economic transformation. By the end of the interwar period the open economic relationships that had symbolized the early twentieth-century trajectory of the area within the world-economy had been decisively shattered.

No simple extrapolation of interwar trends into the postwar period occurred however. Curiously enough, the very success of South African advance, coupled with new world economic tendencies, was to lead to closer ties between the various parts of southern Africa. South African economic prominence by the early postwar period allowed an aggressive penetration of all southern Africa, with the novel character that it established for the first time center-hinterland relations within the area itself and not just with overseas core areas. This was a fundamentally new structural feature, giving rise to its transformation into what we have termed a "region" of the world-economy. Part and parcel of this new historical process were the conditions and alliances of the new world order established under unchallenged United States hegemony. As the world-economy entered a period of sustained prosperity, the "regionalization" of southern Africa accelerated, with South Africa slowly but surely becoming the regional base of advanced production processes implanted by foreign as well as by local capital. Meanwhile, before that, South Africa was a founding member of all the major new interstate institutions of the postwar world, which seemed to ensure the political conditions for its regional domination.

As we all know, political upheavals in the 1970s and 1980s placed in question South Africa's political domination of southern Africa. At the same time, the world-economy went into a period of economic stagnation, seriously challenging not only peripheral areas but also the semiperipheral zones of the world-economy of which South Africa had become a stable member. The situation faced by both South Africa and new independent states in the region thus took on a very complex character in the 1970s and 1980s. At their base remained, however, the set of core-periphery relationships developed during the postwar period. These were radically different in character from those that had obtained thirty years earlier, and have proven to be more intractable to transformation than most have expected. If one could have imagined as of 1945 separate relationships between different parts of southern Africa and different core areas, the deep structural foundations of southern Africa as a region subsequently developed have precluded any simple extraction from regional core-periphery relationships that mediate ties to overseas core areas. In this context it makes little sense to speak of national development plans or bilateral security arrangements. Given the distinctive entrenchment of core-periphery relationships within the area, antisystemic struggles and hope for economic progress immediately engage regional forces. It is within this framework that we must assess the overall conditions for radical social and economic change in the contemporary period, and in this regard it is crucial to gauge the shifting trajectories of local and world powers within the current phase of the development of the capitalist world-economy.

The further political transformation of southern Africa will be directly affected by the reorganization of the balance of forces in the interstate system which is currently occurring. Regionalization of southern Africa had occurred during the period of the United States' hegemony after the Second World War and was facilitated by the enormous expansion of the world-economy which could therefore easily absorb the expanded industrial production of South Africa.

The period of the United States' full-fledged hegemony came to an end, however, in the late 1960s. It was undermined essentially by three concurrent phenomena: the rise in absolute volume of production and relative efficiency of Western Europe and Japan, which eroded many of the United States' most profitable monopolistic sectors; the rising costs of the United States' production, resulting primarily from the need to maintain internal social peace; within the United States, the erosion of the state's financial solidity caused by the enormous costs of imperialism, exacerbated especially by the Vietnam war.

By 1967, the Kondratieff A-phase of long-term economic expansion had ended and a long contraction of the world-economy had begun, one that continues to the present. In terms of capital accumulation in the world-economy, the contraction led to acute rivalry among the principal producing countries. In particular, it led to a trilateral effort by the United States, Western Europe, and Japan each to foist the immediate costs of contraction (unemployment, low profit rates, balance of payment difficulties) upon the other as well as to maneuver to control the new innovative and monopolistic sectors (e.g., microprocessors and biotechnology) which promise to be the central foci of capital accumulation in the next wave of world-economic expansion.

This acute intracapitalist rivalry plus the internal political and economic difficulties of the socialist countries loosened considerably the structure of political alliances in the interstate system. The automatic reflexes of the 1950s and 1960s gave way to a situation in which many political battles and line-ups were ideologically difficult to explain. This is quite normal after the breakdown of hegemony, and it should be emphasized that we are only at the beginning of this process which ultimately, no doubt, will lead to new, even radically new, political alliances at the level of the interstate system.

It is therefore no accident that in the period of United States hegemony, southern Africa, which was an area relatively sheltered from the full effects of decolonization because of geographic remoteness, the hard line of the South African and Portuguese governments, and the indifference of the United States (unlike in many other areas), found itself suddenly an arena of acute antisystemic struggle. The most dramatic precipitating factor was the politico-economic collapse of Portugal which could no longer bear the social and economic costs of the struggle, given the downward conjuncture of the world-economy. It is clear that 1974 was a political turning-point for all of southern Africa. The effects of world-economic change were also felt, however, within South Africa. The growing strength of the African urban waged working class was in part the consequence of South African capital's need to remain competitive in a tighter world-economy. But this in turn was the basis of the militant trade-unionism that emerged in the 1970s, and the wave of strikes which opened the way for the resurgence of the open urban political conflict which we are seeing today.

When the president of Anglo-American Corporation meets with the leaders of the African National Congress (ANC) in Lusaka and they meet with him, when there is an Nkomati accord and when it is inoperative, when the United States oscillates between sending aid to Savimbi and agreeing to some sanctions against South Africa, we can of course explicate these developments in terms of the short-term tactics of the various actors. But one element that should not be overlooked is that it is the fact that the interstate system is being slowly restructured which conditions these actions, makes them more possible and more important. It is the fact that it is not yet clear what the political and economic line-up in the world-system will be circa 2000 that impels a good deal of the ground-testing that is going in.

Of course, the ANC wants to end apartheid and come to political power. But it wants then to be able to achieve significant economic transformation and expansion in South Africa itself. Whether southern Africa continues to be or not to be a "region" in the world-economy is relevant to ANC's objectives. And, of course, most of the White urban middle class in South Africa wants a minimum of real political change, but not at any price. We have seen already in other parts of the world (e.g., France in the early 1960s, the United States in the late 1960s, Portugal in the early 1970s) how behavior can change substantially when the price becomes too high. Anglo-American is afraid that change might go too far for its tastes, but it also has to plan its survival as a corporation in the conditions of those changes that seem unavoidable. And the various members of the Southern African Development Coordination Conference (SADCC) would all like the South African monkey off their back, but none wishes to remain an obscure backwater of the world-economy.

From a narrowly economic point of view, should the 1990s continue to be a period of armed struggle in southern Africa, the region risks being left behind in the economic restructuring of the world-economy. During these fifteen years, there will be a big worldwide race for the location of some of the more important economic activities of the next wave of economic expansion and, given the choice of a number of zones in which identical activities could be located, it is likely that a zone of strife will be bypassed. That is the one thing which could lead certain capital interests to favor a relatively speedy transition to majority rule in South Africa—the prospect that such a speedy transition, and only this, might stabilize economic activity in the region as a whole and thereby ensure their continued high profit levels.

In terms of the potential politico-economic realignments on a world scale, southern Africa seems to be less central (despite its mineral wealth) than the Middle East, south Asia, and the Central America-Caribbean region. In this sense, the movements of the region remain and will remain, relatively speaking, more on their own and will only achieve what they can achieve by their own struggle. There is little that will be available by default, so to speak. In the last analysis, for the five major power centers of the contemporary world—the United States, the U.S.S.R., Western Europe, Japan, and China, while there is no geographic zone to whose politics they are indifferent, developments in southern Africa nonetheless are not the top of their agenda. This is at one and the same time the region's fortune and its misfortune. That this is so is probably more fortunate for southern Africa in political terms and less fortunate in economic terms, as we move into the next round of economic expansion.

The degree to which the "regional integrity" of southern Africa can be a fortunate or unfortunate characteristic for its various peoples very much depends on how the diverse movements will relate to each other. It is doubtful that the ostensible SADCC objective—a southern Africa region minus South Africa—is feasible. Nor will a region constructed as South Africa was able to construct it in the post-1945 period be able to meet the aspirations of most of the states and peoples of the region. On the other hand, a breakup of the integrity of the region may undermine the economic hopes of a majority-rule South Africa without necessarily benefiting other countries in the region. The question may rather be: "How can the movements in the region, once the ANC is in power in South Africa, use their region's cohesiveness as a weapon in their struggle for economic transformation rather than succumbing to the constraints its structure has historically placed on such transformation?" It is clear that sensible economic maneuvering by the peoples of the region in the next period of the world-economy will require more common planning by the movements than has been the case thus far.

Chapter 5

CONFRONTATION AND THE CHALLENGE FOR INDEPENDENT DEVELOPMENT: THE CASE OF LESOTHO

Sibusiso Nkomo

Introduction

T HE ATTAINMENT of independence by Lesotho from Britain in 1966 was heralded by many as a step toward eradicating the regional hegemony established by the Republic of South Africa (RSA) in the southern Africa region. The South African domination of the region politically, economically, and socially became apparent when the first southern African countries gained their independence. Countries like Lesotho which share a border with South Africa, the subimperial power, have not had the opportunity to operationalize their independence to the benefit of their citizens.

South Africa, through the use of its political, military, and economic power, has been able to subjugate and strangle the political economy of Lesotho. On the political front, in January

1985, a bloodless coup d'état was successfully orchestrated by the South African regime. In 1983, "[South Africa] kept the boundary with Lesotho partially closed. By thoroughly searching all freight shipments, South African customs officials seriously interfered with [railway] traffic so that many stores in Lesotho ran out of supplies" (Reitsma, 1983-84:22). The latter economic strategies were also used to create an opportunity for the coup d'état in this geographically surrounded independent southern African country.

The independent southern African countries must move into the 1990s and twenty-first century with a stronger commitment to eliminate political-economic arrangements that allow the exploitation by South Africa of labor and other resources in countries like Lesotho. In addition, when southern African countries participate in political economic arrangements with other countries, their most pressing objectives must be development, rather than dependency or dependent development.

Lesotho's political economy is under siege. Its economy is heavily dependent upon income generated by more than one-half of its labor force which is employed in South Africa at any given time. Because of its dependent relationship with South Africa, Lesotho's development strategies are undermined. As Bardill and Cobbe have observed:

> For Lesotho, this dilemma is exacerbated by four considerations. First, permanent migration, producing a lower home population and the possibility of higher GDP per capita—the classic adjustment mechanism for peripheral regions within single national economies—is not permitted by South Africa, is inconsistent with national aspirations, and is not even desired by the majority of current migrants. Second, the formalization of integration with South Africa into agreements such as those covering the Customs Union and the Rand Monetary Area greatly constrains the policy possibilities for disengagement. Third, Lesotho's weak resource and infrastructure base and the very wide exposure of its population to South Africa income levels and methods make it very hard to find activities that both are profitable in Lesotho and meet the population's expectations of what is "modern" and represents

"progress." Fourth, it seems plausible that the short-to medium-term interests of almost all influential groups within the country are better served by continuation of the status quo or something close to it, rather than by radical change that in the long run may be necessary for the national interest as a whole (Bardill and Cobbe, 1985:81-2).

Development predicated on a relationship of this kind has negative implications for national development. Lesotho remains very dependent and underdeveloped, and South Africa on the other hand continues to flourish as a subimperial power. Emphasizing Lesotho's dependency dilemma: "Current income is maximized by promoting integration with and labor flow to the developed core, but long-term development of self-sustaining nature requires some disengagement and the imposition of barriers to the free flow of goods, services, labor, and finance" (Bardill and Cobbe, 1985:81). Given the above, development in Lesotho in the 1990s and twenty-first century must emphasize national political and economic independence and non-perpetuation of regional hegemony by the South African regime. For Lesotho, then, by national development is meant the structural and institutional transformation of the political economy and social conditions of the country. This transformation is intended to create a political economy that is internally directed and social wants of the society are integrated in economic development. There must also be internal integration which covers sectoral integration (i.e., integration between the agricultural and industrial sectors), spatial development with an urban and rural balance, and congruence between the needs of the people and what is being produced.

Placing an emphasis on this form of development, Lesotho must cooperate with the Southern African Development Coordination Conference (SADCC). This regional body has the objective of freeing the political economies of the independent southern African countries from the hegemonic power of South Africa. To date, SADCC has given priority to coordinating and selectively integrating member nations' efforts in the following sectors: agriculture, energy, finance, industry, manpower development, transportation, and communication. When SADCC was established, however, the migrant labor situation was not explicitly identified as a major pillar of regional economic and political hegemony for South Africa. Thus, critics of SADCC challenged the regional body's objectives of freeing the independent countries from South Africa (Setai, 1988b:24).

Currently, Lesotho's development strategies are predicated on its dependence on the migrant labor system (MLS) dominated by South Africa. Some individuals hold the view that some benefits can be derived from the migrant labor system. These benefits are summarized as follows:

1.   Migrant labor wages are sources of income for the households of the migrants and revenue for the government of the sending country, thus contributing to an increase in the GNP (JASPA, 1979:53).

2.   The MLS opens up job opportunities for persons in the sending country which otherwise would not be available and allows the acquisition of occupational skills which can be subsequently applied in the economy of the sending country (Reyneri and Mughini, 1984:32-3).

3.   Income generated from migrant labor can be invested to develop the physical and human capital and the transformation of the economic structure into one which is no longer dependent on the export of migrant labor (Bardill and Cobbe, 1985:81).

Furthermore, Bardill and Cobbe (1985:83) conclude:

. . . close to 30,000 young people enter the labor market annually; only 2,000 to 3,000 at most can hope to become legal migrants, and a comparable number might get formal sector wage jobs according to recent trends. Over 20,000 people a year cannot be absorbed indefinitely in the informal sector and rural areas, with incomes grossly inferior to migrants or junior civil servants, without some form of disruption. South Africa's policies represent a useful, and real, scapegoat for economic difficulties in Lesotho . . . .

Given the arguments as presented, several questions can be posed in terms of Lesotho's dependent development. One set concerns whether or not these income efforts occur and, if so, are they in an amount and form that benefit development independent of South Africa or do they perpetuate dependent development? The second set relates to whether or not there are also costs associated with supplying labor to the MLS which reduce or negate ostensively positive income effects.

Migrant Labor Incomes and Expenditures

Perhaps the most obvious benefit to one nation supplying labor to another is the income generated in the latter and remitted to the former. As has been indicated, remitted wages constitute the single most important source of income for Lesotho. Further, no one would question that, given the present structure of its economy, many of these workers could not find jobs within Lesotho (Setai, 1988b:24); in those cases where employment was available it would not be for as high a wage (Bardill and Cobbe, 1985:82).

The earnings of about 140,000 Basotho migrant workers have contributed 40 percent of the country's GNP (Edlin, 1983:43). Also remittances have been increasing since 1975. In 1979 it was estimated that at least 30 percent of government revenue was generated from expenditures of migrants through the custom union agreement between South Africa and Lesotho (JASPA, 1979:53). In 1979 the government of Lesotho generated revenue of about $2.5 million, accruing also from a Basic Tax of about $7 per miner and an attestation fee of $12 per migrant contract (JASPA, 1979:53).

Basotho workers in the gold mines of South Africa have generated higher wages, paid in rands (R), than at home. As wages for Africans in the gold mines increased in 1984 by R901 per annum giving them an earned income of R23,972 per annum, so did the earnings of the Basotho workers (Levy and Mbali, 1987:311). Basotho migrants by 1985, were on the average earning $2,000 (U.S.) per year, which collectively was over $200 million (U.S.) (Bardill and Cobbe, 1985:81). One must note, however, that the earnings in the gold mines are still differentiated between whites and blacks even with these increases. For example, in 1984 whites earned an average of R21,369 per annum (Levy and Mbali, 1987:311).

At the insistence of the government of Lesotho, South Africa has agreed to the mandatory remittance of 60 percent of the wages earned there by Basotho workers. Income earned by Basotho workers is remitted by their South African employers to the state-controlled Lesotho Bank as deferred pay (Setai, 1988b:28). The rationale for this is that the families of the workers should have access to these incomes while the major wage earner is away (Setai, 1988b:28). The remaining 40 percent of the wages are paid to the worker while he is in South Africa.

In practice, however, the direct contributions of these two sets of funds are not as they appear. According to Gordon, a man is expected to have utilized the 40 percent of his earned wages provided as cash before requesting that his family have access to the deferred portion. As she states:

> . . . [A man] may be asked what he did with his cash that makes it necessary for him to arrange such a withdrawal. He may be told to make regular remittances from his monthly wages or send extra cash, rather than to bother the office with the more complex procedure. It can be made clear to the miners that requests of this nature will not be tolerated more than once or twice a contract; after more frequent requests he may be viewed as a troublemaker . . . (Gordon, 1981:119).

The result has been that over one half of the miners' earnings are untouched by the miner and his family until his contract ends (Gordon, 1981:118). This means, then, that 60 percent of the wages are not infused into the Lesotho economy by the families as consumers for a significant period of time after it is earned.

The deferred migrant labor pay as controlled by the government is supposed to be used in the form of investment and other domestic outlays. The following observations have been made, however:

> . . . although it is known that some of these funds are invested in the Johannesburg money market it is not

known what happens to the remainder... In the short
run, the best strategy would appear to be to invest in
projects of social development in the rural areas of
Lesotho . . . (Wallis, 1977:20-1).

Even in the case of the 40 percent paid directly as cash, there
is no guarantee that it will be spent in ways that contribute to the
national development. Much of this purchasing power is diverted
away from Lesotho's domestic economy (Setai, 1988b:28). This
diversion can be understood as a case in which South Africa gives
with one hand in the form of incomes and takes away with the
other hand because it is either spent in South Africa or in Lesotho
on goods manufactured in South Africa. This makes it difficult,
if not impossible, for the income earned by Basotho migrants to
turn over within Lesotho's economy for its own development
purposes. Eckert and Wykstra (1980:7) conclude that the
penetration of the Lesotho economy by South Africa's goods and
services has resulted in a high propensity to import on the part of
Basotho and strong disincentives for domestic production. Thus,
every rand of additional income earned in the MLS is matched by
one of additional imports.

Eckert and Wykstra indicate that during the decade of the
1970s each R1 million increase in national income contributed by
migrant labor incomes was offset by an increase of R1.05 million
in imports from . According to Setai (1982:24), "Imports increased 6-fold between 1972-73 and 1979-80 it reached a value of
$28 million (R244m). 72 percent of these were consumer goods,
15 percent intermediate goods and 13 percent capital goods."

Since 99 percent of Lesotho's imports were from South
Africa, it would appear that there was a substantial leakage of
benefits to the domestic economy from the purchasing power
provided by the wages of migrant workers. Furthermore, the
incomes generated from the migrant labor system have been offset
by the deficit of the country. The total debt service grew in 1979-
80 to 5.1 percent of the GNP and 29.7 percent of revenue just
three years later in 1982-83 (Bardill and Cobbe, 1985:78).

The leakage of migrant labor earnings in terms of purchasing
South African-produced commodities is directly linked to the fact
that the consumption patterns of Basotho migrants and general
citizens are determined by wage rates and marketing techniques

(e.g., advertising, distribution, etc.) operating within South Africa. With South Africa having absolute control over migrant laborers' incomes and marketing techniques, the economy of Lesotho does not have the advantage or opportunity to plan and respond to the income changes occurring in the latter country. For example, when South Africa increases migrant worker wages without prior notice, Lesotho's industrial and agricultural sectors are usually unresponsive to meet the demand for consumer goods. Consequently, the increase in demand can only be met through the importation of South African goods and services. This is confirmed by Eckert and Wykstra (1980:11):

> ... the mine wage increase elevated incomes in Lesotho much more rapidly than the domestic economy could accommodate. The result was very heavy growth in imported goods of all kinds, a serious imbalance in trade deficit and a dramatic increase in dependency of Basotho consumers on market ...

Also, a dependence on foreign incomes does have the tendency to work as a disincentive to production in the industrial sector and the agricultural sector. Indeed, at one level the MLS is a source of pecuniary benefits but at the other level empirical evidence demonstrates that the system acts as a disincentive, resulting instead in more dependence on imports.

Lost Surplus Labor Value and Venture Capital

There is another aspect of the value of the labor supplied in which is not reflected in the wages received but has implications for national development in Lesotho. The value of labor from Lesotho, utilized by South Africa, is not accurately reflected because of South Africa's longstanding policy to exploit black labor, regardless of origin. Rather, the wages paid are deliberately suppressed by employers in collusion with the South African government. The result of this is to increase the profit margins of South African producers by reducing labor costs. Two subsequent effects can be discerned. The profits realized by the undervaluing of Basotho labor strengthen the economy of South Africa and reinforce its regional domination. This means that, among other things, the profits contributed by the migrant workers are available for investment and innovation in South Africa rather than Lesotho. It is obvious that not all of the migrant workers going to could be employed in Lesotho or at the same wages. For those that could be, however, the contributions of their labor to profit would be potentially available for investment in Lesotho for the innovation which is a necessary element of development. As McConnell (1978:669) noted:

> . . . It is profits—or better the expectations of profits—which induce firms to innovate. An innovation stimulates investment, total output, and employment. Innovation is a fundamental aspect of the process of economic growth, and it is the pursuit of profit which underlies most innovation . . . . Indeed, profit rewards are more than an inducement for an industry to expand; they also are the financial means by which firms in such industries can add to their productive capacities . . .

Humanpower Development and Utilization

Beyond the question of remitted wages, there are a series of other issues growing out of having a large portion of the workforce participating in the migrant labor system which have consequences for development. These relate to Lesotho's inability to effectively compete with South Africa for utilization of its own workforce and in the process lose the benefits of educational investments which have been made in workers who migrate during their prime years. For example, in 1988, 140,000 citizens from Lesotho were employed in South African mines. This figure accounts for 60 percent of Lesotho's workforce (Setai, 1988a:69).

According to researchers at the National University of Lesotho (NUL), it was reported that 92 percent were single, 2 percent were widowed, 4 percent were divorced, and the remaining 2 percent had not recorded any marital status. The ages of migrant workers varied between 15 and 40, although in 1974 and 1977 it was found that there were males who joined the migrant

labor system at the age of 13 (JASPA, 1979:53; Gordon, 1981:60).
A breakdown of the age structure of Basotho migrants indicates
that 3 percent are age 15 to 19, 32 percent are between 20 and 29,
and 58 percent are between the ages of 30 to 39 (JASPA, 1979:53).

The average period of time spent by the migrants in South
Africa is estimated to be just under 14 years. Frequently, then, by
the time a migrant worker is ready or is forced to return permanently to Lesotho, he has reached the retirement age or his
productive capacity is on the down slope. There are no retirement
benefits for the worker and the socio-economic costs that arise
must be absorbed by the family, voluntary sector or government in
Lesotho.   This life cycle pattern was well stated by a migrant
worker who is quoted as reflecting: " . . . Now is the time that
Lesotho ought to learn to do these things for herself . . . .   My
knowledge and wisdom are being wasted in the Republic, and I
shall be sent back home once I can no longer do anything. I will
have become (useless) with my wisdom used up there . . ."
(Spiegel, 1980:127). The lost opportunity to utilize its workforce
during years of highest productivity cannot be fully measured by
the time spent in South Africa. People who wish to participate in
the MLS spend a considerable amount of time seeking employment, waiting and hustling to be recruited. This is time lost to
national development, for potential personpower does not involve
itself in any productive activity but is concentrated on struggling
to obtain South African work. A waiting recruit (Anonymous,
1984:4), explains how thoroughly institutionalized this process has
become:

> We wait for a long time to be employed but the
> "employer" will go to their village first to collect
> people who want to go to the mines. When they come
> back here, they only take a few. Sometimes you wait
> for such a long time thinking that you will be recruited;
> then you are told that you are too old to work in the
> mines or that you do not look well . . . even before you
> see the doctor. This is so painful because after waiting
> for such a long time you do not have any money to go
> back to your family . . .

Another type of loss in personpower due to the MLS
affecting national development in Lesotho is government spending

in education and skill development which end up being used in South Africa. JASPA (1979:216) explains this loss as "one of the crucial manpower problems in the country . . . the seepage of skilled and trained manpower to the RSA . . ." Both use of the skills acquired and a return on the educational costs are lost by Lesotho. Since independence, education has expanded greatly and yet there is very little evidence showing a major benefit. The expected private return to education for males has been zero except at university level (Bardill and Cobbe, 1985:81).

The seepage of personpower in Lesotho has largely been occurring with individuals who have attained primary education, high school education and technical training. The government educates these individuals with the expectation that the return would be the utilization of the acquired skills to help the country toward national development. It is estimated that in 1977, the government's average cost per student-year was R20 (approximately $22) for primary level, and R95 ($97) for secondary students (Cobbe, 1982c:11). The Ministry of Education allocated not more than 2 to 3 percent of its budget toward technical education in 1977-78 (JASPA, 1979:214).

A NUL study found that 43 percent of those who were involved in the migrant system had never been to school, whereas another 53 percent had attained the varying basic levels of education. One could easily conclude that those who have been unable to acquire more education become part of the migrant labor system. Empirical evidence, on the other hand, demonstrates that some who have higher education and acquired professions, e.g., school teachers, have abandoned teaching and become migrant workers.

Overall, government expenditure on training Basotho in technical skills has benefited South Africa through the MLS rather that Lesotho's national development. JASPA (1979:217) observed the following in terms of the leakage of trained personpower:

> . . .The country has been producing craftsmen for the last 80 years. During the last 15 years, 1962-1977, the Lerotholi Technical Institute itself has produced more than 650 craftsmen/artisans, but the 1976 Census recorded only 81 males and females with vocational education perhaps there were others mixed up in other

group-headings, such as persons with junior certificate, lower primary teachers certificates or equivalent. However the fact remains that a large number of skilled workers have gone and continue to go to RSA, denuding the country of the critical manpower needed for its own development. A tracer study conducted in Lerotholi Technical Institute (LTI) in 1977 found that of its total trainees since 1973 about 75 percent were not working in Lesotho. Another study in 1977 recorded that out of 54 students interviewed in three technical institutes 30, or about 56 percent, were thinking of going to the RSA.

The low wage structure for skilled and professional work in Lesotho in comparison to mine work in South Africa has drawn Basotho with education out of the former country, and has also acted as a disincentive for other Basotho to acquire education. Cobbe (1982b:6) presents the propensity to oscillate in this manner:

> . . .Admittedly, minework is unpleasant, physically demanding and dangerous, involves separation from families, and requires life under the apartheid South African regime. Nevertheless, remembering that mine employment involves free board, lodging, and medical care in addition to cash wages, if we focus on pecuniary returns only the implications are striking. In 1975, even a novice mineworker on the surface could earn the Lesotho minimum wage in 9.9 months, while underground novice could earn the starting salary of a recruit with JC (junior certificate—three years of secondary school) to the Lesotho public service in 10.9 months. The average migrant mineworker in 1975, if he spent the whole year in RSA, could earn 4% more than the starting salary of the highest entry level COSC (Cambridge Overseas School Certificate-High School) recruit to the Lesotho public service! In 1978, the picture was not much different; a surface novice could earn the Lesotho minimum in 11.8 months, an underground novice could earn the JC entry salary in 9.7 months, and despite the large increase in COSC entry

salaries, the average mineworker in a full year had earning only some 11% lower than the top entry rate for COSC in Lesotho public service.

These wage benefits to individuals are offset, however, by the loss of personpower for development purposes and loss of return of the educational costs incurred by the government.

To the individual with skills, he is underemployed and unable to develop and improve on the skills acquired through government investment. The latter point is worsened by the fact that no educational credentials are required by migrant mine work in South Africa, only physical qualifications (Cobbe, 1982a:6).

Socio-Demographic Effects

Beyond the question of the contribution made by wage remittances, there are a number of additional effects of the MLS which are relevant to national development in Lesotho. These relate to the way in which the MLS interacts with the socio-demographic and spatial structure of the country. They include general patterns of population distribution within Lesotho, the male-female ratios, the composition and functions of the household, and labor power utilization. As will be seen, these matters have spatial as well as structural dimensions which are particularly significant for the agricultural sector.

Macro Patterns

There are certain general demographic consequences of the MLS which are immediately apparent. The 1966 census indicated that 42 percent of all males aged 20 to 59, and 51 percent of those aged 20 to 39 were absent from the country. A decade later, in 1976, the census recorded that 44 and 52 percent of these respective age groups were absent as migrant workers (Murray, 1981:40). Murray (1981:41) reports that most mine workers continuously oscillated during their participation in the MLS which, in most cases, lasted a decade and a half. Drawing upon van der Wiel, Murray (1981:41) states "these years of absence are concentrated in early manhood and middle age" and that: "On the basis of a survey of Bàsotho who had completed their migratory careers . . . 'the real average length of his working life that a migrant worker spends outside Lesotho is estimated to be 16 years for those coming from the lowland and 13 years for those coming from the mountain zone.'"

Participation in the MLS not only affects the characteristics of the population within Lesotho by causing the absence of a significant portion of males but also influences how the remaining population is distributed. Many of those involved in the MLS move from the hinterland to Maseru, which has the attribute of a primate city, albeit on a small scale, and then to South Africa. As Wilkinson observes, migrants to Maseru are typically young and better educated (Wilkinson, 1983:221). This means that the more resourceful individuals, including males and females, migrate from the periphery to Maseru. Eventually, however, the majority of the males join South Africa-Lesotho MLS because of the lack of adequate opportunities and low incomes when jobs are not available in the capital city. This reinforces the role of Maseru as a recruitment center for labor whose productivity contributes to South Africa's development.

One result of the MLS-influenced pattern of migration is reflected in the ratio of males to females within Lesotho. Gordon, using Lesotho Department of Labor figures for 1976 which indicated that an average of 121,161 Basotho were in South Africa at any given time, came to the following conclusions by applying a marriage rate of 70 percent to those absent:

> . . .the miners leave behind close to 85,000 wives living in Lesotho. If the wives of 30,000 to 80,000 men working as migrants in agriculture, construction, and other industries are added, the number left behind reaches more than 100,000 and may approach 150,000. The 1976 census indicates that 234,159 married women reside in Lesotho. Thus it appears that 40 to 60 percent of married women in the country live as wives of absent migrants at any one time (Gordon, 1981:60).

There is a spatial dimension to these aggregate figures on the ratio of males and females. Within the urban areas of Lesotho, particularly Maseru, one aspect of this imbalance can be shown.

As noted above, both males and females migrate to Maseru in search of opportunities not available in the hinterland. While the males tend to move on to South Africa, the females do not because South Africa's influx controls bar them from doing so. In combination, then, the effects of these male and female migration patterns result in distorted sex ratios in Maseru and other secondary urban centers, as well as the depletion of labor from the hinterland.

Wilkinson (1983) observed that the large number of young females among urban migrants was, in the context of Africa, unusual. He cited Monyake who found that: ". . . a large number of females in the range 15-39 years (but more especially 15-29) are flooding the town (Maseru) . . . in the urban areas there is what Monyake calls a 'grotesque imbalance' between the sexes (Wilkinson, 1983:217)."

Family and Household

Several other types of more specific socio-demographic "distortions" follow from these general ones. The family is a basic unit in Basotho society. In the absence of the welfare infrastructure which Western nations incorporate into the public sector, the household serves a variety of critical socio-economic and normative functions. However, there are a number of ways in which the MLS negatively affects the viability of the extended family in these roles. Barker, as cited in Murray (1981:101), states that:

> It is at the family level that the most pain is felt, and we cannot forget that the African cultural heritage enshrines a broader, more noble concept of family than that of the West. The extended family has proved a marvelous security for those for whom, otherwise, there was no security at all. The extended family is a net wide enough to gather the child who falls from the feeble control of neglectful parents, it receives the widow, tolerates the batty, gives status to grannies. Migratory labour destroys this . . .

The concentration of Basotho males in the MLS means that they will be absent from their families for a considerable part of their productive lives. In turn, this has required a significant change in the traditional distribution of responsibilities within the family and in the role the wife must play. A study done by Elizabeth Gordon (1981:66) provides the following data on the attitudes of females toward the effects of having husbands participate in the MLS:

1. Some 75 percent of the females felt that when husbands are away as migrants the burden was too much for them to take care of the agricultural sector;
2. Some 60-66 percent of the females felt that when the husbands are away, they carry too much of the family responsibilities;
3. Some 74-75 percent of the females were of the opinion that the sharing of the responsibilities in their children's upbringing would be effective if their husbands could be home all the time.

The assumption that remitted wages from young migrant workers can be expected to provide for the old, in the absence of any retirement benefits from prior employment in South Africa, also creates a strain upon the extended family. Spiegel (1980:141) has noted that when a young wage earner marries, "he and his wife regard his remittance as the means to their nuclear family's growth." However, Spiegel (1980:141) continues: "If, as occurs in some cases, older households treat remittances from younger wage earners as a sustenance resource, conflict may arise resulting eventually in the segmentation of the household with the younger nuclear family setting out on its own."

Negative effects of the MLS can fall on the quite young as well as the old, particularly in rural areas. As working-age males in a family migrate to the mines and other work places in South Africa, school-age male children frequently must replace the absent personpower. JASPA (1979:189) reported that:

Enrollment in 1,058 primary schools in 1977 was 226,019 of whom 59 percent were girls. During the last 10 years (ten years prior to when a study was done) enrollment has grown by around 2.3 percent per annum which is about the same as the annual rate of population growth. The dropout rate from one standard to another is ranging from 9 to 21 percent of the total enrollment . . . . *The dropout rate is much higher in the case of boys . . . being the result, it is said, of boys having to herd cattle in the absence of adult males who go to the Republic of South Africa for work . . .* (emphasis added).

The extent to which this occurs is reflected in the statistics from 1977 which indicated that 47 percent of Basotho migrant workers had never attended school and 53 percent had never attained a high school certificate (JASPA, 1979:54). The fact that participation in the MLS has no educational requirement reinforces the likelihood that the option will be chosen. This disincentive to continuing or returning to school has longer term consequences for labor utilization in Lesotho, particularly in terms of the agricultural sector.

Human Labor Power and Agriculture

Most migrants work in South African mines. Lesotho has no mining industry. The skills that are developed, then, relate to South African personpower needs and have little relevance to those of Lesotho. The result is that when these workers can no longer be employed in South Africa, there is little transferability of their knowledge or experience to productive use in Lesotho. Further, individuals who once had agricultural skills seldom retain them after a life of migrant labor.

The long-term decline of the agricultural sector has been an important factor in the underdevelopment of the country. One has to consider that about a hundred years ago Lesotho had a highly productive agricultural sector and was regarded as "the granary of the Free State and parts of the Cape Colony" (Murray, 1980:3). As Lesotho became a British Protectorate in the middle 1800s, however, it was incorporated into the developing South African migrant labor economy (Murray, 1980:5). As a result, the British and South Africa policies have been prime factors in forcing Lesotho into South Africa's migrant labor market, and have also contributed to agricultural decline and continued deterioration.

The agricultural sector also seems to have suffered due to lack of sufficient labor power. Much of Lesotho's male labor force participates in the South Africa-dominated MLS. Hence, it is estimated that 85 percent (211,000) of the female labor force is involved in agriculture, while only 13 percent (32,000) of the male labor force is actively involved in agriculture (Wykstra, 1978). In further elaboration of our analysis of the disequilibrium in the division of labor, Wykstra (1978:5) makes the following observation:

> . . . the aggregate male labor supply "potentially" available for both the crop and livestock sectors of agriculture approximates 81,000 persons. However, this does not imply in any way that full employment in farming while on leave is a reasonable expectation of the 49,000 miners on home leave. The on-site labor force of 32,000 or so *men* aged 15-59 not employed on an off-farm basis is very small, relative to (a) some 900,000 arable acres of fragmented cropland, and (b) 3 million head of livestock in Lesotho's agricultural sector.

Therefore, Lesotho's agricultural sector has not been able to maximize its utilization of the available male labor force. The decline in this sector has made it even more difficult to attract male labor power.

Conclusion

Central to Lesotho's independent development is its identification of its commanding heights, strengthening its cooperation with the development strategies articulated by SADCC, and formulating development strategies that take into account the total liberation of South Africa. First, Lesotho must harness its major leakage to South Africa, its labor force. This leakage has a detrimental impact on Lesotho's development. Income generated by migrant workers in South Africa is spent disproportionately in that country, not in Lesotho; profits extracted by the extreme exploitation of Lesotho's mineworkers are used to reinvest in the South African economy, and personpower that could be utilized for the development of Lesotho is nearly completely lost to South Africa, in some cases after significant investments are made in skills development by the Lesotho government. The agricultural sector in particular suffers from the loss of personpower, and accordingly this critical sector has declined in Lesotho in recent years. Family structures have been severely damaged by the MLS, no doubt with longlasting repercussions for the future of the country's social and economic development.

These difficulties demonstrate that first, Lesotho must identify the major resources the country has that can be used to create jobs. Second, the situation created by the MLS shows the essential importance of Lesotho's continued cooperation with SADCC. This is so in terms of SADCC's perceived strategy for regional structural adjustment, addressing the elements necessary for the recovery, rehabilitation and sustained growth of the regional political economy. Even though SADCC operates under the difficult conditions that are created by South Africa, the regional body is still a viable alternative for Lesotho and the region.

Chapter 6

REALIGNING BOTSWANA'S TRADE STRUCTURE: CONSTRAINTS AND POSSIBILITIES FOR SADCC

Renosi Mokate

Introduction

SINCE its formation, the Southern African Development Coordination Conference (SADCC) has been engaged in the process of creating greater linkages among its members. One of the requirements for the success of the regional effort being undertaken by SADCC is the ability of the individual countries to restructure their economies and, hence, that of the region. This restructuring requires that the member states of SADCC realign their economies in such a way that internal development is achieved, dependence on the Republic of South Africa is eliminated and regional development facilitated. An important element in this process is the realignment of the trade relationships in the region. This entails increasing intra-regional trade, use of local resources through intra-regional industry and market linkages, and more efficient utilization of regional resources.

Realignment of the trade structure for any African country carries with it certain constraints and costs. In conventional customs union theory, the costs identified are those pertaining to trade diversion which occurs when, as a result of the formation of a customs union, union members are forced to purchase their goods from a high-cost producer rather than the least-cost producer. The costs and constraints which must be examined by the SADCC countries in order for them to be effective in their endeavor, however, go beyond the question of trade creation and trade diversion. Of more significance is the challenge facing SADCC regarding how to realign the regional trade structure in the presence of South African regional and economic hegemony and the participation of some of its members in the South African Customs Union (SACU). The constraints and opportunities for SADCC in realigning the trade structure within the region away from South Africa to one where the SADCC countries have greater interaction with each other bear examination. The case of Botswana is analyzed here for the purpose of drawing some generalizations as well as demonstrating differences in the challenge facing the various countries depending on their economic relationship with South Africa.

Before current issues concerning the trade sector of Botswana are discussed, it is appropriate to review the historical processes which contributed to the present integration and subordination of its economy to that of South Africa. Botswana's trade relationships with the southern African countries are such that its major trading is done with South Africa. There is very little trade with the other southern African countries. This condition is a consequence of the colonial history of the region, whereby Botswana and other countries in the region were created as peripheral entities of South Africa. In the case of Botswana, Lesotho and Swaziland (BLS) this condition has been ensured and perpetuated by their membership in SACU. The BLS countries, in fact, form a subset of SADCC because of the historical linkage of their present economies to South Africa.

The History of Trade Links in Southern Africa: Botswana and its Membership in SACU

The South African Customs Union is a trade institution made up of Botswana, Lesotho, Swaziland and South Africa. This institution dates back to 1910, when the British and the Boer colonialists in control of the respective territories made a customs agreement. In 1910, the four colonial provinces, Cape Colony, Natal, Orange Free State, and Transvaal combined to form the Union of South Africa, now the Republic of South Africa. During this same year, the colonialists of South Africa signed a Customs Union Agreement with the British authorities in the three British neighboring protectorates, Bechuanaland (Botswana), Basotholand (Lesotho) and Swaziland. This agreement was designed to the clear advantage of South Africa, since British interests in the protectorates were only marginal.

In its basic form, the agreement covered customs and excise duties, and financial arrangements. The points agreed upon were (Hudson, 1981:131-2):

A.   Customs and Excise Duties
   1.   No customs duties would be levied on goods moving from one country within the customs union to any other member country, except that the three protectorates could collect duties themselves on South African beer, spirits and wines.
   2.   The members of the union would charge the same rate of customs duty on goods entering a member country from outside the Common Customs Area (CCA) and the same rate of excise duty on dutiable goods produced within the CCA.
   3.   Any member could in principle initiate a change in the rate of duty, but in practice these would be set by South Africa.

B.   Financial Arrangements
   1.   South Africa would act as the custodian of the duty collected, including duty paid at South African ports on goods destined for Basotholand, Bechuanaland and

Swaziland; and all duties collected would go into a
revenue pool.

2.   Annually, each member would receive a fixed percent-
     age of the amount of duty collected out of the common
     revenue pool.

3.   These percentages would be based on estimates of duty
     consumed in each country during the period April
     1907-March 1910.

4.   The percentages could not be changed even if patterns
     of consumption on dutiable goods among the members
     changed since there was no statement to the contrary
     in the agreement.

Since 1910, the agreement has been amended twice, once in
the colonial era (1965) and then in the post-colonial era (1969).
The 1965 amendment concerned the percentage of revenue each
country was supposed to receive. When the economies of the
members of a customs union are unequal, there is a tendency for
the strongest partner to benefit disproportionately from the union;
such integration exacerbates rather than relieves the economic
problems of the weaker states. The experiences of Africa and
Latin America with regional integration have been such that trade
diversion from the industrialized countries occurs as import-substitution industries are established. Jaber (1971:258) noted that
when this occurs, the customs union/common market members
have a choice between "trade diversion in favor of the domestic
producer at any cost and trade diversion in favor of the most
efficient producer in the region."

Since with the free operation of the market forces no
automatic mechanisms exist for equitable distribution of costs and
benefits, it is the economically strong partner with a well established industrial complex and infrastructure that will attract the
most investment. The case of southern Africa has demonstrated
this clearly. South Africa has a stronger economy than those of
the BLS countries. South Africa has been able to attract virtually
all the investment in the region due to her well developed
infrastructure and availability of cheap labor. Thus, she has
developed a complex industrial infrastructure through import
substitution while the other members have not been able to do so.
In addition, South Africa through the control of the tariff

structure has been able to use this trade diversion process effectively to further its own development at the expense of the other members.

This fact is clearly demonstrated in the case of the BLS countries where the direction of trade is skewed in favor of South Africa. The BLS countries hardly export anything to South Africa, while on the other hand they are dependent on South Africa for over 80 percent of their imports. Thus, the absence of trade barriers has not necessarily encouraged increased trade toward South Africa from the BLS countries.

Botswana's dissatisfaction with the customs union agreement is cited in the country's first development plan. In the post independence period, Botswana showed dissatisfaction with the customs union arrangement on several grounds (Landel-Mills, 1971:266). One problem was that the revenue accruing to her from the arrangement did not reflect the economic growth that had occurred within Botswana. Second, the high protective duties imposed by South Africa tended to reduce imports and hence the total revenue collected. It also diverted consumption from cheaper overseas imports to more expensive South African manufactured products. This effectively amounted to a subsidization of South African manufacturers by Botswana consumers. Thus, Botswana sought to build into the arrangement some automatic redistribution of resources towards the disadvantaged partners that would lead to a more equitable customs arrangement.

When Botswana and the other former protectorates met with South Africa in 1969, several changes were made in the 1910 agreement. The important changes as outlined by Hudson (1981:134) were as follows:

1. The revenue-sharing formula was made to depend on current patterns of import consumption.
2. The revenue-sharing formula was revised from being asymmetrical in favor of South Africa.
3. In principle South Africa would no longer place non-tariff barriers on BLS products; meaning that, the latter now ostensibly have guaranteed access to the large South African market.

4.   Each country could maintain its own separate import quotas on goods from outside the CCA.

5.   The BLS countries can impose additional duty against South African products competing with their infant industries, while S.A. may not do likewise for BLS products.

6.   South Africa should consult other members before changing the tariff and give consideration to their interests as well in doing so.

Since the renegotiation of the customs union agreement, Botswana has been receiving more and more revenue. At present it is estimated that the 1.42 multiplier alone gives Botswana a gross benefit of 30 million Pula a year (Tostensen, 1982:146); in 1982, 1 Pula was equal to $0.9788 (U.S.). Table 1 shows the marked increase in revenue that has occurred as a result of the customs union agreement. As indicated in Table 1, after 1969-70, the proportion of Botswana's revenue from the customs union increased by almost 100 percent from the previous decade, to constitute one third of the revenue source. As a result Hudson (1981:146) states that:

> There can be no question that the BLS countries have benefited substantially from the new agreement. Those people who would like to reexamine Botswana's membership in the Southern African Customs Union will have to put in a fair amount of serious study and produce tangible evidence to change the general view that Botswana is better off inside the customs union than outside it.

The question of whether or not Botswana is "better off" remaining in the customs union goes to the heart of the issues that are important in considering how the realignment of its economy is to be undertaken to fit the goals and objectives set forth by SADCC. While the answer to the question itself depends on what qualitative and quantitative measures one is looking at and the time frame being considered (i.e., short-term or long-term), the issues the question raises, demonstrate the challenge SADCC faces in attempting to meet its goals.

Table 1
Contribution of Customs Revenue to Botswana's
Total Recurrent Revenue

Financial Year	Customs Revenue	Total Recurrent Revenue	Percent from Customs
		(million pula)	
1899-1900	0.012	0.12	10
1909-1910	0.021	0.15	14
1919-1920	0.042	0.16	26
1929-1930	0.062	0.29	21
1939-1940	0.081	0.48	17
1949-1950	0.190	1.10	17
1959-1960	0.610	3.80	16
1969-1970	5.100	17.00	30
1979-1980	79.000	210.00	37

Note: 1 pula was equivalent to $1.4000 U.S. in 1960 and 1970, and $1.2871 U.S. in 1980.

Source: Hudson, 1981, p. 147

Realigning Botswana's Trade Structure

The consequences of Botswana's membership in SACU in terms of its trade structure and relationship with other countries is easily demonstrable. Tables 2 and 3 contain data on direction of trade. Botswana trades mainly with South Africa, the United States, the United Kingdom and other European countries. However, South Africa alone has the largest share of the trade volume (over 50 percent) particularly with respect to imports. In 1981 it accounted for 87.6 percent of Botswana's imports. Most of Botswana's exports go to other European countries (over 40 percent in 1981 and over 50 percent in 1979 and 1980). Botswana's exports to South Africa amounted to 16.6 percent of its total exports in 1981, an increase from 13.6 percent in 1978 (Botswana, 1981:27).

Table 2
Imports From Some Major Trading Partners, 1981

Country	Total Trade in '000s UA	Trade Volume as Percent of Total
CGA	608,594	87.56
Zimbabwe	42,250	6.07
USA	14,565	2.09
UK	7,867	1.13
Zambia	629	0.09
Malawi	623	0.09
Other	20,531	2.90
Total	695,059	100.00

Note: 1 UA = 1 Rand

Source: Botswana, External Trade Statistics, 1981, p. 27.

Botswana trades very little with the other SADCC countries. In 1981 only 9.2 percent of Botswana's total exports went to any of the SADCC countries, with Zimbabwe accounting for 6 percent of that trade. With respect to imports, only 7.9 percent of its commodities came from SADCC members, with almost all (6.1 percent) from Zimbabwe.

Botswana's imports include foodstuffs, petroleum, machinery, vehicles and apparel. The chief import is machinery and electrical equipment. This is explained by the increase in mining and construction activity. Thus, Botswana imports mainly consumer durable and non-durable manufactured products. On the other hand, exports are dominated by mineral exports, diamonds and copper-nickel matte, followed by meat and meat products. These are exported mainly to the United States and the EEC countries. Its exports to the SADCC countries are principally meat and textiles.

In summarizing Botswana's trade situation, Tostensen states that:

Table 3
Exports From Major Trading Partners, 1981

Country	Total Exports in '000s UA	Trade Volume as Percent of Total Exports
Switzerland	141,087	40.56
USA	84,247	24.42
CGA	47,649	16.57
UK	23,185	6.66
Zimbabwe	20,949	6.02
Mozambique	7,149	2.05
Angola	2,549	0.73
Zambia	1,371	0.39
Other	9,650	2.80
Total	347,836	100.00

Note: 1 UA = 1 Rand

Source: Botswana, External Trade Statistics, 1981, p. 28.

On the export front, Botswana has managed to diversify market outlets so that principal products which were previously largely marketed in the Republic [of South Africa] (beef and animal products, diamonds and copper-nickel matte) now find their way to markets overseas, primarily U.S.A. and EEC .... In terms of sensitivity dependence Botswana is clearly in poor straits when it comes to imports and increasingly so. Vulnerability dependence also seems to be high; the cost of diversifying imports will be high no matter how radical policy changes might be .... Given time it is unlikely that Botswana may be able to practically phase out the Republic as a market, except for a few items (Tostensen, 1982:32).

In spite of some changes that have been made on the export side, Botswana's trade structure continues to be skewed in favor of South Africa. This has been an issue of continuing concern for the government of Botswana since independence. The major types of questions raised in this regard concern the gains and losses Botswana derives from the SACU membership, and the costs of withdrawal from the union. Four studies that have been done since independence regarding these questions will be reviewed. The first study done was commissioned by the government of Botswana. The second was undertaken by Landel-Mills in 1971 to examine whether or not under the new CU agreement of 1969, the cost-benefit situation had changed for Botswana. In 1978 two studies were done, one by Paul Mosley and another by Peter Robson. Finally, there was a study done by James Cobbe in 1980.

Financial Costs of Pulling out of SACU

One consequence of being a member of SACU and importing such a substantial proportion of goods through South Africa is that Botswana gains a large amount of revenue. In light of this, since the 1969 agreement, attempts have been made to assess whether as a result of this agreement the SACU members now benefit from continued membership in the union.

The earliest study done to assess whether or not Botswana gains by its continued membership in SACU was commissioned by the Botswana government soon after independence. The government was not satisfied with the British colonial office's claim that the 1910 agreement was essentially beneficial to Botswana, and that its renegotiation would most likely result in worse terms for the country. The results of the study commissioned by Botswana were published in the 1967 Customs Administration Report. The study stated that:

> . . .A simplified tariff, controlled by Botswana and tailored to her economic needs, could be administered for an annual recurrent cost of about R150,000. By contrast, it was estimated that an annual revenue could thus be raised in excess of R3 million or approximately double what was being received under existing customs

agreements. Although the proposed tariff would have involved higher duties, the increased burden on consumers would have been greatly offset by the freedom to purchase all goods in competitive world markets, where many goods would be cheaper than the highly priced South African products (Landel-Mills, 1971:265).

Thus, the report refuted the colonial office's rationale that Botswana would incur excessive administrative costs by establishing its own customs institutions, which the British often cited as a reason why Botswana should not revert to using its own protected market as a model. Since South Africa agreed to renegotiate the customs agreement in 1969, the conclusions drawn by the 1967 customs administration report were not followed.

Landel-Mills' 1971 study addresses the question of whether or not under the new agreement the BLS countries are compensated for the negative effects of being SACU members, specifically fiscal discretion and having to import goods from South Africa at a multiple of world market prices (Mosley, 1978:31). Landel-Mills concluded that if Botswana had pulled out, it would have had to levy much higher duties on imports in order to achieve the revenue level accruing to it at the time. Such higher duties would have raised the cost of living in Botswana directly or indirectly. Botswana would also have had to impose higher duties on investment goods such as imports of plants, machinery and building material needed for mining development, thus raising the cost of development.

Furthermore, under the new agreement Botswana is guaranteed free access to the South African market. In terms of long-term development this could turn out to be advantageous since, according to Landel-Mills:

> If BLS were to leave the Customs Union, their chances of creating a sizable manufacturing sector, which must be based on the production of export goods rather than import substitutes would vanish. It is most unlikely that trade agreements with other countries in Africa could provide opportunities even remotely equal

to free access to the large and rapidly growing South African market (Landel-Mills, 1971:280).

Clearly, then, there are financial costs to be incurred by withdrawal from SACU. The validity of Landel-Mills' latter statement becomes questionable, however, in the context of the formation of SADCC, which now opens new opportunities for Botswana.

Another cost constraint that Landel-Mills discusses is possible retaliation by South Africa should Botswana and other countries withdraw from SACU. Such retaliation would create considerable economic difficulties for Botswana. Thus far, South Africa has demonstrated its willingness to retaliate against the southern African countries for undertaking economic and political actions of which it does not approve.

In the context of the formation of SADCC, the key question with regard to costs is whether, under the new revenue formula, Botswana does in fact get compensated for the opportunity foregone to form a more integrated economic relationship with other SADCC members and/or whether the revenue benefits derived are an acceptable rationalization for remaining in the SACU. Furthermore, does continued membership in the SACU preclude effective realignment of Botswana's economy?

In 1978, two separate studies were done reappraising Botswana's role in the customs union agreement. The first study, done by Paul Mosley, attempted to evaluate the costs and benefits to Botswana, Lesotho, and Swaziland of membership in SACU. Mosley looked at industrial development, exports, government revenue and the cost of living. Thus, he tried to go beyond the question simply of whether the revenue formula compensates the BLS countries. He sought to determine whether or not the existence of the customs union hinders growth of industries in the weaker countries, and to identify various factors that are important in assessing costs and benefits of seceding from the customs union.

Mosley asked two primary questions: "If the [SACU] were dismantled, and replaced by four separate national markets, each protected against import duties of appropriate magnitude, what gains and losses in real income would the BLS countries sustain? Balancing these gains and losses, would there be any benefit to the BLS countries from leaving the customs union?" The gains and losses he considers pertain to the domestic market, export market, governmental revenue and the cost of living.

With respect to the domestic market, the author looks at what Botswana would gain if certain economic activities presently located in South Africa "shifted" to Botswana, and an increased local market became available for local manufacturers. Botswana would gain the most from a shift to a protected market based on the total value anticipated added. Assuming that some of the industries can be shifted to Botswana, one can conclude that the production by these industries will equal the value of imports from South Africa and that each plant's ratio of value added to output will equal the average ratio for that industry. Mosley then used the estimated increment in national value added from "shifting" the industry under a protected market as an estimate of the gain from seceding from the customs union.

In addition to the above costs, Mosley examines other factors. One is the demand for BLS export products, once South Africa puts up tariffs against them. *In extremis,* South Africa could react to secession by blocking the transport of exports overseas through her territory, in which case the effect would be even more adverse.

On the revenue side, the net revenue cost of withdrawing from the union would consist of three factors. First is the administrative cost of establishing a new customs administration estimated at 5 percent of existing tax yields. Second, would be the loss of the multiplier effect of 1.42 presently included in the 1969 customs agreement. Third, the yield of import duties might change.

Also likely to occur is an increase in the cost-of-living due to a rise in tariffs and the prices of outputs of industries shiftable to Botswana. The extent of the damage done to Botswana would depend on South Africa's reaction, the extent to which Botswana can find alternatives for exports and/or imports, and the extent to which alternative investment could take place. Mosley concluded that:

> In all custom unions, freedom of trade encourages specialization, and specialization implies dependence; but in no other customs union is the disparity in income levels and social philosophies between partner states so great, and in no other customs union, there-

fore, is the specialization so damaging to the development of the weaker partners nor their dependence so
deeply resented (Mosley, 1978:39).

Peter Robson's study was done as a response to Mosley's
article, and also to highlight other issues he felt Mosley did not
consider. Robson's critique of Mosley's presentation centers first
on the methods Mosley used to calculate gains and losses; these
included his calculation of loss in revenue from export, his
inclusion of the cost-of-living component as a real income change
rather than simply as a transfer from consumers to the national
budget, the use of the concept of shiftable industries and, finally,
the calculation of the costs of a separate customs administration.
According to Robson, Mosley's study indicates which industries
one might do prefeasibility or feasibility studies on, but cannot be
used as a basis for formulating specific economic policy for
industrialization. Furthermore, he argued that the calculation of
costs of administering a separate customs union understates the
costs BLS countries would incur. Based on these criticisms, he
recalculated the gains and losses to Botswana.

With the above in mind, Robson contends that Botswana and
the other countries can industrialize while being members of the
customs union. The need for economic growth and development
does not, according to Robson, necessarily point to secession. He
states:

> There can be little dispute with the proposition that
> there are good reasons, both political and economic for
> promoting growth—inducing industrial development in
> BLS—and this is clearly an important objective of
> public policy. But the crux of the matter is whether
> the pursuit of this objective points to withdrawal rather
> than the initiation of more positive industrial develop-
> ment policies already capable of being pursued within
> the letter and spirit of the agreement. At least since
> the new agreement was introduced in 1969, no convinc-
> ing case has been made out that pursuit of industrial
> development and income growth yet points to with-
> drawal . . . . If industrial development has been less
> rapid, than the basic situation would permit, a possible
> explanation may be that the [governmental] industrial

promotion agencies have not been given sufficient support and backing for their task (Robson, 1978:465).

Therefore, Robson does not support the idea of withdrawal from the customs union, either because it will cost too much or because, in his estimation, the BLS still have leverage, even within the customs union, for development.

Robson's contentions, however, are contradicted by the socio-economic reality in the region. Namely, that South Africa's regional strategy is incompatible with his suggestion that the BLS countries can achieve independent economic development in the context of SACU. Indeed, the formation of SADCC is testimony to the negative effects of South African economic hegemony under which the BLS countries and other SADCC members have suffered.

James Cobbe's 1986 study of SACU produced conclusions similar to those of Robson although for different reasons. Cobbe, in appraising the studies done by Mosley and Robson, argues that since there was another agreement made in 1976 concerning percentage revenue shares, one cannot really predict or know precisely how much the 1.42 enhancement or compensation factor will be. This makes it difficult to calculate any gains and losses. Thus, Cobbe takes a different approach concerning what the important issues to address are with respect to SACU.

According to Cobbe, the Mosley and Robson approaches ignore two important questions related to the effects of the customs union on the overall development of BLS countries. These are income distribution in the BLS and the "long-term structural objectives and possibilities of development in BLS and the effects (if any) of membership in the customs union on them." Cobbe states that under the SACU, the customs duty, sales duty, and excise duty as determined is regressive. Thus,

> . . .the southern African indirect-tax structure is regressive, and the relative price structure in southern Africa favors the consumption patterns of high-income groups (in South Africa, largely white and voters) relative to low-income consumption patterns much more than in other parts of Africa (Cobbe, 1980:332).

For example, customs on durable goods such as air conditioners, vacuum cleaners, fans, and pianos is 5 percent; cameras 15 percent; cassettes and domestic-type sewing machines 20 percent; household refrigerators 25 percent; radios priced over R14 30 percent and those below R14 40 percent; textiles and apparel at between 25 and 40 percent. As a result of this indirect-tax structure, income distribution becomes less egalitarian in Botswana, in spite of what the government's objectives are. More importantly though, the government has no power to adopt a more progressive excise and sales duty, because under the agreement these are determined by South Africa.

The second issue that Cobbe discusses is the effect on consumption patterns, preferences and aspirations of Botswana as a result of being in the customs union. These are factors that can influence general perceptions about development and production possibilities. In terms of consumption effects possibilities are that Botswana will prefer imported goods to locally produced ones, and there will be a tendency to favor mass-produced goods which do not fit into Botswana's economic structure rather than more "appropriate" substitutes, as a result of exposure to the South African market. On the production side, there might be a tendency to utilize production techniques used in South African mass-production industries that are large-scale and capital-intensive. The consequences of this are inappropriate choice of products and processes, neglect of possibly profitable projects, and pessimism over possibilities of ever being able to produce on the South African level. Therefore, beyond simply the question of gains and losses as discussed by Robson and Mosley are broader issues relating to the integration of BLS into South Africa's economy.

In terms of what can be done with the problems above, Cobbe argued that in the medium-term and possibly in the long-term, Botswana will continue to be adversely affected unless there is a radical change in South Africa. Experience has shown that South Africa is not willing to tolerate any large- scale development of manufacturing in the BLS (Cobbe, 1980:331). Cobbe concluded nonetheless that any radical change on the part of Botswana under the prevailing conditions would be detrimental. This is because of the resource constraints she faces in terms of shortage of physical and social infrastructure, dependence on foreign manpower in technical and managerial positions and her complete integration into the South African infrastructure. Finally, since the 1976 agreement provides a substantial source of revenue, and provides room for creation of infant industries, Cobbe argues that Botswana has more to gain by remaining in the customs union.

From the discussion presented in these various studies, there are clearly several facets to Botswana's membership in SACU that must be considered. First, is the loss of revenue that Botswana would incur as a result of withdrawal from SACU. Second, are the costs of establishing her own import-substitution (IS) industries in an attempt to reorganize her economy. These costs would come in the form of high-priced goods produced behind high tariffs and tax incentives to attract private foreign investment. These measures would be necessary to counteract competition from South African industries. Third, there are the economic and social costs of retaliation by South Africa. Finally, there is the cost of administering a customs union department.

For Botswana, unlike other SACU-BLS countries, the financial costs of loss of revenue may be possible to overcome, as can those arising from the additional cost of administering a customs union department. With the new Jwaneng diamond mine, the financial position of Botswana has been expected to improve. Diamond revenue should be large enough to enable the government to dispense with all or part of the SACU income. Botswana's primary need involves redirecting resources away from dependence on the cattle industry and on the civil service toward diversification and development of other sectors.

Botswana should be able to cope with the financial costs involved. The more complex problem is that of diversification of other sectors of the economy in order to overcome other aspects of dependency. To understand the complexity of this, in the next section the constraints of being a member of SACU and SADCC are discussed simultaneously.

The constraints to be discussed relate to South African imported goods and the establishment of IS industries. Beyond the question of financial costs due to loss of revenue, Botswana may want to remain within SACU, in order to take advantage of the goods it imports from South Africa. This may be an interim strategy while selected IS industries are being established in the country in conjunction with SADCC.

Regional Implications

Constraints Due to Botswana's Membership in SACU

The constraints arising from continued membership in SACU that need to be seriously considered will come in two forms. One is trade barriers existing between Botswana and other SADCC members due to its membership in SACU. The second is competition from South African industries for any projects by SADCC that are likely to be established in Botswana, and for goods originating from other SADCC members to Botswana. When these factors are considered, one finds that they essentially stifle any meaningful trade that can occur between Botswana and other members of SADCC.

Trade Barriers

The trade barriers that one is concerned with here are in the form of tariffs on goods being traded. Under the CU agreement, any goods entering Botswana from other SADCC members except Lesotho and Swaziland are subject to duties. These duties are essentially set by South Africa, and Botswana has little say over what they are. Clearly, this is to the disadvantage of any trade that has to be undertaken.

This issue of tariffs is further complicated by the fact that the customs tax is regressive, as Cobbe (1980) states. The taxes are higher on non-durable goods than they are on durable goods. Considering the economic structures of SADCC countries, the former are the goods that will most likely be traded, and these are the goods that account largely for Botswana's import dependence on South Africa. Therefore, unless these constraints are seriously considered, SADCC will exist, but in fact very little trade will occur between countries like Botswana and other members.

Another important aspect of trade that will be affected by tariffs is regional inter-industry trade. One way to utilize resources efficiently and effectively in the region will be to engage in intraregional interindustry trade. This will encourage a pooling of resources and create viable possibilities where they did not exist without SADCC. This cannot be efficiently undertaken with barriers existing as is the case in Botswana. The barriers would increase the cost of raw materials and make the goods produced less competitive.

The above constraint presented by trade barriers is further complicated by the fact that South Africa has the power to veto any concessionary agreement in which Botswana can engage with countries outside the customs area. For example, South Africa can veto any proposed tariff reductions between Botswana and other SADCC members. Therefore, Botswana's options and leverage in innovating ways to overcome the above-mentioned trade barriers are limited.

Competition From South African Based Industries

Botswana's continued membership in SADCC means that other SADCC industries that might want to export goods to Botswana will have to compete with South African manufacturers. First, the trade barriers are such that on that basis alone, South African-made products will be cheaper to import. The price of other goods will be increased by the import customs tariffs placed on them. Second, most of the southern African countries do not have well established industrial sectors. Being predominantly import substitution industries they tend to have higher input costs and hence higher priced goods. These industries will not be able to compete with South African industries which are not only well established but also have at their disposal cheap African labor.

Therefore, Botswana's continued membership in SACU will have the effect of stifling the establishment of new industries within SADCC, in spite of SADCC's plans; unless creative ways of dealing with the situation are found. At the moment these issues have not been addressed within the SADCC program.

Conclusion

There are several conclusions to draw concerning the pattern and structure of Botswana's trade and its regional implications. First is that the pattern and direction of trade is clearly oriented towards South Africa. Thus, Botswana trades little with other SADCC countries. Second, Botswana's trade structure is dominated by the import of large volumes of manufactured goods from South Africa and the export of primary products to South Africa, the EEC and the United States. Third, this trade pattern is perpetuated and exacerbated by Botswana's membership in the SACU, due to the tendency of customs union arrangements to favor the country with the more powerful economy and South Africa's historical dominance of the region. In addition, this pattern of trade has affected the structure of Botswana's economy in that there is no congruence between the structure of demand and structure of supply within the domestic economy. Therefore, for Botswana and other SADCC member countries realignment of their economies will entail a complex process. In this process, the regional goals set by SADCC cannot be achieved without the concurrent internal structural transformation of the economies of the constituent countries. Part of this restructuring concerns an evaluation of BLS countries and their membership in the SACU.

Chapter 7

THE POLITICAL ECONOMY OF STATE-OWNED ENTERPRISES IN THE THIRD WORLD: THE CASE OF TANZANIA

Joseph J. Semboja and
Lucian A. Msambichaka

Introduction

I MMEDIATELY after gaining political independence, most African states opted, for many reasons, to rely more heavily on state-owned enterprises (SOEs) (Nellis, 1986:12-7). First, for most of these economies government involvement in economic affairs was a common practice. Colonial governments had involved themselves in wage and price determination, agricultural marketing boards and investing in industrial enterprises. Second, for most of these economies whatever important activities that existed were in the hands of aliens. In many countries, colonial exploitation was linked with ownership and control of economic activities and the concept of nationalization and state control was appealing.

Even countries whose ideological inclination has not been socialism included the issue of ownership in their agenda.

Third, SOEs received attention in the years following independence because the private sector simply wasn't there or was not doing enough of what was hoped for by the new governments. The indigenous businessman was quite weak, involved mainly in brokerage, not investment. Foreign private capital was not forthcoming, either; weak infrastructure repelled foreign investors. The role of the state in the infrastructural activities such as communications, transport, water, electricity, finance and certain branches of heavy industry was not seen as an act to replace a competitor but as a complementary move aimed at stimulating the small, weak indigenous private sector.

A fourth reason was related to the state's desire to control savings and investments. Assuming that the state knows the priorities of the economy and that private investors and brokers consume wastefully, invest in low priority areas or invest abroad rather than domestically, development will be maximized by adopting a public sector oriented strategy. A fifth reason is related to the economic ideology of the country. In Tanzania, for example, the economic strategy embedded in the Arusha Declaration of February 1967 sought to lay greater emphasis on self-reliance and the attainment of rapid economic development and of an equitable and just society. Two principles of the declaration were socialism and self-reliance, the former defined to include the absence of exploitation and the people's control of the economy. Further, the people's control was essential for the implementation of the policy of self-reliance. The expansion of SOEs was a precondition for the implementation of the pronounced economic strategy.

The international donor community has also been fond of creating autonomous institutions to manage its activities. This partly results from the donors' lack of confidence in domestic institutions although in many cases competition and show-off among donors may result in duplication of activities.

Once SOEs are created they become important sources of power. Even poor performing parastatals find justifications for existence. For instance, they produce sensitive items for the army, they provide employment, not only to the low-income workers but also to political supporters, allies and retired servants, etc. On a few occasions, institutions are created and maintained to accommodate personality changes.

Recently, the sacrosanct mission of the public enterprise sector enterprises has increasingly come under critical scrutiny. There are several reasons for this.   One, the success of the advocacy for SOEs has resulted in such enterprises increasing their share in the economies of the developing countries. Not only do public enterprises represent sizable and increasing shares of the Gross Domestic Product (GDP) but they are also represented in many activities outside the "traditional" areas of natural monopolies, public utilities and large scale heavy investments like mining, steel and coal. The second development is the recent deterioration in the economic situation, with increasing debt burdens, budget deficits, slowing or negative growth rates.

Both circumstances have made the discussion of the role of the state in developing countries timely. The existence of public enterprises in many developing countries provides the opportunity and the challenge to researchers to examine their role. The strained economic circumstances and the alleged contribution of the public enterprises to the deterioration provide the urgency for the exercise. Further, developments in the economics profession and other social sciences suggest increased attention to the theory and experiences of SOEs.

This chapter attempts to place the public enterprise sector debate within the political economy framework. Once this is done it becomes quite obvious that several constraints have to be attended to whenever discussions on the future of SOEs take place. In the following section a review of policy instruments which have been used to support SOEs is given. The resource allocation implications of these actions is also provided in order to set ground for discussions on the future of SOEs. In Section III the growth of this sector, in terms of the contribution to Gross Domestic Product (GDP), investment, employment and wage bill, is briefly outlined.   Sections IV and V of the chapter contain a discussion of the issues of performance and constraints which arise from the interdependence of the SOEs, government and private sectors. In Section VI, the issues of divestiture and SOEs reforms are discussed.

Policy Instruments in Support of State-Owned Enterprises

The above reasons, and probably others, have led to the adoption of policies, explicit or implicit, which have favored growth of SOEs. A review of some of these policies as applied in Tanzania will provide useful examples.

Major nationalizations took place in 1967, the year of the Arusha Declaration. Almost immediately, the government announced the nationalization of banking, insurance and eight milling firms. It also acquired up to 60 percent of the shares of seven industrial firms under the Industrial Shares (Acquisition) Act. Eight months later, 60 percent of the shares of most sisal estates were acquired under the Tanzania Sisal Corporation Act. The government then created the National Bank of Commerce (NBC) to take over the activities of the nationalized commercial banks, the National Insurance Corporation to take care of the insurance portfolio, the State Trading Corporation (STC) to replace the nationalized export-import firms, the National Milling Corporation (NMC) to replace the nationalized milling firms and, the Tanzania Sisal Corporation (TSC) to undertake the activities of the nationalized sisal estates. The National Development Corporation (NDC) was created in 1965 to serve as a holding company for the shares owned by the government in commercial enterprises. The NDC, which had shares in about 43 enterprises in 1966, had this number raised to 64 and 142 in 1967 and 1974, respectively. Clark (1978) has observed that between 1967 and 1971 the government nationalized assets amounting to 888 million shillings, of which 41 percent was acquired in 1967; between 1960 and 1972, one Tanzanian shilling was equal to $0.1400 (U.S.). Major nationalizations continued up to 1971 when buildings valued at 100,000 shillings and above were taken over by the government under the Buildings (Acquisition) Act. There were no significant nationalizations after 1971 and whatever took place in this area was done on an ad hoc basis.

According to Clark (1978) between 1964 and 1971 the government invested 2,098 million shillings in the SOEs of which 48 percent went to new areas/firms. During the 1966-71 period SOEs' investment was 22 percent of total, compared to 12 percent in 1966. Most of the new firms were in manufacturing (54 percent), transport (29 percent) and tourism (13 percent). The issue of government investment in the SOEs will be dealt with further in the next section. It suffices at this point to say that government investment policy was becoming that of direct involvement in production and distribution.

Once state institutions got involved in production and distribution, fears of competition for markets and resources with some private enterprises began to emerge. The fears were expressed in terms of adopting policies which gave preferential treatment to SOEs as is discussed below.

Under the Regulation of Prices Act, No. 19 of 1973, the National Price Commission (NPC) was established with the principal objective of keeping prices low and stable. Price control does not discriminate on the basis of ownership arrangements and its main weakness lies in the extent to which it enhances distortions in the allocation of scarce resources and its relationship with other discriminating instruments. The method used by the NPC in determining maximum prices is "cost-plus" which sums all the costs of production and distribution plus a margin. The method ensures that all firms whose output prices are fixed by NPC earn a profit, regardless of the performance of the firm. Indeed even firms producing similar products will be allowed to fix different prices if they experience different average costs. This procedure has the effect of discouraging cost minimization, as efficient firms are not rewarded. The implication of this procedure is to retain resources in activities which are less productive. Furthermore, this method raises costs of production of activities which use inefficiently produced outputs as their inputs. This arises if there are no competing sources of supply. The consumers eventually bear the burden.

Price control enhances discrimination between privately owned enterprises (POEs) and SOEs in favor of the latter, when other policy instruments directly or indirectly discriminate. As we shall see shortly, policy instruments which have discriminated against the private sector include foreign exchange allocation and exchange rate policies, credit and interest rate policies, taxation and subsidy policies. Discrimination arises when: foreign exchange is allocated to SOEs at the low official rate and the private enterprise sector has to do with the high unofficial rates; credit policy favors SOEs who receive more funds at the low official rates of interest; SOEs apply for and are granted tax exemptions and relief on their inputs and the favor is not extended to the private sector; and SOEs receive subsidies when they are in financial trouble while the private enterprises have to do with high interest rate bank credits. All of these actions have direct cost implications. Under a sellers' market situation, price control will not penalize the private enterprise if every seller adopts the official price which will be different for each producer. In a buyers' market, as is currently the case for some products, the private producer will be penalized, since producers may choose to adopt cost pricing rather than scarcity pricing.

The current move to decontrol some prices will serve to reduce discrimination and resource misallocation. Care should be taken, however, with monopolists in order to avoid attempts to adjust their output downward with the intention to raise prices. Adopting a policy that may force monopolists to fix their prices at the level which is, at most, as high as those that would be charged by a competing importer, would be useful. Furthermore, competition should be encouraged where appropriate.

Foreign exchange has long been the most constraining resource. The government, after assuming that it knows the priorities of the economy better than any other agent, decided to ration the resource in accordance with the established priorities. Priorities for rationing the FOREX from free resources start with imports of petroleum, medicines, foodgrains and defense needs. Revenue generating products such as beer and cigarettes have also received special attention. Due to severe shortage of FOREX and lack of detailed guidelines on its allocation, however, the actual allocation has become affected by a bargaining process which takes into account past import patterns, the need to alleviate perceived short-term crisis and the socio-economic and political strengths of various applicants. According to a World Bank study (1987), in 1982 administrative allocation of FOREX gave 88 percent of the official allocation to SOEs. In 1983, 1984 and 1985 the percentages were 93 percent, 91 percent and 92 percent, respectively. This study has also revealed that administrative allocation of FOREX has favored economically inefficient firms at the expense of efficient ones. In 1982, administrative allocation gave 49 percent of the official allocation to extremely inefficient firms, i.e., those which produce negative value when all inputs are valued at world market prices. Only 23 percent of the FOREX was allocated to efficient firms. In 1983, 1984 and 1985 the figures were 48 percent, 50 percent and 52 percent allocated to inefficient firms against 34 percent, 22 percent and 24 percent, to efficient firms, respectively. Furthermore, in the SOEs more extremely inefficient firms got official FOREX than in the private sector. The reverse was the case for efficient firms, i.e., in the private sector efficient firms got more official FOREX than in the SOEs.

Starting in 1984 the government allowed individuals earning FOREX to import any item as long as it fell under the list of permitted items. The list has included transport equipment, some consumer goods, building material and equipment, electrical goods, fishing equipment, a large number of industrial goods and inputs for the manufacturing sector. This scheme can safely be considered to be largely aimed at the private sector.

By allowing own funds imports the government by implication has legalized the use of a dual exchange rate. Since the use of the high unofficial rate is almost entirely relevant for the private sector, the system is discriminatory. A continuing devaluation which has been taking place until now has worked to bring the two rates together, a positive move toward eliminating this discrimination.

The retention scheme was introduced by government in 1984 to allow private and state owned firms to retain a portion of their export proceeds for their own use. This measure has done much to resolve the problem of obtaining FOREX from unofficial sources at high exchange rates.

State owned enterprises also had privileged access to technical assistance and donor funds at concessional rates. At the same time, the private enterprise sector had difficulty attracting expatriates since they could not offer them an arrangement whereby they could convert a portion of their salary into foreign exchange, as could SOEs directly or indirectly by receiving donor funds. Furthermore, at the Bank of Tanzania (BOT) foreign exchange applications for dividends and interest payments overseas are given low priority, making it virtually impossible for private firms to raise foreign equity or loans.

Recently, however, as a result of their advantages in obtaining foreign loans, SOEs have found themselves saddled with a financial difficulty. Since firms are generally required to assume the foreign exchange risk of loans passed on to them by the government, recent devaluations have hit firms with large foreign debt and little chance to increase prices.

The other source of discrimination between importers arises through import tariffs and sales tax. Imposition of duty and sales tax on imports is equivalent to adopting a multiple exchange rate system, unless all imports receive the same rate. Two kinds of discrimination exist when imports are taxed. The first applies to importers and the second to products. In the former case, certain categories of importers (e.g., diplomats, charitable organizations and the government) receive automatic exemption on their imports. Although SOEs do not normally receive automatic exemption, experience has shown that these institutions apply for the favor and get it, through gazetted exemptions, once the Minister of Finance is satisfied that their imports serve the interest of the economy. During the fiscal year 1985-86, 829 million shillings in import duty were exempted under the gazetted exemptions. In 1986-87, 3,221 million were exempted and in the first half of 1987-88, 2,440 million were exempted. The Tanzanian shilling was equal to $0.0572 in 1985, $0.0305 in 1986, and $0.0156 in 1987. It is believed that most of these exemptions were granted to SOEs. As import duty adds to the costs of production and therefore lowers protection of the using activity, any discrimination on granting exemptions that is based on ownership has implications on resource movements in favor of the sector that receives the exemption.

Sales tax has a similar effect on protection if it is levied on imported inputs. Sales tax, however, cannot be exempted through the minister. The practice has been for SOEs to apply for payment by installment or postponement of the whole lot into a future period. In both cases, the result is equivalent to receiving a government loan on which no interest is charged. If this favor applies more to the SOEs than to the private enterprises, as is believed to be the case, the result on resource flows is the same as in the case of import duty.

The current efforts by the government to reduce granting of exemptions with hopefully the intention of reaching a point where gazetted exemptions no longer have significant repercussions on costs is an important move towards correcting these distortions. In the event reductions to this desired level are found to be impractical, the second best solution would be to extend the favor to the private sector in order to minimize discrimination by ownership. Then the government must confront the other type of discrimination, that which applies to products. We do not wish to dwell on it here because it has no direct bearing on ownership, unless it is assumed that the structure of imports is based on ownership. Otherwise, it suffices at this point to say that discrimination on the basis of products has resource allocation implications and has to be dealt with in order to minimize misallocation.

On the opposite side of taxes are subsidies normally paid to commercial institutions that face financial difficulties. These should be distinguished from grants and subventions which are defined as payments to non-commercial public sector institutions such as universities and government health centers. Most subsidies are paid to state-owned crop authorities. Before July of 1984, they were given mainly to cover differences between purchasing and selling prices of crops. Since 1984, when the government decided to stop providing subsidies, subsidies have been provided to cover past debts and interest obligations, particularly for the National Milling Corporation.

While it is true that official subsidies have been restricted to a few crop authorities, in recent years, loss-making SOEs have found ways of surviving through implicit subsidies. These include resorting to excessive overdrafts, unpaid loans and unpaid purchases. In some cases the government has bailed out loss-making SOEs. For example, the fertilizer plant has survived despite charging unrealistically low prices for their product because the government has agreed to make up the difference. The government loses revenue as a result. Moreover, in a number of instances, the government has put pressure on financial institutions to extend overdrafts to SOEs, particularly crop authorities, even when these enterprises have surpassed their credit ceilings but have not accounted for the previous overdraft. The government may do this even when it is known that the SOEs involved will not be able to repay the loan.

Table 1
Subsidies to SOEs, 1981-82 to 1985-86
(million shillings)

1981-82	958.1
1982-83	1,333.5
1983-84	1,322.1
1984-85	734.4
1985-86	714.6

Note: The Tanzanian shilling had the following U.S. dollar equivalencies: 1981 - $0.1207; 1984 - $0.0654; 1986 - $0.0306

There is no official discriminatory policy on credit applicants. The influence of platform statements by senior politicians on credit allocation and access to guarantees by SOEs have resulted in SOEs getting the bulk of the credit made available at official interest rates.   Such rates have been negative in real terms. Available figures on commercial bank deposits and lending show that while the private sector has been the major depositor it has been the minor beneficiary in terms of borrowing (Table 2 below). In 1966 the private sector contributed 75 percent of the commercial bank deposits and borrowed 94 percent of total lending. In 1970 its share in total deposit was 57 percent against 47 percent of the borrowed funds.   In 1981 the two shares were 74 percent against 14 percent.   Thus, over the period 1966-81 the private sector was increasingly financing the public sector, as is indicated by the declining ratio of private sector borrowing to deposits.

In 1986 the National Bank of Commerce (NBC) gave 65 percent of its total lending to SOEs, 21 percent to the cooperatives and 13 percent to the private enterprise sector. It is not clear how the private enterprise sector finances its activities, particularly those of a short-term nature, given what can be referred to as "crowding out" by the financial institutions. One possibility is the informal private credit network where extended families of entrepreneurs, residing in Tanzania or abroad, lend funds at market clearing interest rates, which are believed to be higher than official

Table 2
**Private and Public Sector's Commercial Bank Deposit and
Lending**

End of Year	Ratio of Private Sector Deposits to Total Deposits	Ratio of Private Sector Borrowing to Private Sector Deposits	Ratio of Private Sector Borrowing to Total Lending
1966	74.9	112.5	94.0
1967	71.1	100.7	87.2
1968	61.2	93.0	79.2
1969	61.2	78.5	67.1
1970	56.5	62.0	47.2
1971	52.3	45.2	33.8
1972	55.4	45.6	40.0
1973	56.9	28.8	27.0
1974	61.9	28.1	21.0
1975	58.7	24.2	19.1
1976	58.2	16.8	14.8
1977	64.0	16.2	15.3
1978	66.4	19.6	15.6
1979	69.1	14.1	15.0
1980	75.8	11.6	15.4
1981	74.3	10.9	14.2
1982	65.1	14.0	17.8

Source: Bank of Tanzania, Economic and Operations Report, various years; National Bank of Commerce, Annual Reports and Accounts, various years.

rates. The other possibility, however, may be that the private sector did not need more than what was allocated to it. A recent study (Semboja, 1987) found that prior to adoption of credit ceilings, the private sector did not find much difficulty in securing funds from the commercial banks; until recently, NBC was facing the problem of overliquidity.

In addition to receiving priority in credit allocations, state owned enterprises have been able to expand credit through arrears to the banking system. At the end of 1986, 73 percent of the Tanzania Investment Bank's (TIB) loans outstanding were accounted for by SOEs and 54 percent of these loans were in arrears, compared to 28 percent for private loans.

Although the accumulation of arrears by the SOEs has become a way of raising more funds, negative implications of this action can be noted. First, the SOEs are drying up funds which could have been used by other potentially more productive users. This is particularly important under the current credit squeeze. Second, these actions can lead to problems of solvency. For example, at the end of 1985, 74 percent of TIB's loan portfolio was affected by arrears. If, as is now the case, these institutions are unable to raise foreign funds, their operations for existing and future projects will be affected.

Under the Economic Recovery Program (ERP) credit ceilings have been instituted. The advantage of this is that institutions are forced to generate more of their own funds or perish. The problem is that some institutions such as the National Milling Corporation (NMC) and the Cotton Authority have their operations predetermined by the Government in such a manner that they cannot break even. Furthermore, as a result of current devaluations, institutions which received foreign loans find themselves hit with foreign debt and little chance to raise prices. The credit ceiling policy did not seem to have considered these special cases. As a result, a few problematic SOEs seem to have surpassed their ceilings, thus affecting the aggregate ceiling for the economy as a whole so that the efficient SOEs and the private firms find it difficult to obtain credits. If this continues for long, the scheme will fail and those who can resort to the informal private credit network will do so at higher interest rates.

Methods must be devised to assure that special cases are not allowed to crowd out other institutions. As some of these are priority institutions, it may be necessary either to raise their individual ceilings or to deal with the root causes of their financial problems. Furthermore, costs of obtaining official credits should be increased by raising official interest rates to market clearing interest rates. The current official interest rates, which are negative in real terms have led to a number of negative results.

First, there are no incentives for people to deposit in official banks. Thus, deposits in real terms have declined,[1] particularly after 1980. Commercial bank deposits fell in real terms, from 2,749 million shillings in 1980 to 2,423 million in 1981, and then to 2,390 million in 1982; the Tanzanian shilling was equal to $0.1207 (U.S.) in 1981. Some analysts have further suggested that capital flight has resulted from low interest rates. Second, negative real interest rates encourage investors to over-invest in fixed assets and, as studies have shown, capacity underutilization is widespread. Third, the level of interest rates charged by banks may not be adequate to cover administrative costs, including adequate provisions for default risk. The government has raised these rates in recent years but they are still negative in real terms.

Before 1984 confinement was one of the major sources of discrimination between the public and the private sector. Under the confinement policy, wholesale trade for some domestic and imported commodities is restricted to state owned organizations. Firms and individuals were required to sell specified items through national and regional public institutions and to purchase many of their imported requirements and some specified domestic products through designated state owned institutions. The Board of Internal Trade (BIT) and BOT administer the policy. Although there was no concordance between the items subject to price control and those under confinement, there was significant overlap. For those items which were not price controlled, the trading companies would negotiate prices with the suppliers, usually on a cost-plus basis; this is a process which led to outcomes similar to those followed by the price commissioner.

The confinement policy has been associated with poor services, lack of payments to suppliers and high marketing costs. SOEs have not been able to develop marketing strategies and have often been unresponsive to consumers' demands. By implication of being monopolies/monopsonies, inefficient buyers/sellers could transfer the rising costs to the producer/consumer and survive at the latter's expense.

---

[1]Here we are assuming that bank deposits vary with interest rate changes only. The aspect of financial intermediation, an important factor indeed, is assumed away.

As we have noted, most, if not all, of the confined items could be obtained at controlled prices either because their prices were controlled by the price commissioner or because they were negotiated using the same procedure, the cost-plus. These prices were usually (and still are) lower than those obtaining in the markets. Confinement policy generally favored SOEs by giving priority to these institutions in the allocation of scarce items such as vehicles, tires, fuel, etc. Thus, in 1984 only 35 percent of the trucks imported through the official system were allocated by the State Motor Corporation (with approval of the prime minister's office) to the private sector. Yet 70 percent of the trucking services are provided by the private sector and state-owned institutions receive the bulk of vehicles imported under aid projects. For example, in the same year 100 trucks were given to the Tanzania Cotton Authority by the Dutch government. Since 1984, when own-funded imports were allowed and many prices decontrolled, there has been a shift towards deconfinement with producers/importers being permitted to distribute their products directly. Today, only a few important items are subject to confinement. Deconfinement has not only reduced discrimination but it has also led to increased availability of consumer goods, particularly in the remote areas, and inputs to producing activities. Resource misallocation has declined and incentives improved. Room for improvement remains, however, particularly in the marketing of agricultural products.

The Contribution of State-Owned Enterprises

In the economy's production account there are public and private firms, noncommercial public institutions, and government. The "public sector," in the popular usage, may refer to both commercial and noncommercial public institutions and to government activities. We shall refer to the public commercial institutions as public enterprises, state-owned enterprises or parastatal enterprises to distinguish them from private firms, noncommercial public institutions as well as government qua government.

In Tanzania, the SOEs are made of parastatal enterprises, East African Community (EAC) enterprises and the local government corporations where they exist (the EAC ran the railways, airways, harbors and telecommunications until 1977 when it broke up and its activities were taken over by parastatals).

The most comprehensive source of data on SOEs is the Bureau of Statistics (BOS) of the Ministry of Finance, Economic Affairs and Planning (FEAP). Notwithstanding the theoretical distinction made above between the private, public and government sectors, there are practical and conceptual problems associated with the use of data compiled by BOS. According to the BOS (1983:2), parastatal enterprises are those "commercial enterprises owned by the government or with majority government participation and are run on commercial principles and whose accounts are not integrated into government budgets." Those subsidiary companies at least half-owned by parastatal enterprises are also classified as SOEs.

The exclusion of minority government ownership understates the presence of SOEs and government control. The impact of this, however, is expected to be reduced or even eliminated by the inclusion of private ownership in SOEs which are not wholly government owned. The second problem with the BOS data relates to the method of data collection. The data is obtained by sending out questionnaires to SOEs in January of every year. Figures reported are usually based on preliminary data before the audited accounts have been prepared. Estimates are made for nonresponding enterprises, normally by adopting the previous period figures, a procedure that cannot capture the inevitable fluctuations inherent in economic variables. Thirdly, there is the problem of including some noncommercial parastatals in the BOS sample. An inspection of the list of parastatals contained in the BOS' accounts of parastatal enterprises shows some doubtful inclusions. For instance, the inclusion of Capital Development Authority (CDA), Tanzania Agricultural Research Organization (TARO), Small Industries Development Organization (SIDO), Rufiji Basin Development Authority (RUBADA), etc., can hardly be justified.

The BOS material will constitute the primary data base for this section. The alternative to this data base would be to comb through the individual parastatal accounts, and having done so, there would be no guarantee of comparability with other national income aggregates.

Gross Domestic Product (GDP)

The total product of the SOEs sector has been rising in absolute nominal terms. The contribution of SOEs in GDP ranged between 9.6 percent and 13.3 percent during the 1974-84 period. SOEs have dominated in finance and electricity and, in some years, in mining and transport also. The significance of SOEs in transport is accounted for mainly by rail, water and air transport. Also, the significance of SOEs in finance arises from parastatal enterprises' dominance in banking and insurance. SOEs have played a minimal role in agriculture, construction, real estate and business services.

Wage Employment

The absolute figures of SOEs' wage employment rose from 107,724 in 1974 to 175,953 in 1984. The share of SOEs in total wage employment ranged between 22.3 percent and 27.8 percent during the 1974-84 period.[2] SOEs dominated in electricity, transport, mining and manufacturing activities; they also contributed significantly in commerce.

Earnings in the State-Owned Enterprises

Following the BOS' accounts of parastatal enterprises, earnings are defined to include wages and salaries (including all payments, bonuses, overtime, commissions, allowances for sick, annual leave and vacations), employers' contribution to provident fund, pension and gratuity in cash or kind. In absolute nominal terms, SOEs' labor cost has risen from 903.0 to 3,360.40 million shillings during the 1974-84 period; the Tanzanian shilling was

---

[2]It should be noted that these shares are not directly comparable with the GDP shares observed above. This is because total output of the economy includes non-monetary contributions, a portion of which is entirely privately produced. On the other hand, employment shares do not take into account non-wage labor. However, fixed capital formation shares are directly comparable with GDP shares.

equal to $0.1401 (U.S.) in 1974 and $0.0654 (U.S.) in 1984. The share of SOEs in total labor cost has ranged between 22.5 percent and 41.2 percent between 1974 and 1984. Data also suggest that SOEs dominated in electricity, mining, transport and manufacturing and, beginning in 1977, in commerce also.

Fixed Capital Formation

Data on Fixed Capital Formation (FCF) are very confusing. They differ by publication, even when they are produced by the same source, the BOS. They may also differ by issue of the same publication. In this section data on FCF in SOEs were obtained from the *Analysis of Accounts of Parastatal Enterprises* while those for the whole economy were taken from *Economic Surveys* and *Statistical Abstracts*.

During the 1974-84 period parastatal enterprises FCF as a share of total fluctuated between 17.3 percent and 33.8 percent. In absolute nominal terms SOE fixed capital formation, which stood at 1,065.7 million shillings in 1974, rose to 2,101.5 million in 1977, fell to 1,484.1 million in 1979 and then rose to its highest level at 3,630.5 million shillings in 1982. In 1983 the variable fell sharply to 2,017.3 million and rose in the following year to 2,751.8 million shillings; the Tanzanian shilling was equal to $0.1401 (U.S.) in 1974 and $0.0654 (U.S.) in 1984. Examination of the composition of investment shows that manufacturing and transport still dominated as indicated earlier for the period 1966-71, although diversification into other areas is observed during the 1974-84 period.

The Performance Controversy

In Tanzania, as in many African countries, SOEs have yielded a very low rate of return on the large amount of resources invested in them. Given the preferential treatment most SOEs enjoyed, the expectation would be for them to earn reasonable returns on their investments. Some SOEs do, but a number do not, and substantial losses are suffered as Table 3 shows.

In 1984 the audited SOEs showed a loss of 83 million shillings. Even during the years which SOEs made profits on the

Table 3
Profits Before Tax (Million shillings[a]) of SOEs whose Accounts were Audited by Tanzania Audit Corporation (TAC), 1983-85

	1983	1984	1985
Profit Makers	3,876.5	2,911.9	3,811.4
	(n=196)[b]	(n=213)	(n=189)
Loss Makers	910.2	2,994.4	1,853.0
	(n=165)	(n=171)	(n=165)
Aggregate	2,966.3	82.5	1958.4
	(n=361)	(n=384)	(n=354)

Notes
a. The Tanzanian shilling had the following U.S. dollar equivalencies: 1983 - $0.0897; 1984 - $0.0654; 1985 - $0.0572.
b. n is the number of SOEs

Source: TAC Annual Reports

aggregate, a significant number of them showed losses; in 1983 and 1985, 46 percent and 47 percent, respectively, suffered losses. Unprofitable parastatals included crop authorities and important commercial SOEs such as National Milling Corporation, Mwanza Textiles Ltd., Kilimanjaro Textile Corporation Ltd., Steel Rolling Mills Ltd. and Musoma Textiles Ltd.

In two studies (Semboja, et al., 1985; 1986) which included over 100 enterprises, it was found that output per worker/man-hour in SOEs was roughly half that of private firms. In the manufacturing sector this result was observed despite the fact that output per unit of capital employed was about the same, an indication of the existence of redundant labor in the SOEs. Furthermore, manufacturing SOEs' employees worked less hours per year although they were being paid more per hour. The state-owned sisal estates received a lower price for their output, probably due to quality differences but also, it has been suggested, because of their poor marketing strategies. In another study (Semboja, 1987) that included over 100 SOEs, the service-oriented parastatals produced better financial results than directly productive SOEs.

On the basis of the World Bank's (1987) report, in 1985, 55 percent of all the SOEs in the industrial sector were extremely inefficient in that they produced negative value added when all inputs are valued at world market prices, compared to 15 percent for the private sector. Using the same criteria, the study found that 23 percent of the SOEs were efficient, in that they used less inputs than the value added of their output, compared to 34 percent in the private sector industrial activities.

On the basis of these findings, and others not reported above, some analysts have linked the issue of performance with ownership. The state is a poor entrepreneur; given the same conditions, resources producing a modest return in SOEs could produce a higher return elsewhere. Pre-investment analyses are not properly made; in a number of cases the assessment of the economic prospects for an enterprise are made by a private agent attempting to sell the plant and equipment, or by a donor agency's representative that takes an optimistic view of prospects in order to advance a politically advantageous project. There are no incentives for the management and workers to perform; no rewards are given to good performers and poor performance is not punished. Resources are not allocated where they are most productive; administrative rather than market signals determine their allocation.

On the other side are those analysts who feel that the issue of poor performance of SOEs can not be explained entirely by the involvement of the state in production. First, the involvement of the state was not a voluntary move, since at independence reliable private entrepreneurs did not exist. The conditions of operating an infant business in an almost nonexistent infrastructure (transport and communication, financial institutions, industrial linkage, etc.) were very difficult. Second, due to the small size of the domestic market these economies could afford to have only one large firm, an automatic monopolist. It can be argued that the replacement of an inefficient SOE monopoly by a poorly regulated or unregulated private monopoly would not raise the welfare of the residents. Indeed, it can be argued that, under conditions of monopoly, divestiture can lead to a decline in the supply of essential goods and services unless effective price control is exercised.

A third argument is based on an empirical observation that some SOEs are performing very well, some even better than private activities in the same lines of production. Tanzania Cigarette Company Ltd., Tanzania Breweries Ltd., National Bank of Commerce and the Bank of Tanzania are a few of the SOEs whose performance has been cited by many. The performance of SOEs has differed within the same line of production suggesting that factors other than ownership may be at play. The quality of management is not the same in all parastatals. It was noted in a study by the World Bank (1987) that SOEs with dynamic management performed better; examples cited were Tanzania Cigarette Company, Ubungo Farm Implements and National Transport Company. It was also noted that some firms may experience special problems which negatively affect their performance. For example, Musoma Textile Mill has continuously faced problems of water and electricity supply.

Using a sample of six textile firms representing 91.1 percent and 89.3 percent of the textile industry's capacity and output in 1976 and 89.3 percent and 77.7 percent in 1984, respectively, Mbelle (1988) found that "the private firms were in 1976 more efficient than public firms, while in 1984 the latter were more efficient. Thus, over time the private firms have become more inefficient." Another study (Semboja, 1987) has shown that for many of the factors which influence production there was no significant difference in their accessibility between SOEs and private enterprises. The study came to the conclusion that a correction of the macroeconomic environment, the use of market signals (in general) and the enforcement of commercial principles in commercial SOEs should go a long way toward improving the performance of SOEs.

A fourth argument is based on the measurement of success. Clearly each of the indicators used to measure economic or financial performance of firms is subject to criticism. But suppose that for each of the financial/economic indicators used the results had shown that all the firms, private and SOEs, have yielded similar levels of performance. Would it then be justifiable to conclude that all firms have been equally successful, or failures? The answer is definitely no. A firm's successes and/or failures would also have to be gauged by the extent to which they performed against their established objectives. On this issue some analysts have underscored the role of the extended public sector in Tanzania in ensuring political stability.

The above views and others (Nellis, 1986; World Bank, 1987; Semboja, 1987) have led to the more moderate view that improvements of the SOEs could be made even under present ownership arrangements. This could be achieved through the creation of an appropriate macro-economic policy environment in order to expand the role of markets, exposing SOEs to the stimulus of competition, clarifying objectives and the relations between governments and enterprises and optimizing managerial autonomy at the level of the firm.

This view seems to be gaining popularity, even within the donor community. The World Bank (1987) study emphasizes rehabilitation of SOEs along the lines proposed above. In a recent issue paper entitled "UNDP Approach to Private Sector in Developing Countries," the UNDP (undated) defines a Private Sector Oriented Strategy (PSOS) to include not only ownership but also the realization of human talent and ingenuity. The latter aspect is given more emphasis than the former and can take place "even in a centrally controlled economy through increasing decentralization of the management and by combining responsibility with accountability."

Symbiosis: A Constraint to Performance and Reforms

In our specific context the condition of symbiosis refers to the association of dissimilar sectors for mutual benefit. Understanding this is important because it poses special problems in dealing with these sectors. The symbiosis is represented in Figure 1 that shows how each of the three sectors receives and provides goods and services to the others.

Some government officials own privately owned enterprises (POEs). They receive dividends, profits and satisfaction from the POEs they own. But their enterprises may have links with other POEs not owned by them. Furthermore, as government officers are responsible for allocation of scarce resources and making important decisions, their services are normally paid for through tangible (money and goods) and/or intangible (loyalty, respect and services) contributions. In a number of countries the private sector has at some point succeeded in shaping their political system by placing their candidates in key political positions.

The private sector, in return benefits from this relationship in different forms. For instance, government decisions on allocation of scarce resources are important in determining how and/or where they will be allocated. Even in situations where government machinery in the allocation of scarce resources is relatively unimportant, however, the private sector still requires government moral support and assurance in order to build confidence for continued investment. In many cases the domestic POEs apply for protection against foreign competition. If the application is accepted, the government will, in effect, have allowed POEs to earn higher profits than they would have otherwise managed.

Some of the reasons which have led to the creation of public enterprises particularly in third world countries were presented in the introduction to this chapter. The government owns these institutions, and government officials make decisions on their behalf. SOEs are in some respect extensions of the government. These officials receive goods and services in return for services rendered; economic assurance, in the form of job security and fees earned by being board members; political stability, through assured loyalty by providing jobs to opponents and retired loyal servants, and control of strategic commodities (including arms and foreign exchange). The SOEs in return receive favorable allocation of resources, support and protection, in the same manner as discussed above for the POEs.

Some POEs are owned by officials of SOEs. They receive dividends and profits from the firms they own. Their POEs are granted tenders by SOEs to perform services. The POEs they own have business relations with those they don't own. Those officials heading very key SOEs such as financial institutions, licensing

Figure 1

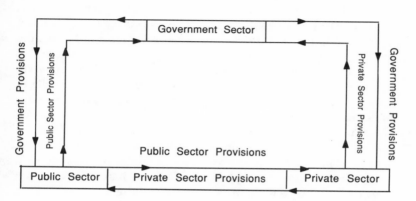

boards, etc., also receive tangible and intangible appreciations from POEs which receive their "favors," particularly during periods of economic hardships. In return the POEs receive support, resource allocation favors and protection from SOE officials. Further, some POEs' owners are board members in SOEs and receive benefits from them.

The symbiosis as described above represents a fairly good picture of what exists in Tanzania, as well as other third world and developed countries. There are, however, differences between third world and developed countries which may account for observed differences in performance. There are differences of size and pressure to perform as shown in Figure 2 below.

The size of the public enterprise sector in developed countries is smaller than that in most third world countries. This observation is important when it is remembered that it is in developed countries where resources necessary to run this sector are more available. Given the limited resources and many public enterprise sector institutions available in third world countries, the tendency has been to spread resources thinly over SOEs. For some of the scarce factors like skilled labor, this has meant the utilization of marginal skills to manage some institutions. As we have already noted, SOEs with good management perform better. Similarly, most SOEs have not been able to replace their worn out capital equipment and have to bear with frequent machine breakdowns and production stoppages.

Furthermore, due to the large number of SOEs, the governments of third world countries have not managed successfully to monitor developments of these institutions and take corrective measures where necessary. This difficulty arises because of the preference for administrative mechanisms in the allocation of resources and price determination rather than the use of market signals. The limited resources that are available to undertake monitoring, controlling and supervision can hardly be of much transparent use given the number of institutions involved. As a consequence it may take quite some time before the results of many of the poor performing institutions can be examined. It may take an even longer period before corrective measures are taken; incompetent managers can be retained because an appropriate replacement cannot be found.

Pressures for SOEs to perform are also more intense and diversified in the developed countries than in third world countries. These pressures come from two sources. The first is political pressure. In developed countries there are open debates (conflicts) about the role of the public enterprise sector. This continuous debate keeps SOEs aware of their vulnerable position; they have to defend themselves by proving to the public that they can deliver. In third world countries these debates take place mainly among groups with similar interests to defend, those employed in the government, the public sector and, very briefly, in the parliament. In some countries this issue is given an ideological connotation making it politically sensitive.

The second form of pressure arises from competition. Competition can originate from domestic producers/suppliers and external producers/suppliers. In developed countries competition from domestic supplies is limited due to the concentration of the SOEs in a few areas, such as in water and energy supply, railways, sewage and postal services. Recent developments in the areas of

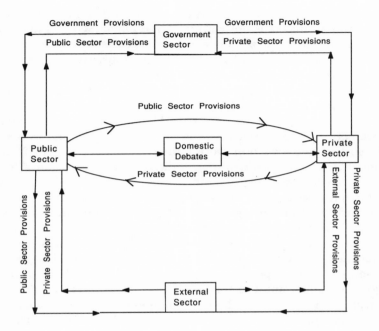

postal services, rural water supply, power supply and railways show acceptance by a number of governments to introduce competition into these areas. Competition within SOEs will increase even further as the concept of "natural monopolies" is being challenged by experience. In third world countries, despite extending into areas which the private enterprise sector also has interest, SOEs have normally been protected from competition. Genuine monopolistic SOEs exist but a number of monopolies are created without justification. Competition among SOEs should be encouraged.

Competition with foreign producers is another feature that is gaining momentum in developed countries. SOEs are involved in the export trade of the goods and services they produce but also, in recent years, in specialized skills. In third world countries SOEs have not only been protected from external competition, but they have also been inward looking.

Furthermore, in third world countries, competition from external producers is not lacking in the public SOEs alone. As indicated before, the private sector is also protected from external competition. As a result, even in this sector, pressure to perform is not strong enough. In developed countries this is not the case as competition for price and quality exists in almost all areas of production.

The importance of the current liberalization is to introduce competition into Tanzania. From the above discussion, this is an important step toward improving the performance of both SOEs and POEs. Casual observation indicates that apart from a few problems here and there, the move has produced positive signs. The question is, can this be replicated in other third world countries? Clearly the amount of imports that come into Tanzania under the liberalization program must be financed by foreign currency that is lying idle somewhere. Furthermore, it is important that this source continues to be replenished so that goods continue to be imported. The issue of the sustainability of this source is important if the process is to continue. Is it practical to assume that all countries have a pool of unused foreign exchange lying idle somewhere? If not, another source has to be found; one which is as flexible as own funds.

Rehabilitation and Divestitures

We have noted that some SOEs had economic justifications for their establishment while others did not. Partly due to government policies and also due to the constraints imposed by symbiosis, both categories of SOEs were retained. The policies ensured that either they were performing well financially or were bailed out when they had financial losses. Our discussion in the previous section would suggest that introducing competition into the SOEs is desirable. Competition is considered fair if it is done on an "equal" basis. It is not true that all SOEs benefited from the old system. Most of the SOEs operating in the distorted market also suffered for a lengthy period; their machinery and equipment are beyond repair, their marketing system is under-developed, they have accumulated debts, their capital structure is heavily indebted, etc. Most, if not all, cannot compete effectively under the new market-oriented macroeconomic policy environment. The question is, should they be left to fend for themselves when it is known in advance that they will not survive for long?

Two lines of argument have emerged in response to this. The first is that the SOEs have had enough of the good time, they were protected long enough, and they should now be exposed to reality. The problem with this argument is that it assumes that government policies favored all SOEs in the same direction and at the same level. If the pattern obtained by arranging in ascending order the economic returns of different SOEs differs from that for financial returns, the adopted policies can be judged to have been discriminatory within the SOEs. Thus, such policies have penalized economically justified SOEs at the expense of un-economically justified ones. On the basis of this, the second argument goes, economically justified SOEs should not be penalized for being affected by these policies. Rather, they should be given a chance to prove their worthiness by being allowed to compete fairly. The game can be considered fair if all the participants start from the same point. With an accumulation of debts, old machines and equipment, underdeveloped market systems, poor capital structure, etc., most SOEs will start the game from different points. This argument is convincing although most constraints arising from government policies applied to both POEs and SOEs. But this does not mean that SOEs and POEs are starting from the same point since, in practice, consistently loss-making POEs cannot be allowed to accumulate debts. What then should be done within the SOEs? Given limited resources, what criteria should be used to allocate resources for rehabilitation?

Perhaps the starting point should be to state the obvious: given the available resources, Tanzania has a very large, diverse and complex public enterprise sector. As one World Bank analyst put it "only in countries as large as Brazil (six times the population and fifty times the GDP of Tanzania) and Mexico (3.6 times the population and 35 times the GDP) does one find more than 425 parastatals" (World Bank, 1987:6). Clearly the number of parastatals that depend on government resources should be limited to a manageable number.

As is the case with all countries, there are activities which have to be under state ownership. This may also include those SOEs which the state is determined to support even if their operation proves to be uneconomic for a short period. This category will include posts and telecommunications, water and electricity supply, rail and air services, harbors and ports, banking and insurance. It will be noted that this list is not confined to "public utilities" or "natural monopolies." This is a list of priority areas which is likely to change with time.

The managements of these SOEs should submit to the government plans which detail rehabilitation of their machines and equipment, financial restructuring, annual cost minimization targets and price targets. These plans should also include a post-rehabilitation program detailing investment expansion plans. The plans should include a program of action. Funds for rehabilitation should be released when the government is satisfied that the proposed plans and programs of action are justified. Competitive pressures could be introduced in this category by encouraging competition among SOEs, where applicable.

The second category includes those SOEs which cannot become economically viable in the near future. Two options are open for this category. First, they could be included in the third category and be permitted to fend for themselves. However, since it is understood that they will not succeed, this decision is equivalent to allowing them to continue wasting resources; it will be more economic to deploy their assets and manpower sooner than later. Thus, the second option is to divest part or the whole to other owners. Analysts find this option to be subject to political objections. They may be correct. Experience from other countries has revealed that there have been concerns on nationality and indigenousness of prospective buyers. In some countries ideological issues involving the extent of people's involvement are also featured. These are practical problems which cannot be ignored, but they should not be an excuse for continued waste of resources. Often these concerns are magnified by misinterpretations which have equated divestiture with privatization. Indeed divestiture does not exclude efficient SOEs or cooperative ventures from expanding by acquiring property of the divested SOEs.

The third category includes the rest of the SOEs. They should be allowed to fend for themselves. In order for the game of competition to be a fair one, these firms should be given freedom to decide their affairs; they should not be asked to serve noncommercial goals without receiving appropriate compensation from the government.

Some temporary initial assistance may be necessary in order to correct the effects of past policies. Due to limited resources, however, assistance should be provided to those who can prove that they will sustain improved performance if assistance is provided. Firms should be requested to compete for funds by submitting proposals for rehabilitation. Funds should be allocated to firms whose proposals provide evidence of a bright future. A panel of experts should be used to scrutinize the proposals and to ensure that requests are realistic; funds should not be spread too thinly. A system of revolving funds could be established by providing these funds in the form of soft loans rather than grants, although this may generate temptations to make this source permanent. It will be useful to define the transition period, after which government assistance should cease. Those firms whose proposals do not qualify for temporary government assistance should be encouraged to look for other sources such as going into joint ventures with more financially healthy firms.

Conclusion

Reasons for state involvement in production and distribution of goods and services have been outlined. State involvement found justification from social, political and economic grounds. At the time of independence, for a large number of countries, state involvement did not come in as a replacement or as a competitor of indigenous private enterprise. Indeed, state involvement was seen as an essential complement to private enterprise growth.

Once the state got involved in production and distribution, fears of competition emerged and protective policies were applied. Although discriminatory policies were not officially documented in most policy instruments, political statements by party and government leaders significantly influenced resource allocation in favor of SOEs.

Despite the practiced favoritism for SOEs it has been noted that a large number of SOEs have been loss-makers, leading some analysts to associate poor performance with state ownership. This association, however, has failed to take into account important issues, including the existence of efficient SOEs, some of them performing better than POEs in the same lines of production or outside. As such, privatization cannot be a quick solution to poor performing SOEs.

Recently the government has adopted policies which are aimed at correcting the macroeconomic environment by expanding the role of markets and reducing the role of administrative mechanisms in the allocation of resources. Positive results are observed but more needs to be done before the productive sector can respond fully.

The discussion of symbiosis outlined in this chapter is aimed at exposing the dilemma that faces Tanzania and other countries with similar economies. On the one hand, symbiosis is not a condition that encourages SOEs to produce efficiently, i.e., there is no pressure for price and quality competition. On the other hand, symbiosis is self-guarding; that is, every sector (government, private and parastatal) benefits from the existence of the other and works for the survival of not only itself but also the other. Any move that is aimed at weakening one of the three actors will be rejected by all, collectively.[3]   This is why reforms tend to be compromising and sometimes contradictory.

The government's decision to correct the macroeconomic environment by expanding the role of markets is commendable. Managerial autonomy in the performance of SOEs is important in order for firms to compete on equal grounds. Before the SOEs can compete effectively for prices and quality, however, a rehabilitation program has to be undertaken that will enable economically viable SOEs to cover their huge debts, repair and/or

---

[3]These decisions may not necessarily be popular to the public. As is usually the case, decisions which matter are those made at the "political centers."

replace their worn out equipment and develop their weak marketing systems.

Chapter 8

DEVELOPMENT BANKS IN THE ERA OF "SOCIALIST TRANSITION": ACHIEVEMENTS, PROBLEMS AND PROSPECTS IN THE ZIMBABWE CASE

Theresa Moyo

Introduction

Z IMBABWE is one of the youngest newly independent countries in sub-Saharan Africa. Independence was attained in 1980 after about ninety years of British colonial rule. The colonial economy as could be expected was characterized by the political rule by a white minority class who owned and controlled the country's rich resources of land and capital. Under the various Land Apportionment Acts, the colonial regime successfully drove off the indigenous black population from the fertile lands of Natural Regions I and II to the dry, infertile lands of the so-called tribal trust lands. This had the immediate effect of impoverishing the black population, consequently compelling it to seek wage employment on settler farms, the mines and emerging industries.

Through exploitation of black labor, the settler class reaped massive profits which were reinvested in the country especially during the Unilateral Declaration of Independence (UDI) period as the economy was under international economic sanctions. The initial impact of economic sanctions imposed on Southern Rhodesia in 1966 was a drop in the real rate of growth in the economy. This, however, was short-lived as the economy took off in 1967, growing rapidly at an average annual real rate of 7.6 percent until 1974. The main sources of growth were diversification and import substitution in both agriculture and manufacturing and expansion of exports which generated the required foreign exchange. The rapid growth soon saw manufacturing overtake agriculture as the leading sector. With the onset of the war of liberation (*Chimurenga*), growth slackened. Business expectations were at a low ebb, resulting in very few new fixed investments. Banking and financial institutions experienced high levels of liquidity.

The advent of peace, the election of a new government and political independence in early 1980 created a favorable business and economic atmosphere that, combined with existing excess capacity in the economy, formed the foundation for the real growth of more than 11 percent achieved in 1980. The lifting of sanctions improved Zimbabwe's terms of trade. High prices for minerals and other exports were largely responsible for the 27 percent surge in export earning. The increase in minimum wages raised aggregate demand and increased growth and employment.

That economic growth trend, however, has been steadily declining since 1980 and, with it, growth in employment as well. The inherited economic and political structure of the country has posed serious and challenging problems to the government. It is these problems which have made socialist transformation almost impossible. First, the predominant role of foreign capital in virtually every sector of the economy has made change difficult because the government did not have the vast foreign exchange resources needed to pay compensation as required by the Lancaster House Agreement. In addition, there were very few Zimbabweans with the managerial and technical skills needed to run those enterprises, once they were nationalized. The second problem relates to the dependent nature of the economy. A producer of primary raw material exports from mines and agriculture, the economy is vulnerable to external shocks of every kind, international recessions, declining terms of trade, growing protectionism, rising prices of its manufactured imports, etc. The third problem is perhaps a more serious one, namely the shortage of skilled local labor. This was a result of past colonial policies of racial discrimination against blacks who were denied good quality education and adequate technical training facilities. The pace of indigenization has therefore been slow although tremendous efforts have been made to expand education at all levels.

The Zimbabwe government's development thrust is most succinctly described in key policy statements such as Growth With Equity (1981), Foreign Investment Policy, Guidelines and Procedures (1982), the Transitional National Development Plan (TNDP) 1982-83 - 1984-85, and the Five Year Development Plan 1985-1990 (FYDP). Government's thinking as laid out in paragraph 3 of the Growth with Equity statement reads:

> The government of the Republic of Zimbabwe, conscious of the basic characteristics of the past and indeed still prevailing socio-economic order of this country, is determined to undertake a vigorous program for the development of the country and within it, to pursue and implement policies based on socialist, egalitarian and democratic principles in conditions of rapid economic growth, full employment, price stability dynamic efficiency in resource allocation and on equitable distribution of ensuring benefits.

More detailed macroeconomics and sectoral objectives are laid out in the same documents. However, the developmental strategy deserves special attention here as this will be the basis for evaluating the performance of the development banks. The development strategy as laid out in the TNDP paragraphs 4.11 - 4.22 is summarized below:

1. The strategy adopted to achieve the objectives of the plan is one of growth with equity and transformation. It is a problem-solving oriented strategy which aims at

providing efficient solutions to the urgent problems of reconstruction, growth, equitable distribution of income and wealth and socialist transformation.

2. Moreover, it promotes rapid and efficient economic growth and development and equitable distribution of income and wealth, is people oriented and aimed at the attainment of full-employment and full development of Zimbabwe's human resources, both as a factor in, and as an end of, development, promotes greater participation in, and control of, the national economy, and over natural resources by nationals, and the state itself, and promotes attainment of a socialist egalitarian society.

3. The strategy requires a comprehensive structural and institutional reorientation of the inherited socioeconomic system to facilitate its eventual transformation. In addition to reorientation of existing institutions it also requires the creation of new organizations which will underpin the new order.

4. In the economic area, the strategy requires increased domestic participation, ownership and control of the economy by nationals and the state, and active worker participation and involvement in decision-making in industry and agriculture. It requires the establishment of state farms and encouragement of the development of co-operatives in both the urban and rural areas.

5. This strategy emphasizes rural development and land settlement schemes, requires the strengthening of backward and forward linkages between light and heavy industry, agriculture and the resource sector.

6. The reconstruction of the economy has to be an integral part of the long-term development strategy, which recognizes certain historical, sectoral and other inherited imbalances.

7. It will be necessary to generate high rates of domestic savings in order to finance the planned investment program and utilize external assistance pledged at ZIMCORD.

8. Legitimate increases in expenditures on social services will be accommodated but these and other services as

well as subsidies will be strictly disciplined. Deficits in [the] central government's recurrent budget will be reduced.

9. Small- and medium-scale industries will be encouraged in the rural areas in order to create large amounts of productive employment and encourage labor-intensive methods of production.

10. Land redistribution and rural development programs will aim at a progressive reduction in the disparities between the modern and rural peasant sectors.

It is clear from the policy documents that the government's objectives are indeed comprehensive insofar as they address basically all the crucial issues in any development planning.

The problem, however, lies in the actual implementation of the planned objectives. This can be attributed to a number of factors such as the declining rates of GDP growth, shortage of foreign exchange, recessions, droughts and bureaucratic inefficiency and planning. In fact, the pace towards socialist transformation has been so slow as to make the use of the term socialist transition almost a misnomer. The land distribution pattern is still highly inequitable despite the resettlement program embarked on in 1981; income distribution is still highly skewed despite the introduction of minimum wage laws. Although the government has bought shares in a few banks and companies, foreign capital still controls and owns over 60 percent of national wealth. Dependency on the Western capitalist world has increased as reflected in the heavy borrowing of financial resources from various Western bilateral and multilateral sources.

Thus, the analysis of the role of the development banks should be viewed in the framework outlined above.

Key Economic Indicators

Economic growth and employment have been on the decline since 1980 and this has added to the constraints hindering meaningful transformation. Table 1 below shows the trends in GDP growth since 1979.

Table 1
Annual Rates of Growth of GDP at Factor Cost
(1980 Prices)

	1979	1980	1981	1982	1983	1984	1985	1986
Material Production	+3.8	12.5	11.2	-5.6	-6.8	1.4	11.0	-1.4
Non-material Production	-3.7	8.2	18.3	9.0	1.2	3.2	5.3	2.7
Total GDP	1.4	11.0	10.7	1.4	-4.2	2.6	9.3	0.2

Source: Annual Economic Review of Zimbabwe, 1986, p. 2.

Foreign exchange shortages and low investment were the major factors behind the falling growth. Trends in Gross Fixed Capital Formation (GFCF) are shown in Table 2.

It can be seen from Table 2 that GFCF has been declining since 1982 with the biggest decline of 22 percent being experienced in 1984. Very little, if any, new investment has taken place in recent years; in fact there could have been an actual decline in capital stock.

Gross national savings as a percent of GDP increased from 14 percent in 1980 to 24 percent at the end of 1985—a rather paradoxical situation of low investment versus high savings. This is explained by foreign exchange (FOREX) shortages which determine the volume of investment.

Table 2
Growth Rate of Overall GFCF from 1980-86 (1980 Prices)

	1980	*1981*	*1982*	*1983*	*1984*	*1985*	*1986*
Growth of GFCF	19.2	36.7	9.1	-6.1	-22.2	-12.8	-7.4
GFCF/GDP %	16	20	22	21	16	13	12

Source: Annual Economic Review of Zimbabwe, 1986, p. 5.

Development Banks in the Economy

The role of banks in general in the development process has been debated among economists. There is a consensus, however, on the positive role they can play in this respect. But of course there is major debate on the extent to which their role will depend on the prevailing mode of production—i.e., that under a capitalism system they will reinforce private ownership and therefore perpetuate the process of labor exploitation.

Development banks play an important role in mobilizing resources and lending them on a long-term basis, i.e., for development purposes. Zimbabwe's first established banks were commercial and merchant banks who tended to lend on a short-term basis. Development banks were therefore established to compensate for the shortage of development finance. The FYDP points to this.

Financial institutions private and public, are expected to be responsive to development requirements as laid down in the plan. These are as follows:

1. Increase availability of financial resources and assistance for increased state involvement in the strategic sector of the economy.

2. Mobilization of financial resources for priority development projects and provision of the necessary financial expertise and assistance to investors.
3. Increase of the level of domestic shareholding in the financial sector, including shareholding by the state.
4. Encouragement of the extension of banking services to rural areas, and in particular to co-operative and small procedures.
5. Assisting local investors and government in establishing joint ventures with foreign partners.

At the second reading of the Zimbabwe Development Bank Bill in parliament, former Deputy Minister of Finance Malianga said:

> A new development bank can be justified in the light of the enhanced Zimbabwean role in business development, in the ownership and direction of enterprises and the desire of Government to ensure a coordinated allocation of overall development finance. Existing commercial and development financial institutions, both publicly and privately owned, could not be relied upon to meet all development requirements effectively because of their orientation and their obligations, as they say it, to shareholders and depositors.

The statement emphasizes the dissatisfaction of the government with the way the banking sector has performed in the past. In the pre-independence period, there were some development banks but they confined their activities to the more successful and well-established ventures in industry and agriculture. They tended to neglect emerging small-scale black businessmen and communal farmers. In addition, they failed to promote rural development through their lending activities.

In short, therefore, development banks since 1980 have been expected to play a significant role in the country's development. They are expected to go beyond the traditional confines of the orientation of pre-independence banks and to spearhead development in line with planned objectives. Yet despite concerted efforts their role appears to have been very small.

The Problem Identified

The establishment of new development banks and corporations after independence was a step forward. There are a number of problems, however, that have reduced their effectiveness and are likely to limit their role in the future.

Although the government holds some shares in the banks, they depend quite heavily on external sources of finance. The question then lies in the ability of the banks to pursue independent decisionmaking in their lending activities or even the extent to which external financiers agree with the implementation of specified objectives of the banks. Can rural transformation be effected by relying on donors whose interests may be at odds with those of Zimbabwe?

Development banks are financed mainly by the government. Due to financial problems of its own, the government was not able to grant the funds which would have enabled the banks to meet the demand for loans. Existing commercial banks and other institutions in the money market have over time established themselves and are able to mobilize large sums of money.

A basic question to raise then is, in view of the government's own financial problems, should it not have either bought more shares in money market institutions or set up its commercial banks or alternatively, require the latter to hold a prescribed amount of its assets in development bank shares/stocks?

The banks have not made a significant impact on rural development. Lending to cooperatives and small-scale producers in rural areas has been small. They have also not been successful in gaining control of the strategic sector of the economy as spelled out in the FYDP. Their main role was to rescue existing enterprises which were in serious problems following the rise in minimum wages, FOREX shortages, falling export prices, etc. The banks merely helped to maintain existing capacity and save jobs. Perhaps the absence of a clear-cut industrialization strategy accounts for the failure of development banks to transform the structure of industry.

Case Studies of the Performance of Development Banks

The Agricultural Finance Corporation (AFC)

The Agricultural Finance Corporation started in Zimbabwe as the Land and Agricultural Bank of Southern Rhodesia in 1924. During the next twenty years, the organization grew slowly, granting 3,850 loans valued at £5.4 million (Whitsun Foundation, 1981:164); the pound sterling was equal to $4.0350 (U.S.) in 1944. Then in the two decades after World War II, spurred by the rapid increase in post-war immigration, demand for agricultural finance grew quickly and 35,000 loans were granted between 1946 and 1971. In 1971 it was officially constituted by an Act of Parliament (Chapter 101) as the Agricultural Finance Corporation (AFC). The act precluded the AFC from lending to communal farmers, the limited amount of financing in this sphere being handled by the African Loan and Development Trust. In 1978, however, the act was amended to allow the AFC to lend to communal land farmers. Despite this, the corporation continued a greater portion of its money to commercial farmers. With the attainment of independence in 1980, the government redressed this so that the AFC could give more loans to communal farmers.

The AFC assigned to promote agriculture by extending credit to all sectors of the farming community of Zimbabwe. The act states that the corporation can make advances to any person directly or indirectly connected with the production processing, storage, packing or marketing of any produce procured from agriculture. The government guarantees all loans of AFC. The corporation has a number of schemes it offers: The Small Farm Credit Scheme assists small-scale farmers in the communal sector; the Resettlement Scheme was introduced in 1982 to lend money to farmers in the government's Resettlement Program as well as small-scale farmers; the Tenant Farming Scheme assists well-experienced young people to acquire capital to purchase their own farms; the Leasehold Finance Scheme assists those farmers who do not meet the conditions of above; the Purchase Guarantee Scheme assists experienced farmers who are unable to meet the AFC's normal lending criteria for purchasing a farm in the commercial areas; the Agricultural Assistance Scheme assists those who show prospects of viability but are undergoing financial difficulty; and the Special Relief Loans rescues drought-stricken farmers. Loans range from short-term (up to two years), medium-term (2-5 years) to long-term (6-30 years). Interest rates vary from as low as 0.9 percent to 13 percent per annum.

Lending criteria emphasize the economic viability of the farmer more than availability of collateral security. Where security is available the corporation will include it as a basis for lending. For the bulk of communal farmers who lack security, the AFC arranges stop-orders with the Marketing Boards so that loans are paid. Therefore, the farmer has to register with the local marketing authority. Many farmers found ways around this requirement, leading to a large number of defaults, thus making operation more difficult.

The AFC obtains funds from the government, external donor agencies, sale of fixed assets and farm properties. Total source of funds for the financial year ended March 31, 1986, amounted to $50.45 million; these and all figures are in Zimbabwe dollars, that had an equivalency rate of 1 to $0.6006 (U.S.). That amount includes about $12 million of loans and grants from donor agencies. (The total signed for was $33,959,534). Table 3 gives a breakdown of the source and value of the loans and grants.

The report notes that the World Bank loan finances the Small Farm Credit Scheme with respect to seasonal and medium-term loans to farmers, together with finance for supporting services such as transport, training, equipment an civil work; small-scale commercial farmers and resettlement farmers are supported by the Kreditanstalt with respect to medium-term loans only; the African Development Bank provides funds for seasonal and medium-term loans for the Small Farm Credit Scheme and Resettlement Scheme; and the Danida and EEC grants are used to finance the Resettlement Credit Scheme. In the case of the EEC, five accelerated resettlement schemes in the Midlands are financed while the Danish Aid supports the Resettlement Scheme as a whole.

A point worth noting is that although the external funds provide a smaller proportion of the corporate's financial require-

Table 3
External Loans and Grants to AFC (1986)
(in Zambabwean dollars)

Donor Agencies	Received during the year	Cumulative to 1986
LOANS		
World Bank	7,380,105	21,132,810
Kreditanstalt	1,540,294	3,222,537
African Development Bank	647,000	2,981,200
Total Loans	9,567,339	27,336,547
GRANTS		
Danida	2,002,779	3,662,075
European Economic Community	419,891	825,891
African Development Fund	108,070	108,070
African Development Bank	26,951	26,951
Total Grants	2,557,691	4,622,987
Total Loans and Grants	12,125,909	31,959,534

Source: AFC Annual Report, 1986

ments, the bulk of the funds are not used to bring about structural change in the sector, but to maintain existing patterns of production. Over 80 percent of AFC's total loans were granted to meet crop and production expenses and only about 5 percent for the purchase of land during 1985-86.

AFC makes loans to four sectors in agriculture: the large-scale commercial farming sector (LSCS), the small-scale commercial farming sector (SSCS), the resettlement area farming sector (RS), and the communal farming sector (CS). The number of loans to the LSCS has declined in the six-year period but their value has increased three-fold from $39.3 million in 1975 to $113 million in 1985. Table 4 shows the loans granted to all sectors in value terms.

It is important to consider the types of loans granted to these sectors. Long-term loans are mostly granted to the commercial sector. Short-term loans account for the vast majority of all loans; in the 1986 season short-term loans extended to the CS accounted for 90 percent of the total number of loans.

Despite the AFC's support of the transformation policy, the commercial sector still receives the largest proportion of the value of all loans. For example, in the 1984-85 season, the commercial sector received approximately $119 million worth of loans out of

Table 4
Loans Granted by Sector

Year	Value in Millions of Zimbabwean $				Loan as Percentage of LSCS		
	LSCS	SSCC	CS	RS	SSCS	CS	RS
1980	86.9	3.7	4.2	—	4.3	4.7	—
1981	88.8	4.6	10.1	0.5	5.2	11.4	0.6
1982	88.7	4.5	13.2	1.5	5.1	14.9	1.7
1983	110.2	8.1	23.4	10.6	7.4	21.2	9.6
1984	110.3	8.7	32.0	10.7	7.9	29.0	9.7
1985	113.0	11.5	38.8	8.5	10.2	34.3	7.5

Legend: LSCS = Large-scale commercial sector; SSCC = Small-scale commercial sector; CS = Communal sector; RS = Resettlement sector.

Source: AFC Quarterly Statistical Digest, Sept. 1986, Vol. 1, No. 1

total loans of $164.8 million, a value equaling 72.5 percent of the total loans. The communal sector received only 20.6 percent, while the resettlement sector received about 7 percent of the total value of loans.

Table 5 shows the allocation of credit by province in 1986. With no specified criteria for lending to provinces, regional discrepancies appear.

The major problem faced by the AFC is the high rate of defaults on loan repayment due to stop-order evasion. Table 6 shows the seriousness of the problem over the period 1980 to 1984. More recent information is not yet available. A related problem is the misuse of loans as some farmers spend the money on expenditures not previously approved by the AFC. Due to shortage of staff, it is difficult to monitor all borrowers periodically.

Table 5
Number and Value of Loans, in Millions of Zimbabwe Dollars, by Province, 1986

	LSCS		SSCS		RS		CS	
Province	Number Loans	Value Z$M	Number Loans	Value Z$M	Number Loans	Value Z$M	Number Loans	Value Z$M
Masvingo	15	1.82	211	2.36	1324	0.86	5728	3.99
Midlands	50	2.94	512	2.24	3129	1.99	9167	5.70
Manica-land	73	6.37	117	2.79	2908	2.48	4207	4.10
Mashona-land E	129	13.36	117	0.38	1391	1.30	1449	110.75
Mashona-land W	280	30.80	393	2.66	1285	0.66	15835	11.09
Mashona-land C	217	24.49	368	2.72	1271	1.42	26402	20.64
Matebe-land	15	0.43	7	0.01	347	0.20	857	0.75

Legend: LSCS = Large-scale commercial sector; SSCS = Small-scale commercial sector; RS = Resettlement sector; CS = Communal sector.

Source: AFC Quarterly Statistical Digest, Sept. 1986, Vol 1., p. 12.

Table 6
Repayment of Loans, 1980-85

Year Ending 31 Dec	Long- and Medium-Term Loans (including Development Loans)			Short-Term Loans		
	Loans	Repaid	%	Loans	Repaid	%
1980	61,721	8,161	13.2	42,844	8,579	20.0
1981	65,055	6,837	10.5	45,708	8,676	19.0
1982	72,632	9,637	13.3	82,239	10,413	12.7
1983	83,807	13,483	16.1	19,107	39,423	33.1
1984	95,928	17,159	17.9	142,952	55,097	38.5

Source: AFC Annual Report, 1985

The Zimbabwe Development Bank

The Zimbabwe Development Bank (ZDB) was established on May 6, 1983, in terms of ZDB Act (1983). It started with a share capital of $20 million. The Zimbabwe government shareholders are the Commonwealth Development Corporation (10 percent); the African Development Bank (8 percent); the Finnish Fund for Industrial Development Corporation (8 percent); the Nederlandse Financierings-maatschappij voor Onwikkelingslanden N.V. (F.M.O.) (8 percent); the Reserve Bank of Zimbabwe (7 percent); D.E.G. Deutsche Finanzierungsgesellschaft feur Beteiligungenin Entwicklungslaendern GMbH (6 percent); and the European Investment Bank (2 percent).

The objectives of the ZDB in terms of the 1983 Act are: to mobilize internal and external capital; to provide capital which is needed for the expansion, modernization or creation of new enterprises; and to engage, alone or with other persons or institutions, in financing loans and bonds, whether medium- or long-term, guaranteeing loans, underwriting and other related activities.

Projects should be financially and economically viable, technically feasible and socially acceptable. In addition the ZDB gives priority to projects which generate or save foreign exchange, utilize or raise the value added of local materials, enhance linkages, provide permanent employment, and promote Zimbabwean ownership and management.

As a relatively new institution, the ZDB has made very few loans, mainly for the expansion of existing enterprises and not new capital. The bank lends to large or established enterprises. The minimum amount to be applied for is $100,000. In addition, the loan should not exceed 50 percent of total funds applied for. It meets the foreign exchange costs of the projects: in the 1986-87 year the bank made an operating profit of Z$619,292.

During the period 1986-87, the ZDB approved loans to eighteen projects with an investment of $17 million. The bank provided $9.3 million.

The Small Enterprises Development Corporation

The Small Enterprises Development Corporation (SEDCO) was set up in November, 1984 following the enactment of the SEDCO Act No. 16 of 1983. Its objectives were to promote and accelerate the development of commerce and industry in Zimbabwe's rural areas and small towns, create employment and generate income for people in economically depressed areas, sustain economically viable enterprises, foster self-reliance and greater participation in economic life by the majority of Zimbabwean nationals via cooperative enterprises, stimulate and increase exports from the small enterprise sector, and creating more wealth via increased productivity in the small enterprise sector.

The corporation's main thrust was to encourage cooperatives and small-scale commercial and industrial enterprises. It provides assistance, management counselling and training, information and advice to cooperatives and small-scale enterprises. Schemes supported relate to reconstruction expansion, better organization and modernization of existing and new enterprises.

Criteria for lending include: projects must be economically viable; borrowers should have a good track record and should contribute 15 percent of required funds; borrowers must attend training sessions or seminars, conferences or workshops on various business aspects; projects must be within a provincial or district development plan; and projects should as far as possible utilize domestic resources.

Table 7
Investment Summary for 1987 (Z$ 000s)

Project	Total Investment	ZDB Financing Local	FOREX	Employment Generated
Manufacture pelletized stockfeed	540		219	22
Manufacture high tensile nuts	440		300	3
Manufacture polypropylene bags, cloth	532		300	22
Process edible oils	4,348		2,009	—
Recycle used plastic	587		313	na
Produce cereal products	524		230	10
Poultry and market gardening	399	195	—	na
Package food stuffs	708		567	na
Manufacture aluminum tubes, enclosures	1,759		1,173	22
Manufacture cotton fabric	1,006		747	na
Manufacture plastic stationery	954	350	—	na
Commercial printing	1,039	394	—	na
Process leather	916		616	na
Manufacture crepe bandages	335		171	—
Manufacture surgical tape and plaster	668		382	—
Produce shoes	737		525	—
Color separation	374		248	na
Produce carbonated drinks	1,828		508	na
TOTAL INVESTMENTS (TOTAL Local and Foreign Currency)	17,694	939	8,308 (9,247)	

Source: ZDB Annual Report, 1987.

SEDCO has applied its criteria very strictly and has therefore made a concerted effort to promote small-scale ventures. It appears, however, that due to its own financial constraint, it has not been effective in promoting structural transformation in the small-scale enterprises sphere. This can be clearly seen in the relatively smaller and declining proportion of loans awarded to cooperatives since the establishment of the corporation. Also, the lending pattern strengthened the commercial rather than the industrial sector. Yet at this stage of Zimbabwe's development, the key to solving a host of the country's problems is industrialization.

During 1985-86, 646 applications were received. Most (83 percent) of the applications were from sole proprietors, 9.1 percent from companies, 4.6 percent from partnerships, and 3.1 percent from cooperatives (SEDCO, 1987:17). Out of a total demand for loans of $14.6 million, 64.1 percent came from sole proprietors, 18.6 percent from companies, 9 percent from cooperatives and 8.3 percent from partnerships. Also noteworthy is the fact that 61.3 percent of the loan demand was from the commercial sector, while the industrial (23.4 percent), service (12.1 percent), and construction (3.1 percent) sectors were less represented.

During 1986-87 there was a slight increase in the demand (by $16.2 million) for loans. Demand sources were 56.8 percent for commerce, 28.4 percent for industry, 13 percent for services, and 1.8 percent for construction. 115 loans with a value of $1.9 million were approved—clearly far below the demanded $16.2 million.

During the period under study, the value of approved loans to cooperatives declined sharply from $0.8 million (1984-85) to $0.1 million over 1985-86 to about $0.05 million (1986-87) while the amounts declined slightly for the sole proprietorships—so it is evident that the corporation's lending has simply encouraged individual private enterprise. Of course, it was also largely because the bulk of loan applications was from that sector. Yet this lending pattern seems to contradict the goals of socialist transformation.

The Industrial Development Corporation

The Industrial Development Corporation (IDC) was established by an Act of Parliament in 1963. Its objectives were to facilitate, promote, guide and assist in the financing of new and old industries; to expand, better organize and assist industries to operate efficiently; and to coordinate industrial activities.

Under the new Act of 1984, the government of Zimbabwe acquired 80 percent of IDC's shares. The other 20 percent is held by Barclays Bank, Grindlays Bank and Zimbank, the South African

Mutual Life Assurance, Anglo-American Corporation, Delta Corporation and Security Nominees. Though predominantly government-owned, IDC operates on business lines.

IDC's lending was largely in the form of providing bridging loans to rescue enterprises in financial straits. Other funds were to increase state participation in industry and to provide expertise, consultancy and technical management services.

IDC's major success lies in that it was able to save numerous industries faced with liquidation and, thus, help retain technology and prevent the loss of employment that would have resulted from closures. It has not been very successful, however, in creating an industrial base as very few loans were made toward the establishment of new enterprises. In fact, it has promoted commercial rather than development-oriented activities. Table 8 shows IDC's investments over selected years after independence.

Conclusion

The foregoing analysis has shown the efforts made by the development banks in Zimbabwe's post-independence economic reconstruction and development. It examined the circumstances under which the institutions were formed, stated their objectives and assessed their success. They were established primarily because private sector banks and financial institutions did not provide adequate finance to provide long-term capital for investment purposes. Thus, the task of the development banks were to identify, appraise, promote, finance and implement investment projects. To this central role can be added other, no less important tasks, namely, the creation of employment, the saving or earning of foreign exchange, the development of small business and the diversification of industry. Clearly, the development bank assumes a wider role than if it were a purely private sector financial institution. It becomes an instrument of government policy, and is generally expected to act in the long-term interest of a country's economic development, a function which may often clash with its criterion as a profit-making institution.

Table 8
IDC Investments in Selected Years

Industry	1981 Z$'000s	%	1984 Z$'000s	%	1986 Z$'000s	%
Chemical	199	0.76	173	0.52	171	0.33
Clothing	366	1.40	971	2.59	1,019	1.95
Electrical, Electronic	64	0.24	77	0.21	122	0.23
Engineering	568	2.17	670	1.79	1,808	5.38
Film	425	1.63	376	1.00	386	0.38
Financial Services	2,147	8.21	741	2.60	11	2.25
Hotels	28	0.11	1	—	—	—
Industrial Property	72	0.28	37	0.09	—	—
Metal Products	1,147	4.39	7,940	21.20	8,337	15.96
Mining	12,654	48.40	11,732	31.30	2,765	24.41
Motor Assembly	4,641	17.75	6,720	17.90	7,952	15.23
Non-Metallic Mineral Products	944	3.61	2,794	7.46	3,057	5.85
Quarrying	—	—	77	6.21	89	0.17
Spinning, Weaving, Finishing Textiles	2,747	10.51	3,945	10.35	3,803	7.28
Tanning and Manu-facture of Leather Goods	94	0.36	30	0.08	4	0.01
Transport	34	0.13	21	0.05	—	—
Furniture	—	—	950	2.54	898	1.72
Pencils	—	—	153	0.41	183	3.50
	26,144	100.00	34,458	100.00	52,225	100.00

Source: IDC Annual Reports, 1981 to 1984-86.

Although the objectives for setting up development banks were "noble," i.e., the government's long-term objective of socialist transformation, the banks encountered a number of constraints which have minimized their impact on development. The first one was their limited capital base which could not meet the demand for long-term finance. This problem could be one reason why in their lending pattern, they have reinforced traditional patterns of sectoral and regional credit allocation. It is quite evident that these institutions take high financial and commercial risks which would normally require high expected returns, according to capital market theory.

The requirement to meet the government's national objectives implies that from time to time they finance projects whose financial return is expected to be relatively low, that is below the return which is acceptable on commercial grounds. So, to operate as "social" institutions they would require a larger financial base. This requirement is rendered even more critical by the lack of collateral security of the bulk of some borrowers, which means the risk facing the banks is consequently greater.

A related problem to that of inadequate finance was the dependency on external funding of some of the banks. This may also have influenced the pattern of lending, although none of the institutions ever alluded to such a problem. The Agricultural Finance Corporation has received a number of loans from the World Bank. These were used to meet operating expenses in the agricultural sector, and not for land purchases. This could well have been due to the reluctance of the Bank to finance such structural reforms.

For the above reasons, development banks in Zimbabwe have a long way to go in effecting socialist transformation. The government should expand its capital base. The banks' staffing must also be enlarged in order to permit closer supervision of projects. There is also a need to decentralize their activities with a more rural spread being essential for monitoring of activities. Above all, there must be a clear-cut industrialization strategy which each development bank is obliged to follow in a systematic manner. Although their role has been limited in the past, development banks have an important role to play in Zimbabwe's future development. But to do that, substantial changes must be effected.

PART THREE

Popular Participation in the Struggle for Peace and Development

Chapter 9

THE KEYS TO PEACE IN AFRICAN REGIONAL CONFLICTS: LESSONS FROM ERITREA AND ETHIOPIA

Basil Davidson

*"Liberta non tradisce i volenti"**
GIUSEPPE GARIBALDI

I T HAPPENED to me, during the small hours of March 17, 1988, to arrive at the headquarters of the Eritrean national movement, the Eritrean People's Liberation Front (EPLF): during the small hours, because travel by vehicle through na-tionalist-held Eritrea has for some years been chiefly at night, so as to lessen the dangers of Ethiopian aerial bombardment which has generally tried to hit anything that moves.

I had come from the Sudan through these northern mountains of Eritrea along roads carved during the past six years

---

*"Liberty does not betray the violent ones"

or so by Eritrean engineers. These roads are efficient, as one sees, and carry nightly convoys of trucks conveying donated food from the harbor of Port Sudan. But they are necessarily rough and tortuous in this abrupt and often precipitous terrain. Travel can be tiring. Having reached the center-point of Eritrean authority I went to bed in a half-underground shelter hut. At about noon that morning I was able to meet leaders of the EPLF including its 42-year-old Secretary-General Isaias Afwerki—an impressively modest personality already nineteen years in this struggle—and so fulfill one of the objects of my journey.

For someone inquiring into the situation of Eritreans as I was, it could scarcely have been a more interesting moment. "This morning," Isaias Afwerki told me, "we have begun a big offensive along our whole Nacfa front, and it is going well." That was to prove an understatement. Two days later, on March 19, it was clear that early signs of breakthrough were much outreached by results; that afternoon, a day earlier than the Eritrean command had thought likely and had planned for, the battle was over with a shattering success for the Eritrean army, including the un-planned-for fall of the Ethiopian army base of Afabet.

A whole army corps consisting of the Ethiopian 14th, 19th and 21st Divisions, plus its 29th Mechanized Brigade and Tank Battalion—perhaps a total of some 20,000 troops—had been encircled on the plateau northwest of Afabet, and then totally destroyed as fighting units. Only a handful of senior Ethiopian officers, including the corps commander, and a few thousand other ranks could escape in flight to Asmara, together with nine of their thirteen Soviet instructors and planners, while three of the latter were captured by the Eritreans and a fourth found dead on the field of battle. They left behind many thousands of prisoners and all their weaponry as well as vast quantities of arms and ammunition inside Afabet. Some sixty cannons and fifty tanks were likewise taken by the Eritreans, many in good condition.

I thought at the time, surveying this debacle, that it must be the most signal victory scored by any anticolonial movement and army since the Vietminh at Dien Bien Phu, back in 1954, dug the grave of the French empire in IndoChina; subsequent events, whether in Eritrea or in Ethiopian Tigray during 1989, have reinforced this opinion. Within days of it, the Ethiopian army abandoned crucial strongpoints which it had long occupied in western Eritrea, and lost the last of its frontline positions. By the end of March the Derg's forces held little save the towns of Massawa, Keren and Asmara; Keren itself was under close siege by the Eritreans. Roads connecting these garrisons were effectively denied to the Derg's forces.

At the same time the Eritrean command forecast to me, on March 21, that in Addis Ababa the Derg's ruler Mengistu Haile Mariam would not accept that he had suffered a decisive defeat but would return to the attack. This was accurate, as we now know. The road from the south, from neighboring Tigray province now largely under the control of the Tigray People's Liberation Front, was likewise denied to the Derg's forces. But Mengistu at once heavily reinforced by air. By mid-April it was credibly reported that many fresh troops had been airlifted to Asmara. A major Derg counteroffensive was launched on May 13, continuing at least until May 23.

It is certain that pitched battles were fought in that period of ten days or so. Today, about two years later, we are still awaiting any authoritative news from the Ethiopian side as to what befell in those battles. Deprived of Ethiopian reports, we are left with reports from the Eritrean side. These are both detailed and official. They state that the Eritrean army was able in May 1988 to repeat its successes of March, and that a three-pronged force of twelve Ethiopian divisions with much supporting armor, attacking in three sectors, was severely mauled and in part destroyed, failing in each case to reach any of its objectives.

Ethiopian aggregate losses in these May battles are said to have exceeded 9,000 men, whether killed, captured or wounded, together with the complete elimination of a paratroop and commando force including its commander, Brigadier-General Temesgen Gemcechu, and twenty-one out of sixty-five attacking tanks. These grim Eritrean claims are, as I said, unsupported from the Ethiopian side, where silence has reigned. This was likewise the case last March, but then Eritrean claims were substantiated by foreign visitors: my own reports, for example, were confirmed a few days later by the footage of a BBC-TV team. These had arrived with Glenys Kinnock, delegate of the British aid and development organization, War on Want, around March 26. They were in time to photograph the debris of the Afabet battlefield. What the Eritreans had claimed was seen to be true.

The Derg's armies in Eritrea, accordingly, may be reliably taken as having suffered a series of most punishing defeats this year, and to have lost much of the terrain they had occupied for many years. The Eritrean army at this time now commands all Eritrea save the three urban centers mentioned above—Asmara, Keren and the port-town of Massawa on the Red Sea—and holds what must now seem to be an irresistible strategic initiative. Sorely crippled in morale as well as in fighting forces, armaments and organizational capacity, these armies of the Derg, or whatever now remains, can have little fight left in them. At the same time the Derg's position in neighboring Tigray is correspondingly disastrous, while fresh revolts among the insurgent nationalities of the Ethiopian empire-state are reported from Wollo and other provinces.

Is this, then, the beginning of the end for Mengistu Haile Mariam and the Amhara-dominated Derg through which he rules? Is the whole region of the Horn now perhaps on the threshold of a new chapter? If so, this will be a chapter in which the long-sustained hegemony of the Amhara nationality of Ethiopia will come to an end. Accordingly, the other and major constituent nationalities may reach at last some of their principal objectives, such as autonomy in self-government and equality of cultural status.

It remains to be seen. But I raise these questions because, as matters look today, they may very soon clamor for answers: because millions of Ethiopians continue to suffer and starve as these wars of the Derg continue; again, because the survival of the present regime in Ethiopia, or of any regime built to the same pattern, depends upon avoiding, in Eritrea, the very defeats which the Derg has not been able to avoid.

If it should prove that the Ethiopian empire-state as shaped by Menelik, enlarged and strengthened by Haile Selassie, and prolonged since 1976 under a guise of revolutionary jargon and militarist imposition by Mengistu Haile Mariam, is now on the verge of collapse—imminent or seen—how has this been made to happen, and with what kind of outlook, if any, for a democratized Ethiopia? Answers must be long and complex. I will attempt something more modest, though still having to tread a path through political terrain both muddled and obscure as well as, one should emphasize, very little studied or recorded by historians, whether native or foreign. The story of past years and of today has been much told from what one may reasonably call the Ethiopian side. I should like to offer a different and, I hope, more balanced view.

The year 1978 is a good starting point because it can be seen to have marked the maturing of the Eritrean national movement in a number of ways. Paradoxically, it is a starting point which began with a defeat. The national movement came of age, it has seemed to me, with the decision of its principal force, that of the EPLF, to concede to Soviet-backed Ethiopian offensives all but one of the Eritrean towns which the EPLF had recovered in 1977. That was a hard decision, but it prepared the way, however harsh that way might be, for survival and subsequent recovery and, as much as either of those, for a major social and cultural development of the nationalism of Eritrea and its methods and objectives. At the same time this decision was not followed by the earlier and rival Eritrean nationalist organization, the Eritrean Liberation Front (ELF), which, in consequence of this and other failures, laid the ground for its self-destruction. By 1982 or thereabouts, the ELF had ceased to exist in any effective form inside Eritrea or had joined its effort to that of the EPLF.

What the EPLF did was to retreat to the northern mountains, carve a trenchline of defense from the eastern lowlands to the borders of Ethiopia, and within this northern bastion set about extending, building and reinforcing its civilian departments as well as its armed forces. Most of that trenchline today is void and silent, for the Derg's besieging forces have been driven far away; but the trenches still offer a grim and extraordinary witness to years of repeated Ethiopian attack by storm, complete with the skulls and bones of Ethiopian dead picked white by vultures while corpses lay for months in the field of fire and could not be buried.

But the Eritreans proved able to hold this front, no matter what fresh supplies of armaments the Soviet Union provided and what new levies the Derg still conscripted from Ethiopian towns and villages. Behind the front the EPLF proceeded to regather its forces, undistracted at last by any serious contention within the ranks of Eritrean nationalism. It opened new roads along which food from the Sudan could be conveyed. It rebuilt its civilian departments and added new ones, so that today these have achieved an impressive effectiveness in crucial fields of everyday life: in schooling for children, in adult education, in vocational training for technicians of diverse skills, in medical care and surgery, and, underpinning all these, in the promotion of valid forms of local self-government.

While working at all this "behind its own lines," as it were, the national movement and its army began, from the early 1980s, to affirm and extend its control of and presence in most of Ethiopian-occupied Eritrea, notably in the central mountains where population is relatively dense. By 1985, at least, most of the population in these central areas had become mobilized within their own forms of self-government. And whereas the army of the EPLF had begun to evolve from guerrilla formations to regular mobile-warfare formations even by 1976, here in the Ethiopian-held areas it continued upon familiar guerrilla lines. Large guerrilla units have been permanently in place within the Ethiopian-occupied areas—today, of course, vastly reduced in their size—and have ambushed and harassed Ethiopian convoys and garrisons more or less at will.

I pass over much detail reluctantly, for these were years of intensive development, whether political or military, about which surprisingly little has been said. In brief, all attempts by the Derg's forces to dislodge the Eritreans from their fixed lines of defense successively failed. And onwards from 1987 the Eritrean forces were able to launch their own counteroffensives. As matters stand now the ten-year frontlines have little more than an historical interest, and the Eritreans command their own country. Their morale is correspondingly strong—just as the Derg's must be correspondingly weak. Their armaments have manifestly advanced to a technological level of near-equality with those of the surviving Derg's forces—if only because most of the armaments, and all their heavy armaments, have been taken from the Derg's forces. Here is one army of national liberation which does and has operated almost independently of any external source of supply, save of course the Soviet Union by way of seizing Soviet arms from the Derg. Politically, too, the Eritrean national movement can be said to occupy a level of sophistication notably higher than that of the society produced and governed by the Derg. This is in some degree because they have had the historical advantage of a process or urbanization and industrialization—going back even to the Italian colonial period—which has been much advanced on that of Ethiopia. Still more, this higher level of sophistication and organizational capacity has drawn its strength from the bracing challenge of the Eritrean struggle for emancipation compared with the consequences of Ethiopia's highly centralized and bureaucratized forms of dictatorship under Haile Selassie and, since 1976, under Mengistu Haile Mariam. Freedom, as was said long ago, does not betray those who trust it.

Travelling in Eritrea today, one cannot but be struck by the inventiveness and creative ingenuity that one finds in a host of different fields of common effort and individual initiative. Eritrean patriotism has been able to call on the skills and devotion of a wide range of emigrants spread around the world. Surgeons come from the United States, engineers from Sweden and Norway, various specialists from seemingly almost every quarter of the globe. I even found an Eritrean specialist in the application of solar heating who was about to leave for a spell in a British research station in Wales. From EPLF headquarters I was able to telephone to London by satellite, much to the astonishment of those who receive the call as well as to my own.

This is thus a national movement, in some ways notably unique in the history of such movements, which has found it possible to do what may be the most difficult thing of all. It has succeeded in combining the active participation of peasants and urban workers, even of a majority of Eritreans, with a far-reaching promotion of cultural and technological modernization. And it has done another difficult thing, something which few such movements have seriously attempted. It has tackled the huge inequalities of status, respect and employment from which Eritrean women—like women in most of Africa—have suffered by habit and tradition. In this respect I will simply note that some 30 percent of all the soldiers in the Eritrean armed forces are women; women are found in command positions up to battalion level. No doubt there is still a long way to go: but what other national movement, in Africa or anywhere else, has gone as far as that?

This is a national movement, in short, which can be said to have passed the point where it can be defeated: a movement, as one sees it today, in the ripening of its success.

What, then, of its political ideas and aims? And if it should now prove true that this Eritrean development points, ineluctably, to the end of an era of Ethiopian domination, of the Amharic nationality's hegemony within that domination, what kind of Eritrea may one expect to see emerge? What, then, will befall in Ethiopia?

The Eritrean national movement, as one finds it matured today in the EPLF, has clearly emerged from circumstances which have their close parallel with the rise of nationalism elsewhere: in other words, its origins and stimulus belong to the colonized condition. This is not the occasion to examine that process; besides, others have already done this in a fairly copious bibliography. Suffice it to say that this nationalism—this concept or consciousness of Eritrea as the arena of an emergent nation—was vigorous and widespread by the time the country was consigned by the United Nations to the status of autonomous self-governing region of the Ethiopian empire. That was in 1952, and was never accepted by the Ethiopian emperor; he intended to get fullscale incorporation, and ten years later, in 1962, he duly annexed Eritrea, suppressed all its organs of self-government, destroyed its autonomy and banned its languages in favor of the Amhara's own. Armed resistance to all this has followed ever since.

Wisdom must therefore recognize—no matter what the evasions or calculations of diplomacy may prefer—that this 28-year-old war in Eritrea is no kind of provincial rebellion to be assuaged by minor concessions, nor is Eritrea in any legal or realistic sense a province of Ethiopia. The war is the outcome of effort of the Ethiopian empire-state—first under Haile Selassie, now under Mengistu Haile Mariam—to destroy an anticolonial resistance. That effort at destruction, one should add, is entirely unlawful in terms of international law as evolved and codified by the organs of the United Nations. Of course legitimacy may be thought easily expendable in such cases: nonetheless the fact remains that the Ethiopian occupation of Eritrea in 1962, and the Ethiopian usurpation of Eritrean authority which followed that occupation, was as unlawful, by all the principles the world has cared to enunciate and recognize, as South Africa's continued occupation of Namibia in defiance of the International Court of Justice. This illegality aside, there is no way in which one can understand the coherence and persistence of the Eritrean rebellion, and the culture of mass resistance to which this rebellion has led, except in the revolutionary terms of an advanced form of anticolonial struggle.

Thus there are many parallels between the developmental processes of the Eritrean movement and national-liberation struggles elsewhere. There are likewise important differences, even while admitting that each national liberation struggle has been specific to itself. The Eritrean road to unity and maturity has been deeply mired in fratricidal bloodshed, and its history is this respect is undoubtedly specific. Broadly, though, one may think that the EPLF grew out of earlier concepts, confusions, conflicts and modes of organization because it was able, though far from easily, to achieve policies and attitudes of unity and action to which the mass of Eritreans have rallied and held firm. All this bears on what one may say about its political principles.

It is important to bear in mind that the EPLF has not attempted to develop into a political party: it has preferred to remain a political arena—a front of common effort—within which the further processes of Eritrean self-identification and self-government may evolve. The central demand that it makes of its members is that they act effectively, however each may find it possible, to further the objectives of the movement's program: essentially, to secure Eritrean control of Eritrea. There are certainly different opinions within the EPLF as to how that control should be used; but what appears to delineate the policies of the EPLF is not so much an ideological preference—in favor of one possible system, let us say, over another—as a general determination to make these policies serve the practical and evident needs of a democratic national development. There are, for example, no familiar ideological slogans of one sort or another to be heard or seen. And the experience of being between the hammer and the anvil of the superpower rivalry—between the claims of "the West" and those of "the East"—has been repeatedly instructive. No external models of development are likely to appear in the least attractive.

This may sound somewhat blandly pragmatic. In fact it is held within the stern limits and teachings of the possible. Here, too, there are probable parallels with other movements of national liberation in Africa, at least with those that have succeeded, and perhaps especially with the movement led by Amilcar Cabral, until 1973, in what is now Guinea-Bissau. And the *possible*, in these circumstances, is what the majority of Eritreans will accept and sacrifice themselves for. If the earlier ELF failed it was in no small measure because its methods and policies failed that test, above all the test of efficacy, rather than any clear ideological divergence.

Thus the ruling principles of the EPLF—its ideology, if you prefer—lie within the limits and along the parameters of a mass participation in self-development by structures of local government and the local exercise of control over that government by mass involvement in all feasible forms of cultural progress, by the persistent effort to lessen the inequalities of women, and by a no less conscious effort to avoid or at least obstruct all trends towards elitism. This interpretation can suggest no kind of utopia. There is an unavoidable and inherent contradiction, always built into struggles of this nature, between the tolerances necessary to the advancement of mass participation, and the intolerances required, just as necessarily, by the tough disciplines without which no such struggle can survive, let alone hope to win. To cope with this contradiction the EPLF has built up a flexible structure of consultation and "reference back" to movement congresses, mass organizations such as those that represent the interests of women and of peasants not only in the areas under full Eritrean control but also in those semi-liberated areas where, up to now, the Ethiopian armed forces have been present in strength. But the contradiction remains, and the further unfolding of democratic institutions must no doubt await the coming of peace.

This helps to explain why the EPLF has refused to develop a political party out of its impressive functional unity and coherence of attitude. Its leaders' response on this point is to say that they anticipate, after independence is gained, the formation of a multiparty constitution based on the realities of mass participation and on the united military effort through which it is winning its war. On the same line of thought the EPLF has made no move towards the proclamation of an independent state, although in most of the practical attributes of a state the EPLF has produced one already. They evidently prefer to wait until their successes force the powerful in the outside world to recognize the fact and existence of Eritrea: what gain, after all, in proclaiming an independent state if the powerful in the outside world will not recognize it?

Here one reaches something very specific to this movement and its leadership. They have taught themselves to expect no good from the powerful of the outside world. Either the powerful have sought to destroy them by neglect, indifference, or directly aiding their worst enemies, or else the outside world has sought to use them as pawns in the game of intraregional rivalries. Better, therefore, to avoid those traps even if there is a price to be paid, a price in isolation from aid and any encouragement. Better to rely upon themselves. The consistent imprint of the EPLF is self-reliance, while of course accepting—and gratefully—all help which threatens no demand for subservience.

This long experience of isolation, of repeated failure to win the least support from great international organizations such as the United Nations and the Organization of African Unity—not to speak of many superpower or middle power—has had its deep and subtle impact. It has seemed to me to have encouraged something of what may perhaps be called a fortress-mentality, perhaps a kind of psychological insurance against disappointment. They have had to swallow so many disappointments! The visitor from the outside world is made welcome, but no one is going to be tempted to see him or her as any messenger of salvation. It needs to be added, as against this, that for some years now the EPLF has put much time and effort into explaining itself to all who would listen, in several European languages, and has maintained an effective representation abroad. All the same, it is perhaps only now—with the successes of early 1988—that EPLF leaders are beginning to think seriously in terms of new long-term initiatives.

When these arrive, as one may think they will, they will be found to rest, politically, on the dual principles to which the EPLF has pledged itself. The first and prior of these is that there must be an unconditional recognition, by all concerned, of the Eritrean right to independence, a complete independence including the right to decide what shall be done with that independence. The second is that this can and must be made to march together with another necessary condition for peace, the democratization of the Ethiopian empire-state: the fulfillment, above all, of the promise of decentralization, of equality of rights among the constituent nationalities that was made by the Ethiopian revolution of 1974 but not kept.

A corollary of this second key to reconciliation is that there need not be and, as the EPLF argues, should not be any dismantlement of the territorial integrity of the traditional Ethiopian entity, no attempt to promote the secession of a cluster of successor-states, of mini-states as these would be. Thus, in an EPLF statement of 1985: "The demand for the secession of Ethiopian nationalities has neither an historical nor an economic basis: nor is the extent of the prevailing national antagonism so acutely sharp as to justify secession" (*Adulis:* I, 11, May 1985). On the contrary, there should be arrangements of a federal type whereby the insurgent nationalities—notably Tigray, Oromo, Somali, Afar, Sidama—could reach a reasonable unity of organization and mutual accord, and could likewise reach the same with Eritrea. For its part, the EPLF "is convinced that the destiny of the Eritrean and Ethiopian peoples is closely linked" (*Adulis:* supra).

The Eritrean successes of 1988 and 1989 may bring this admittedly very difficult perspective somewhat nearer to reality: if only because Amharic hegemony within Ethiopia seems unlikely to be able to survive the Derg's eviction from Eritrea. However that may turn out to be, the Eritreans have exerted some effort at reaching common ground with the insurgent nationalities, and have had some success with the TPLF, although little, so far as one can tell, with the other insurgent nationalities. What the EPLF leaders now say they hope for, in any case, is to secure a conference of all the nationalities, including themselves, with the aim of reaching at least a minimal program for united action.

On this score, as matters stand, there seems no reason for optimism, not least because there appears, as yet, to be no sign at all of a coherent opposition to the present Derg among the

Amhara themselves. Progress towards a democratized Ethiopia will accordingly be very problematic. At the same time, that progress seems the only sure key to any durable stability in the region. This being so, the EPLF has been asking—so far in vain—for an intelligent and disinterested initiative from an appropriate outside power-source. In January 1988, the journal of the EPLF's foreign relations bureau, *Adulis*, urged that "Europe can play a prominent role in bringing about peace and stability in our region. The positive step is for Europe to use its influence as a third power to help in the consolidation of a constellation of nonaligned states in a nonaligned zone in the Horn of Africa" (*Adulis*: V, 1, January 1988). Europe is seen, in short, as a power which could step usefully between the superpowers in such a way as to remove acute superpower rivalries from the region, and thus assist these various peoples to reach common ground among themselves. The OAU and the UN having refused any such mediating role; perhaps Europe can play it instead.

If something of that order should come about, then the apparently insoluble conflicts of today might be moved towards solution. Within a nonaligned Horn there could be some hope for intelligent reconstruction, for an end to inter-nationality conflicts, and, not least, for rescue of the pastoralist peoples to whom famine and war have proved, are proving now, a veritable genocide.

But what if nothing like that should come about? If no intelligent and disinterested initiative comes forward to set in motion the process of reconciliation? In that case, as it appeared in 1988, there can be no bottom to the pessimism and despair that must ensue. The degradations of natural and human failure will plunge to still more ferocious depths. And in this respect one has to note, with acute regret if not surprise, that among the zones of actual or potential conflict between the superpowers, to the reduction of which the American and Soviet leaders now say they are pledged, there has thus far been no mention, no mention at all, of the Horn of Africa. Yet the Horn of Africa is surely one zone of conflict-inducing rivalry between the super powers that should be relatively easy to disarm, once given, that is, the useful mediating action of what *Adulis* has called a "third power."

Neither superpower would find a nonaligned Horn hostile to its interests; neither has any large economic interest there.

It remains that no such evolution is now in sight. Present sufferings will therefore worsen in Ethiopia. By 1988, there were solid reasons for fearing that a new and massive famine would shortly threaten the lives of millions who are already near the starvation line; these fears were tragically confirmed toward the end of 1989. But here one has to make distinctions.

There need now be no starvation in central and southern Eritrea, just as there is no starvation in northern Eritrea where the EPLF has exercised control for many years, provided, that is to say, that the Eritreans—meaning the Eritrean Relief Association—receive adequate supplies of food by way of Port Sudan and their own road networks. In 1987 the ERA received enough food-aid to distribute some 68,000 tons of which about one-fifth could be channeled into the areas nominally controlled by the Derg's forces. Today the ERA can distribute food-aid in practically all of populated Eritrea save the Asmara-Keren-Massawa "triangle." For that purpose they have the necessary organization, experience, and road transport (of the latter, some 200 trucks before the recent battles which yielded many more); but at present they do not have the necessary food. In March 1988 ERA estimated that they would need an additional 100,000 tons if starvation were to be averted in areas up to now held by the Derg's forces.

In Ethiopia, however, the prospects seem grim. So far, the various international agencies upon whom relief has depended have had to function under restrictions and obstructions imposed by the present Derg. Perhaps these may now be reduced. But once again only the end of the wars can offer any guarantee of averting another huge disaster to these persecuted populations. Here is another reason why intelligent and disinterested outside initiative seems required.

None of this can be easy; one puts these views with hesitation. Yet all the essential facts support these views. Let the superpowers reach a standoff settlement between themselves. Let all these nationalities have time and opportunity to reach their own settlements among themselves. There could then be a real prospect of movement towards durable peace. And peace alone, for these peoples, has become the only alternative to death.

These considerations could be said to have achieved a certain historical validity by the outset of the 1990s: so far as the Horn is concerned, the slogans of "decentralization and democratization" have indeed come to indicate the only available route to recovery, above all for the pastoralist populations who have suffered so much more than any others. It was still far from sure that the meaning of the slogans would be realized in the 1990s. If not, fresh disasters would evidently follow. But the slogans had emerged from a stubborn experience. The lessons they speak for had been harshly taught. Do they, one may ask, have value for the rest of Africa?

Pondering this question, one sees that the Horn, as a region including much of the republic of Sudan, is in this connection a microcosm of the continent. It displays, repeatedly, the institutional failures of the post-colonial nation-state that compose Africa's major political problem now. It portrays the destructive types of relationships so far installed between Africa's new nation-states and the powers of the outside world.

Till lately secretary-general of the OAU, Professor Edem Kodjo has written that Africa's present condition of "nullity" derives from "two obstacles: the nation-state and an obscure despotism" which is, of course, a product of this nation-state. The post-colonial state has become "a shackle on progress" because it prefers the material interest of small sectors of society, above all those who control and profit from urban-directed economies, to the interests of the great majority of citizens, who are rural producers. The "unequal terms of trade" between the industrialized world and the former colonial world are thus reproduced, but still more destructively, between urban controllers or profit-takers on one hand, and rural multitudes on the other. To this situation, decentralization can alone offer a remedy. The transformation of the Ethiopian empire-state into some form of democratized federation, in short, may be an example of solution that other regions could find useful for themselves.

"We need to strive," said King Mosheshoe of Lesotho a couple of years ago, thinking above all of southern Africa as a whole, "to develop open and participatory forms of economic and political planning, wherein people can take part in public debate about the main production and development issues, and then have a direct say in the final decision." In the measure that organizations such as the Eritrean and Tigrayan movements prove really able to devolve to local organs of democratic control, the powers they have wrested from the centralized Ethiopian state, from the old empire-state renamed but not reformed in its systemic structures, such organizations will hold the future in their hands.

Much of the Horn, furthermore, has been ruined by militarism and its indispensable external supports, whether in West or East. Here, too, there are close and painful parallels with the southern region of the continent. The post-colonial regimes of Angola and Mozambique were quite possibly bound to plunge, after 1975, into confusions of their own making, given the problems they had to face and their lack of experience in facing them. But the murderous banditries of the counter-revolutionary forces of UNITA and RENAMO are what have brought about the dire miseries of today. And these banditries could never have begun, or if attempted could not have persisted, without external promotion and support. These subversions in southern Africa can be put in parallel with the destructive impact of the Soviet weaponry and technicians in the Horn.

In 1989 we were long past any point where words of this kind would make much difference. What will do that, and bring these interventions to an end, is their manifest bankruptcy. The interventions have not prevailed. They persist only because reputations and careers are linked to their persistence. This will change: no great power can afford in the long run to hock its credit to personal or private interests, no matter how "embedded" these may be. And as the interventions fall away, and good sense begins at last to prevail, so will the lessons of nonalignment be more and more accepted. Optimistic? For myself, I can see no other way that history can be written at the end of our blood-stained century. What has lately begun to happen in Eastern Europe should have been impossible, let alone optimistic, on any orthodox view. But happening it is; and it is the peoples, not the governments or the parties, that have made it happen.

Any long-term solution to Africa's moral and institutional crisis is going to be written along the same lines: along the lines, that is, of what is loosely but realistically called "people's participation." This has to mean the systemic devolution of debating and executive power to local assemblies and their elected executives, together with an appropriate—that is, constitutional and legal—structure of local influence on non-local issues such as large-scale budgetary matters. Every positive sign of socio-political renewal during the 1980s has confirmed as much, whether in a relatively great case such as Nigeria or a relatively small case such as Cape Verde. And this applies equally to the biggest case of all, to the absolute test-case of Africa's future welfare: to the reorganization and therefore democratization of the whole vast southern region, once racist South African rule is out of the way. Just as the peoples of eastern and central Europe are in the course of shifting mountains of coercion and prejudice, even while all our "authorities" have assured us that they were able to do no such thing, so will the peoples of Africa, in their own place and time, do the same.

Chapter 10

FROM TRADE UNION TO WORKING-CLASS MOBILIZATION: THE POLITICIZATION OF SOUTH AFRICA'S NON-RACIAL LABOR UNIONS

Gay Seidman

Introduction

T HEORETICAL discussions of trade unionism in newly industrialized countries (NICs) have often assumed that emergent labor movements would follow patterns apparently established in earlier industrializers: legal unions, it has often been argued, will tend to seek immediate gains for their members, rather than articulating broader working-class goals or building strong coalitions with popular movements outside the factory.[1]

---

[1]A version of this paper was presented at the American Sociological Association meeting, Atlanta, August 24, 1988. For comments and

Especially in societies marked by high levels of unemployment, industrial workers are generally expected to behave as a labor aristocracy, whose organizations will try to protect members' narrow economic interests rather than foster class mobilization. Indeed, the possibility that labor organizations could help construct a radical movement for social change has all but dropped out of development literature: even Marxist theorists have tended to look toward peasant movements rather than to trade unions as the probable basis of resistance to capitalist development.

Most sociological analyses of South Africa have focused on the historical elaboration of apartheid, examining the peculiar interactions of race and class which produced a system that simultaneously protected white supremacy and created and maintains a supply of low-paid black workers for white-owned industries, mines and farms. These analyses, in general, have not been greatly concerned with the dynamics of black resistance: they emphasize the obstacles to and repression of worker organization. Since the late 1970s, as the nonracial labor movement emerged, many writers have drawn their assumptions about how unions behave from broad theories about labor in developing societies. It has been suggested, for example, that the recent rural background of black workers would retard industrial unionism, because a class analysis would be incomprehensible to recent peasants; that industrial workers are relatively privileged in the South African context, and that instead of confronting the state, the new unions might focus on private employers, seeking to win immediate material gains for their members. Further, it has been proposed that even if the new unions did take up political demands, they were unlikely to prosper: they would face immediate repression, and would be unable to win the shopfloor gains so clearly important to retaining members' loyalties. According to such rather superficial discussions, it seemed unlikely that the new unions, divided by industry and separated from the political

suggestions on earlier drafts, I would like to thank Michael Burawoy, Barry Goetz, Pierrette Hondagneu, Heinz Klug, Tomoji Nishikawa, Kim Voss and Rob Wrenn.

system, could articulate political demands for a broadly defined working class.

Over the past few years, however, the South African labor movement has moved to a prominent position in the struggle against minority rule, to such an extent that by late 1988, barely a decade after legalizing unions for black workers, the government passed a law aiming to close most unions down. Does the growing militance of the labor movement, which by the mid-1980s drew its strength as much from black townships as from shopfloor organization, mean that South Africa is different from all other newly industrialized countries? Is what Webster (1988) has termed South Africa's "social-movement unionism" simply a reflection of South Africa's peculiar political arrangements?

If theories of economic development led some observers to ignore labor movements' potential role in the construction of radical social movements, discussions of trade unions in South Africa have sometimes lent in the opposite direction. The growing radicalization of the South African labor movement over the past fifteen years has sometimes been viewed as a unique phenomenon, shaped by the state's apartheid policies rather than by structural factors. Arguing that "normal" unionism is impossible in an abnormal society, some writers have simply assumed that the black workforce would almost automatically support a broad political movement, using shopfloor organizations to back demands for political change. A sleeping giant—the black workforce—would suddenly awake to its ability to bring production to a halt, challenging the state's control through some kind of general strike combined with "violent social confrontation" (Ehrensaft, 1985). This approach would suggest that the South African case contains no implications for our understanding of the nature of labor movements in other NICs, because its working-class movement would have become radicalized simply by its relationship to an unusual form of racial capitalism.

The recent history of the nonracial labor movement in South Africa suggests that neither set of theoretical assumptions is adequate for understanding emergent labor movements in general, or the South African case in particular. The labor movement has neither been an expression of the demands of a labor aristocracy, nor an automatic outlet for black political frustrations. Until very recently, most broad generalizations about emergent unions were based on the experiences of labor in early industrializing societies, during the initial stages of industrial expansion. These generalizations vary according to theoretical paradigms; whatever the assumptions on which they were based, most discussions of labor in the NICs overlooked the very different international context, and the resultant differences in industrialization patterns, in which working-class organizations emerge and grow. On the other hand, dependency theories, which took these differences into account, have tended to focus on international and elite interactions, and to overlook possible opportunities for worker mobilization. Dependency theories have only very recently begun to explore the role of working-class organization, and to examine the possibility that workers in newly industrialized societies face a very different set of opportunities and constraints than those faced by labor unions in nineteenth century Europe and North America.

The process through which the South African labor movement emerged prompted workers to articulate class interests through shopfloor organizations; but the context in which the labor movement operates has forced unions increasingly to articulate broad political demands. The South African labor movement's emergence on the shopfloor, and its growing politicization, is clearly related to South Africa's industrialization patterns. Rapid, highly stratified industrialization under an authoritarian government created new possibilities for workers organized at the shopfloor; once organized, these unions gradually shifted to take up the political demands of the communities in which workers lived, while community goals were increasingly expressed in terms of working-class interests. The South African labor movement's emergence on the shopfloor, and its growing politicization, is clearly related to South Africa's industrialization patterns. Rapid, highly-stratified industrialization under an authoritarian government has created new possibilities for workers organized at the shopfloor; once organized, these unions gradually shifted to take up the political demands of the communities in which workers lived, while community goals are increasingly expressed in terms of working-class interests. From the late 1950s, the South African state sought to promote industrial growth, attracting foreign capital and new technologies. By the 1970s, this industrialization strategy had reshaped the industrial working class.

Semi-skilled industrial workers challenged employers directly, winning key changes in labor legislation. Black workers brought the class analysis developed in shopfloor organizations into the community groups formed in segregated townships; as the economic impasse deepened into a crisis, and employers and the state failed to make structural reforms or concessions, trade unions strengthened their alliances with communities, expanding their appeal to include a broadly defined working class and redefining political change to include economic redistribution as well as universal franchise.

The dynamics which pushed nonracial unions toward the popular movement, and which strengthened the class character of the popular political movement, may have important theoretical implications not only for our understanding of the struggle in South Africa, but for our understanding of labor movements in other NICs. South Africa's political unionism has been largely shaped by factors that exist in a number of NICs; repressive governments are hardly unique, any more than are rapid changes in the composition of the workforce or the creation of working-class communities excluded from political participation and denied access to social services. Viewed from this perspective, the South African case offers some insights into the strategies available to unions in such cases, and suggests that labor unions in NICs may play a more important role in mobilizing movements for broad social change than has usually been assumed.

National Structures

Most analysts agree that changes in the composition of South Africa's industrial labor force laid the basis for the emergence of a strong labor movement. Rapid industrialization in the post-war era, relying heavily on imported finance capital and technology, changed the country's economic base: manufacturing production rose from about 5 percent of the total national income in 1911 to some 24 percent in 1970. Changes in the workforce were even more dramatic: by 1970, about 18.5 percent of the economically active population worked in industry. The number of blacks in manufacturing rose from 228,000 in 1951 to 567,200 in 1970. By

1982 the number of African workers in manufacturing had reached 800,500, with 311,200 more working in construction and 32,100 in electricity; and 619,251 Africans working in the mining sector (Jones, 1986:13,18; Lipton, 1986:139 fn, 143). By the mid-1970s, even the South African government acknowledged that black workers were no longer the unskilled miners, farmworkers and service sector workers of previous decades: "job reservation" laws, which previously barred black workers from officially occupying most skilled positions, were relaxed, at least in part because of employer concerns about shortages of skilled labor for the positions opening up in new, more capital-intensive industry (Mann, 1988:59). While white workers moved into clerical and supervisory positions,[2] many black workers moved up into semiskilled and skilled jobs; between 1969 and 1981, African women and men increased by 144 and 26 percent, respectively, their share in the manufacturing workforce, while white women and men's shares dropped by 7.2 and 9.5 percent (Prekel, 1986, Table 3).

Changes in the workforce alone cannot explain the rapid rise of union organization among black workers in the 1970s and 1980s, however. As a liberal South African policy group warned in 1972, economic growth and opportunities for training "will not necessarily lead to black workers organizing themselves effectively;" individual firms and the government frequently adjusted apartheid regulations to overcome skills shortages without reducing workplace racial discrimination (Randall, 1972:68-70). Legal restrictions on black unions from the early 1950s left black workers without representation; legislation prevented racially mixed unions, and white workers' unions generally refused to consider black workers' interests in negotiations with employers. Indeed, white workers' unions generally continued to oppose employer recognition of black workers' organizations into the 1980s (Lewis, 1984; Jochelson, 1985:27-9).

---

[2]By 1970, one out of four white workers worked directly for the state, often in white-collar positions tied to the administration of apartheid policies. Another ten percent worked for state-owned companies (Greenberg, 1980:403).

During the 1970s, however, several strike waves swept through South Africa's black workforce, beginning with a relatively spontaneous strike wave in 1973 that involved nearly 100,000 black workers. Building on the legacy of earlier, repressed unionizing drives,[3] as well as on employers' increasing recognition of the costs involved in repressing spontaneous strikes or replacing a semi-skilled workforce,[4] activists began to organize unions outside the state-controlled, racially-divided industrial arbitration system.

By the late 1970s, strikes by black workers had become a standard feature of South African society: between 1973 and 1979, an average of 33,316 African workers annually participated in officially acknowledged strikes, up from an annual average of about 2,000 in the preceding decade (See Table 1). Many of these strikes—as well as overtime bans and go-slows, which do not appear in official statistics—began on the shopfloor, with striking workers calling in union representatives only after an initial refusal to work (Cooper, 1982; Levy et al., 1986; Sitas and Webster, n.d.). Intellectuals and community groups mobilized support for the emergent labor movement, but the new unions won few concrete gains for their members. Employer resistance to unions combined with state repression to such an extent that most union efforts in the 1970s went toward protecting union members from unfair dismissals, and into winning immediate wage increases. Before 1979, only four companies had formally recognized "nonracial"—primarily black—unions (Friedman 1987a:147 fn).

Nevertheless, by 1979 even conservative employer associations supported changes in labor legislation to allow black workers to

---

[3]For a history of earlier attempts to organize black workers, see Ken Luckhardt and Brenda Wall, *Organize or Starve! An Official History of the South African Congress of Trade Unions* (London: Lawrence and Wishart, 1980); and Eddie Webster (ed.), *Essays in Southern African Labor History* (Johannesburg: Ravan, 1978).

[4]See, for example, comments from an employer's representative immediately after the 1973 strikes in the Institute for Industrial Education, *The Durban Strikes 1973* (Durban: IIE and Ravan, 1974), pp. 144-5. The representative pointed out that increasing skills levels meant that employers would be reluctant to increase turnover, as "it is too jolly difficult to get a labor force as it is."

Table 1
Officially Registered Strike Activity in South Africa, 1950-87

Year	Strikes	Workers	Mandays Lost
1950	33	2,399	
1955	102	9,863	
1960	42	5,500	
—			
1973	370	98,378	
1974	384	59,244	
1975	274	23,323	
1976	245	28,013	
1977	90	15,304	
1978	106	14,160	
1979	101	22,803	
1980	207	61,785	174,614
1981	342	92,842	226,554
1982	394	141,571	365,337[a]
1983	336	64,469	124,596
1984	469	181,942	379,712[a]
1985	389	239,816	678,274[a]
1986	n.a.	n.a.	1,300,000[a]
1987	n.a.	n.a.	5,800,000[a]

Note

a. These figures do not include explicitly political work stoppages. These stoppages would increase the number of mandays lost in 1986 to about 3,000,000, and in 1987 to about 9,000,000 (WM, 2/5/1988).

Sources: Department of Labor, official year-end reports; National Manpower Commission, cited in Lambert (1983:220; NPI, 1987:10-1; Director General of Manpower, quoted in WM, 3/18/1988)

register their organizations: their representatives told a state commission that spontaneous strikes by black workers posed a greater threat to industrial peace than would incorporation into a strictly controlled arbitration system (Afrikaans Handelsinstituut, cited in Friedman, 1987a:153-4). In 1979, in a much-vaunted reform move, the South African government announced it would offer black workers collective bargaining rights. Although the new legislation limited black workers' organizing rights, and employers and police continued to resist organizing drives, by the early 1980s union organizers had managed to expand workers' legal ability to challenge employer prerogatives. Faced with growing worker organization and militancy, employers began slowly to accept nonracial trade unions as a permanent fixture in industrial relations (SAFCI, n.d.).

One of the most interesting aspects of union organizers' early internal discussions, both in new labor periodicals and in union meetings, was the tendency to stress the class interests of black workers rather than focusing on the racial exclusion of South Africa's political system. Recognizing that apartheid involves both racial domination and control over the black workforce, unionists in the "nonracial" movement argued that factory-based labor organizations should articulate members' demands in terms of class position, using strikes to push employers and the state to recognize the collective bargaining rights for workers of all races. The Black Consciousness Movement, which argued that all blacks were equally oppressed by white minority rule, dominated political discussions inside the country in the early 1970s. In contrast, activists in the nonracial unions emphasized their belief that democratic shopfloor organizations would bring workers together *as workers*, as distinct from the larger category of all blacks. Apartheid was seen as a systematic attempt to reinforce employers' control over workers; while racial aspects of apartheid were certainly recognized by organizers—particularly in terms of apartheid policies that reserved better-paying jobs for white employees—the labor movement itself stressed economic exploitation and workers' class position. The emphasis on nonracialism was not simply rhetorical: in at least one case, a black organizer who described internal frictions in terms of racial splits was expelled from the nonracial movement.

Over the first decade of emergent unionism, this analysis would become increasingly hegemonic. While the nonracial unions grew, two racially divided federations—one composed of all-white unions linked to "parallel" subsidiary unions for workers classified as "nonwhite," and another whose all-black unions were committed to a black consciousness perspective—weakened steadily. By the early 1980s, unions in both these federations had shifted to a nonracialist position, arguing that workers' identity and class interests should be more important in determining union strategy than racial classifications.

The 1979 change in nonracial unions' legal status—which coincided with a brief economic boom in 1979-80—helped unions to grow rapidly. Major industries such as metalworking and textiles were hit by successive strikewaves in the early 1980s: in 1982, some 290,482 workers participated in officially acknowledged strikes, generally focusing on wage demands, plant-level union recognition, and unfair dismissals.[5] The focus on shopfloor struggles undoubtedly reinforced union members' understanding of apartheid as an economic system. Organized as workers within the plant, workers clearly learned through union activities to analyze their situation in terms of working-class interests and identity (Sitas, 1983). Although community support for union struggles—expressed through donations to strike funds, consumer boycotts and the refusal to replace striking workers—often appeared to be motivated by a rejection of racial discrimination,[6] union activities focused on economic exploitation as a primary dynamic.

Official membership in the nonracial unions reached 400,000 by 1982, but this figure certainly understated the number of workers affected by the new militancy. By 1983, African union membership had reached 741,194, and total union membership reached 1,545,824—about 12 percent of the total economically

---

[5]This figure includes the nearly 100,000 workers who participated in a half-hour work stoppage protesting the death in detention of union organizer Neil Aggett (Lambert and Lambert, 1983:220).

[6]See, for example, the literature published by support groups during the 1979 Fattis and Monis strike, which emphasized the racial solidarity among workers as the reason the strike deserved support. South African Institute of Race Relations Archives, "Fattis and Monis Strike," at the University of Witwatersrand.

active population.[7] Far from remaining concentrated among the semiskilled urban industrial workers who had seemed to show the most potential for workplace organization, the new movement had spread to less-skilled migrant workers from rural areas, who faced a real threat of expulsion to rural areas if they lost their jobs. Organizing drives among municipal workers, among migrant black mineworkers, and even among farmworkers showed that "the church of the union" would not be limited to the manufacturing sector's relatively privileged workers (Keenan, 1981; Friedman, 1987a:355-92).

The new labor movement changed significantly as it gradually built a national organization. At the individual union level, the growth of industry-wide unions meant organizers could move beyond plant-level bargaining. By 1982, organizers in some industries had begun to develop industry-wide bargaining powers. The 1979 legal reforms gave black workers' unions access to national industrial councils, previously restricted to white workers' unions. Recognizing that the state-run industrial conciliation councils might strengthen employers, nonracial unions nonetheless began to argue that plant-level negotiations alone could not resolve pressing problems facing workers, including industrial working conditions, industry-wide pay scales, and retrenchments (Sideris, 1983:10-3; Webster, 1983:14-8). After much debate over whether participation in these bodies would reduce shopfloor militance, several nonracial unions began trying to negotiate national contracts in the previously-shunned industrial councils in the early 1980s.

Perhaps even more importantly, however, the labor movement's growth gave political issues new urgency. The shift from a regional patchwork of struggling independent unions to a national federation committed to industry-wide unions forced the unions to take up broader issues than those which had dominated plant-level negotiations. A national campaign against a proposed

---

[7]Other estimates of African union membership are higher, but may be somewhat inflated. Even this figure for 1983 may be misleading, however, as it includes 800,000 mainly white members of traditional, racially divided unions (Webster, 1985:80; Lewis and Randall, 1985:60,87 fn).

change in legislation affecting pension plans showed in 1980 that black workers recognized, often spontaneously, the impact of white political domination on working conditions and labor relations (Moyle, 1981:4-7); nevertheless, unionists in the 1970s tended to downplay political involvement as they emphasized the struggle for collective bargaining rights.

As the organized labor movement spread, however, mid-level union activists began to articulate political demands related to issues outside the workplace. In several important urban areas, regional shop steward councils brought together union activists from various industries. Although they came together as workers, these shop stewards tended to take up common issues affecting their communities: pass laws, forced removals of urban squatter settlements, high transport costs for residents of black townships and black disenfranchisement all became targets for joint local union campaigns (Baskin, 1982: 42-53; Lewis and Randall, 1985b). In retrospect, it may have been inevitable that union members coming together in regional groupings would take up issues linked more to black communities than to the shopfloor: any effort to improve workers' living conditions under apartheid will have to include improvements in the large black townships and hostels where most industrial workers live. Demands for improvements in those areas invariably challenge the state's failure to provide services to all blacks, and focus on the denial of political access as a basic cause of black impoverishment. In the relatively few areas where regional shop stewards' councils functioned, they quickly moved to political issues.

Nevertheless, the early 1980s were marked by major divisions within the labor movement over how the nonracial unions should relate to political opposition groups. When new unions representing black workers first emerged in the 1970s, many organizers were keenly aware of the practical dangers of political alliances. Although any unionizing drive was likely to meet repression, ties to political groups increased the likelihood of state intervention.[8]

---

[8]The most obvious example of this phenomenon was the severe state attack on organizers of the South African and Allied Workers' Union in 1983. At the time, SAAWU was probably most union most explicitly allied to political groups and the underground ANC; its involvement in an

As the unions grew, however, this fear of close ties to a broad popular movement turned into overt distrust: several unionists argued that the "petit-bourgeois" leadership of student and community groups might persuade union members to support demands that were not in workers' objective interests (FCWU, 1982:54-8; WIP, 1981:6-12).   Others pointed to nationalist movements elsewhere on the continent that used the rhetoric of national liberation to obscure different conflicting interests within popular movements, but which would abandon workers' demands on attaining decolonization (Erwin, 1985:54-7; Plaut, 1987:62-72). Finally, some organizers argued that only a focus on shopfloor organization would build unity within the labor movement and increase internal democracy, creating strong black working-class leadership (Foster, 1982:81-2).

In a widely discussed speech in 1982, the general secretary of what was then the largest grouping of nonracial unions, the Federation of South African Trade Unions (FOSATU), argued that industrialization offered black workers a new capacity for shopfloor organization. With specific class interests and an obvious ability to challenge employers, black workers now constituted a independent political force, separable theoretically and strategically from the broader population. While he acknowledged South Africa's long tradition of a national liberation movement—carried on primarily through the illegal African National Congress (ANC)—Joe Foster (1982) argued that political organization based in democratic shopfloor unionism would ensure that the transition to majority rule would be led by workers with a clear vision of their objective interests. Factory-based unions, free of murky class compromises, were needed "to ensure that the popular movement is not hijacked by elements who in the end will have no option but to turn against their worker supporters."   Following this reasoning, FOSATU resolved in 1982 to work toward creating a national workers' party, clearly separated from the broad national liberation movement.

This "workerist" perspective was challenged throughout the 1970s by union organizers who called for a "popular-democratic" alliance with a broad anti-apartheid movement. These "populist"

Eastern Cape bus boycott, along with its political affiliations, certainly made normal union functioning difficult.

unionists argued that black workers' primary opponent is the apartheid state; shopfloor organization, while important, would not be sufficient for political transformation. Only a popular political movement could give black workers the support they needed to demand fundamental change: community protests and consumer boycotts could strengthen unions' bargaining positions vis-à-vis employers, while workers' strikes could be used to back up political demands. Unlike Foster, "populist" unionists argued that South Africa's industrialization process had affected all blacks. A factory-level focus would leave out workers' families, unemployed workers and people who were restricted to bantustans (Mufamadi, 1984:19-22; Toussaint, 1983:42). Further, the national liberation movement's call for political rights reflected workers' demands as well as those of the tiny black elite; a refusal to join in the broad movement would leave the trade unions isolated and vulnerable. "The economic struggle cannot be successfully conducted...if workers have not won elementary political rights such as the freedom to organize without threat of bannings, detentions, and the violent breaking of strikes" (Njakelana, 1984:32). Unions could bring workers together and stop production, but they could not articulate political demands (MGWU, n.d.; Toussaint, 1983:35-46). Unions with this perspective tended to focus on building a community base, organizing as much through mass meetings in black townships as on the factory floor (Maree, 1982:34-49).

This debate over the relationship between trade unions and the political opposition hinged on two strategic questions: first, whether workers' interests would be submerged within a broad political alliance against the state; and second, whether blacks outside a narrowly defined industrial workforce could be considered working-class. The controversy over whether the unions should join a multiclass coalition began to intensify in the early 1980s, as new political opposition groups sprang up in black townships. In some areas, community groups were initially stimulated by efforts to organize consumer boycotts in support of union recognition drives at particular factories (interview, Capetown, 1987). Most of these groups brought black township residents together over specific local issues, such as rising fares on buses carrying blacks into city centers or rents on government-owned township houses. A few groups, especially students protesting inferior education, had a national constituency. These groups quickly adopted a national structure and political tone.[9] In 1983, some 500 of these politically oriented groups came together in the United Democratic Front (UDF), an umbrella coalition with obvious loyalty to the ANC. This loyalty was expressed through symbolic choices, such as naming jailed ANC prisoners as UDF patrons, and through ideological positions associated with the ANC. Like the ANC—and like the nonracial unions—the UDF rejected the Black Consciousness Movement's insistence on black-only organizations, and sought instead to involve "democrats" of all races in the opposition. The UDF launched a campaign demanding full political participation for all South Africans and an end to apartheid structures—to bantustans, pass laws, and segregated unequal facilities.

Although the UDF (1983) urged the nonracial unions to join the new coalition, and stated its belief in "the leadership of the working class in the democratic struggle" for political rights, union leaders generally agreed that the coalition's loose structure would not give adequate weight to working-class demands (Lewis, 1983). A few small "populist" unions joined the UDF alliance, but most nonracial unions remained aloof, simply sending congratulatory messages to the launch and promising to encourage individual members to participate in UDF-affiliated groups (Barrell, 1984:13-4). The UDF's focus on political rights was considered to be at odds with unions' emphasis on economic change; as Moses Mayekiso, a well-known metalworkers' organizer, said, "The enemy is only one—capitalism—and all other things like [apartheid legislation] are merely appendages" (FWN 25, 1983). Similarly, Chris Dlamini, another important union leader, warned that workers could not join a popular liberation coalition before they had built strong workplace organizations, because "worker liberation can only be achieved by a strong, well-organized worker

---

[9]Steven Friedman has argued that many community groups were created in imitation of shop stewards' councils, but no other evidence suggests this. Interviews with activists in 1987 suggested that the structures of community groups during the uprising beginning in 1984—usually of street committees and block representatives—were instead designed in response to the immediate exigencies of township resistance (Friedman, 1987:61).

movement," independent of broad political alliances (FWN 22, 1983).

The decision to stay out of the UDF was not universally popular, either within the labor movement or outside it. Members of one of the strongest nonracial unions resolved that, despite the decision to reject the invitation to join the UDF, the labor movement should "combine with other democratic, progressive trade unions and community organizations in opposition" to the state (SFAWU, in FWN 27, 1984). In 1984, the metalworkers union split, partly because some organizers charged that union leaders were ignoring workers' needs as community members.[10] In late August 1984, a leading unionist told workers that rent increases and bad school conditions affect workers, too; workers could not afford to isolate themselves in the struggle. "We must unite to fight the bosses in the factories, and we must unite in the communities" (Dlamini, in FWN 32, 1984). Outside the labor movement, student and community activists who had previously mobilized community support for union struggles tended to turn away from worker organizations; disappointed in the bid to gain union support for directly political campaigns, UDF activists focused on building their own organization.

In the early 1980s, then, the nonracial union movement appeared to be following a trajectory close to the labor-aristocracy pattern predicted by most development theories. During its first decade—from about 1973 to 1983—the emergent unions focused on shopfloor organization and workers' most immediate interests, generally defining members' interests in rather narrow terms. Far from immediately joining in a broad multi-class movement for black rights, the labor movement resisted calls to use its strike weapon for political ends: most, although by no means all, of its important leaders explicitly rejected attempts to redefine their struggle in terms of national liberation, or attempts to redefine the labor movement's constituency to include workers outside the

---

[10]Two aspects of this particular split are worth noting: first, that one of the more prominent members of the splinter union had been a vice-president of FOSATU before the split; and second, that after the split, the organizers who led the splinter were charged with defrauding the parent union (Swilling, 1984; Obery and Swilling, 1984).

factory gates. Rather than putting their organizations and their ability to halt production at the service of political campaigns, they turned away to focus on creating a single federation of nonracial unions, where workers would articulate a pure class interest. The shopfloor organizations that marked workers' new awareness of their power to halt production had changed South Africa's political scene: as one observer put it, "For the first time in decades the possibility exists of the working class imprinting its specific demands and perspectives on the South African social and political process" (Hindson, 1984:105).

Changing Context

The labor movement of the early 1980s chose to emphasize economic aspects of apartheid—the economic exploitation of blacks as workers, and the state's close ties to capital as the basis for capitalist development. Indeed, its leaders argued that the movement drew its very strength from the industrialization process, as black workers moved into the industrial labor force and developed a new capacity for challenging capitalist employers. In that sense, labor leaders could, and often did, claim that their unions differed from labor movements in other NICs only in the peculiarities of South Africa's political system: the basic class structure of their society, and the repressive alliance between state and dominant classes, was more similar to Brazil or other NICs than to former African colonies whose national liberation movements grew out of rural peasant movements or broad multiclass coalitions (interview, Johannesburg, 1982).

Within five years, however, the major figures of the nonracial labor movement would reverse their strategy: by 1987, more than 5 million mandays would be lost to explicitly political strikes, and the union movement would take a leading position in the popular political struggle against the state. Abandoning the earlier call for an independent working-class organization and factory-based campaigns, the leaders of the Congress of South African Trade Unions (COSATU) would emphasize their support for political campaigns, viewing a nonracial, democratic South Africa as a prerequisite for any meaningful improvements in the situation of the working class. Although COSATU was not the only labor federation in the mid-1980s, it was by far the largest labor federation in South Africa's history, bringing together more than 1,000,000 workers in 1985. Its shift toward increasing politicization was reflected in an increasing political involvement on the part of other unions, including both the black consciousness-linked National Azanian Congress of Trade Unions, with some 250,000 members, and UWUSA, the union grouping linked to the leader of the KwaZulu bantustan, whose membership is somewhat vague.

The shift in political positions was dramatic. By June 1987, COSATU had completely reversed its 1985 charter principle rejecting political alliances. Adopting the Freedom Charter—the document containing the ANC's basic principles for a future South Africa—the federation implicitly joined a multiclass coalition, in which union members would be an important minority. The Freedom Charter calls for a social democracy, with a mixed economy and social welfare for all; it is hardly a call for an independent workers' movement (Suttner, 1984). Describing the Freedom Charter as "a guiding document which reflects the views and aspirations of the majority of the oppressed and exploited in our struggle against national oppression and economic exploitation," the 1987 COSATU Congress rejected proposals that the labor movement draw up an additional workers' charter; union leaders argued that such a move could threaten the unity of the broad opposition movement (Carrim, 1987:11). Rather than focusing on shopfloor organization, the COSATU Congress placed political goals at the top of its agenda: re-emphasizing the call for international economic sanctions against South Africa, delegates from across the country spoke of the need to put pressure on the state, despite warnings from some economists that such sanctions could erode member unions' bargaining power (Gelb, 1985; NN 7/23/87).

The 1987 Congress' obvious support for the ANC was certainly a far cry from the unions' 1983 tendency to stay outside the UDF. Explanations for the shift in COSATU's relationship to the ANC and the broad opposition movement sometimes focus on workers' traditions and culture. Loyalty to the illegal ANC, whose underground structures certainly played an important role in the growing political opposition, is said to have prompted rank-and-file workers to insist on joining the populist alliance, regardless of the threat to working-class purity (Von Holdt, 1987). Put more negatively, COSATU's move into a broad front is sometimes attributed to manipulation by "populist" unionists, whose true loyalties lay with underground ANC structures rather than to the labor movement (Levy, et al., 1987:5-7,27). Both these explanations contain an element of truth: many older union members participated in ANC-linked unions in the 1950s, or in the ANC itself, and many union members have long viewed the ANC as the main and most important source of opposition to the apartheid system.[11] Similarly, some union activists were undoubtedly linked to underground ANC structures, and sought to push the unions toward a closer alliance with the national liberation movement.[12] During preparatory negotiations for COSATU's launch, "populist" unionists supported candidates for leadership positions who would be sympathetic to more overtly political unionism, rather than adopting a narrowly defined working-class constituency (interviews, Johannesburg 1987).

The nonracial labor movement's shift toward participation in a multiclass alliance cannot be understood simply in terms of individual unionists and changing leadership, however. Too many prominent unionists have changed their opinions for an explanation based on individual loyalties to hold. Instead, COSATU's position must be understood to have emerged through a lengthy process, in which the national leadership was forced to redesign its strategies, and to adopt a different perspective on the nature of the South African working class. That process, in turn, can only be understood in terms of changes in the context in which the labor movement operated, and of the strategic options available to union leaders.

---

[11]Webster and his research associate, J. Khuzwayo, found that 11 percent of unregistered union members were willing to admit they had been members of unions in SACTU, the ANC-affiliated union federation destroyed in the 1960s (Webster, 1979:51).

[12]For example, see testimony at 1987 Durban trial of C. Zama and S. Phashe, who claimed they had left South Africa in 1983 for training as trade unionists ("Military Training: Two sent to jail," *New Nation*, Dec. 17-22, 1987).

Two basic phenomena shaped the context in which the nonracial labor movement operated after 1983. First, a severe economic recession since late 1982 changed the options open to labor leaders by undermining the relatively privileged position of semiskilled industrial workers in a booming economy. Second, and relatedly, the ongoing uprising in black townships since the early 1980s profoundly affected union members, like all black South Africans: it became increasingly difficult for union leaders to stand outside of political upheavals, since an attempt to do so would certainly have weakened community support for union campaigns.

South Africa's economy went into a tailspin in late 1982. As a manufacturing economy that remains reliant on exporting minerals and importing capital goods, it is—like most NICs— extremely vulnerable to international recession. Briefly, its dependence on exported primary goods, whose world prices fluctuate outside South Africa's control; its reliance on imported capital goods and technology; and its inability to expand its domestic consumer market have created enormous structural obstacles to growth. A growing balance of payments deficit, combined with government expenditures on apartheid administration and repression, has worsened the problem. Rising inflation— reaching nearly 20 percent by 1985—gained momentum in 1985, when the currency's value plummeted following a government moratorium on international debt repayments. By the mid-1980s, an estimated fifteen companies went bankrupt daily, and the executive director of the Federated Chambers of Industries warned darkly, "The rule of the day is the survival of the fittest. Manufacturers are concentrating on managing the recession and coming out leaner and fitter" (van Zyl, quoted in Von Holdt, 1986:312).

As manufacturers "managed the recession," workers lost their jobs. South Africa has long registered high black unemployment, but the current recession has raised figures to astronomical heights. In the metal industry alone, 84,000 workers were laid off between 1982 and 1984, while 23,000 general manufacturing jobs were lost in roughly the same period (Von Holdt, 1986:314; Keenan, 1985:138). By early 1987, official unemployment figures reached 1,198,000, or 19.2 percent of the officially recognized labor force (Central Statistical Services, quoted in WM 7/10/87). Unofficial estimates ran as high as 3.3 million unemployed, or nearly a third of the actual economically active population (WM 7/17/87).

From 1982, analysts within the labor movement recognized that declining employment would hurt their members, both by reducing the number of potential union members and by increasing employers' ability to withstand strikes. With clear evidence that employers were using retrenchments to weed out militant union activists, unionists sought to protect previous union gains and to distribute the recession's impact fairly among members by reducing the workweek and insisting on equitable lay-off plans (Jaffee and Jochelson, 1986). As the recession deepened, however, the leaders of the new labor federations recognized that job protection clauses alone would not defend members' jobs or wages. Weakening unions at the point of production, the recession forced unionists to consider new strategies that involved building strong community alliances to protect workplace organization. Organizing unemployed workers had long been a high priority for "political" unions, who saw their constituency in terms of a broad black population rather than simply in terms of industrial workers.[13] By 1987, however, organizing the unemployed in their communities was a priority for the entire labor federation (COSATU, 1987:9). At the same time, in response to galloping inflation, the union federation called for "a living wage" for all South African workers, both employed and unemployed. Rather than focusing on single-factory or even single-industry negotiations, COSATU began to call for a reasonable living standard, undertaking a nationally coordinated campaign for a minimum wage automatically linked to an inflation index.[14]

---

[13]The ANC had apparently long sought to organize unemployed workers—not surprisingly, since it had long held that industrial workers alone did not constitute the entire working class in South Africa. In 1982, Barbara Hogan was convicted of treason for membership in the ANC; her main activity for the ANC had apparently been an attempt to set up a union of the unemployed.

[14]It has been argued that this demand is fundamentally different from SACTU's demands in the 1950s for a basic minimum wage (Jack 1987) but the distinction seems vague at best, since it ignores the different inflation rates of the two eras.

The recession, then, greatly increased unions' involvement in community and political struggles. Not only did increasing unemployment threaten union strength, but rising inflation and economic stagnation threatened to undercut previous union victories. Under these circumstances, even unionists previously convinced of the necessity of focusing on workplace organization were forced to look toward broader forms of organization—in effect, toward popular coalitions with groups outside the factory— simply to protect workplace gains of the previous decade. Finally, the structural nature of the recession reinforced "political" unionists' arguments that black workers could win no lasting gains without political rights.

While the recession pushed the South African labor movement to reach into black communities for support, the spread of a popular community-based movement against the state forced organized labor to focus on political demands. By September 1984, one year after the launching of the UDF, South Africa's black townships were on the verge of a major uprising. The government's promises of reform had been roundly rejected by community groups; the new constitution—offering limited political participation to Asians and Coloreds and political rights only at the township and bantustan level to Africans—provided a target for unified opposition. At the same time, the rising cost of living added a measure of desperation to protests; on top of inflation and unemployment, new taxes and increased rents on were imposed to pay for the promised reforms. On September 1, 1984, rents on government-owned black housing were raised across South Africa: the new Constitution required that township councils finance themselves through increased rents and utility charges. The demonstrations that erupted that month were protests not only against the rising cost of living, but also against black disenfranchisement. Particularly in the area around Johannesburg, these demonstrations were met by virtual military occupation of townships.

Community activists renewed their appeals to unions for strikes backing political demands. In late 1984, a national student group begged workers for support in high school students' struggles for improved, nonracial education.

Workers, you are our fathers and mothers, you are our
brothers and sisters. Our struggle in the schools is your
struggle in the factories. We fight the same bosses
government, we fight the same enemy .... Our
boycott weapon is not strong enough against our
common enemy, the bosses and their government.
Workers, we need your support and strength in the
trade unions. *We students will never win our struggle
without the strength and support from the workers' movement*
(emphasis in original) (COSAS, n.d.).

Workers could hardly ignore community pressures, particularly
from their children. Within two months, leading Transvaal
unionists joined community activists in organizing a general
stayaway—a general boycott organized on a regional rather than
industrial basis. Condemning detentions and repression, the
stayaway's organizers called for the suspension of rent and busfare
increases, the institution of democratically elected student
representative councils in high schools, and an end to the high
school age limit. The stayaway supported community, rather than
workplace, demands; but as a union newspaper editorialized, the
action had "its origins in the growing discontent in the country's
black townships" where workers lived.

Worker parents are naturally sympathetic to their
childrens' struggle and in many townships joint parent-
student committees have been set up to offer support.
On top of this, workers are having to meet ever-increas-
ing rent, food and transport costs at a time when
employers are using the recession as an excuse to block
wage increases (FWN 33, 1984).

Detentions of important union leaders involved in the stayaway
only increased the identification of worker and community
interests.

While the uprising was far bigger than any single event, the
two-day Transvaal stayaway in November 1984, with roughly 60
percent of workers participating, sent shockwaves through South
Africa (LMG, 1985). Stayaways had been a well-used tactic in the
1950s of the then-legal ANC; in the early 1980s, however, some
unionists had opposed community-based demonstrations, arguing

that stayaways' broad character meant such actions would never have the organizational strength of shopfloor actions, and could be misused by nonworker leaders (Webster, 1981). Mass firings of unionized workers at a few government-linked companies following the November stayaway reinforced fears that stayaways could hurt workplace organization. In March 1985, however, a stayaway in the Eastern Cape—in which over 90 percent of African workers participated despite union leaders' strong objections—underlined a growing realization that unions could lose support if they stayed out of popular mobilizations (LMG, 1986). Although regional variations remained important, the initiative seemed by the time of COSATU's 1985 launch to be shifting from the factory floor to community-based political groups, and from factory-based demands to political issues. By mid-1985, unions joined political groups in calling for a national consumer boycott against the imposition of a state of emergency, military occupation of black townships and detentions without trial, and demanding full political rights for all (SAIRR, 1985:184), a campaign that could not be organized within factories, and which was called in support of popular black demands.

The increase in community-based resistance was parallelled by intensified repression. Several trade unionists and other activists were killed. When Transvaal union organizer Andries Raditsela died in police custody in May 1985, a national work stoppage in protest was widely supported by political organizations such as the UDF as well as by unions (SAIRR, 1985:185). Between 1984 and 1987, thousands of activists were detained without trial, arrested for subversion or killed by shadowy death squads. In early 1987, about 10 percent of detainees were estimated to be trade union members (DPSC, 1987).

The uprising, then, changed the conditions confronting unionists in black townships: increased community organization and heavy repression made it difficult for individual unionists to retain a primary focus on shopfloor issues and organization. Pressures from within their communities to coordinate campaigns began to make the attempt to keep the labor movement distinct from community politics seem divisive and dangerous. Two years into the uprising, many unionists had abandoned their previous insistence on separate spheres for community and worker organizations. Many had taken on key roles in community groups in addition to their union work: the metalworkers' Moses Mayekiso, who in 1984 had insisted that workers should build a separate movement, led Alexandra's civic association in 1986, and in 1987 faced treason charges for his community work.

Thus, dramatic changes in conditions changed the options available to unionists. In 1982, in a relative vacuum of community organization and at a time of relative prosperity, union leaders could call for the creation of a pure working-class movement, and reject class coalitions—although, paradoxically, the unions themselves were just beginning to grow. By 1985, the nonracial union movement had developed a national structure; a severe recession had pushed the union federation to develop links to community groups, and to place a high priority on political solutions to workers' problems. Simultaneously, existing community groups appealed to workers as community members, while government repression of black townships turned militant workers' attention from employers to the state. Increasingly, union leaders would adopt a different definition of the working class, and of working-class interests: instead of emphasizing shopfloor organizations, the labor movement began to argue that black workers could not stay outside of the broader movement for black political rights.

COSATU as a Political Force

COSATU was launched in late 1985, with nearly 1 million members. After years of debate, several principles were accepted as the basis of unity: unions would reform themselves into national industrial unions, dividing up members on the principle of one-industry, one-union; member unions would use nonracial membership criteria; and member unions would reject political affiliations (Hindson, 1984; Lewis and Randall, 1985b). The initial principles of the federation thus appeared to reflect "workerist" concerns about multiclass coalitions; this was apparently the structure of an independent working-class movement, organized through industrial trade unions, which would remain distinct from the growing political opposition to the state.

The new federation's elected leadership was surprisingly outspoken on political issues, however. COSATU's first president, Elijah Barayi, was an older mineworker with a history of involvement in ANC-affiliated unions; at the launch, he called for mandatory international sanctions, placing political demands above shopfloor organization. "We make no apologies about connecting issues on the shopfloor and issues facing workers in society as a whole," he has said. "Politics, and especially the lack of even the most basic democratic rights for the majority of our people, is a bread and butter issue for the working class" (Barayi, quoted in WM 7/17/87). Some months after COSATU's launch, the federation's general secretary met with ANC representatives in neighboring Zimbabwe; a statement published jointly following the meeting described the ANC as leading the national movement, with COSATU as "an important integral part" of the opposition (ANC n.d.). On his return, the general secretary linked workers' struggles against employers and the broader struggle against the state, and called for "disciplined alliances" between trade unions and black communities. Workers, he warned, could neither afford to remain isolated from the broad movement, nor to be subsumed into it (Naidoo, 1986).

At the federation level, the political content of the labor movement's demands was unmistakable by early 1987. COSATU's leaders no longer sought to separate workers' political campaigns from the broad opposition, and no longer emphasized workplace organization. Instead, national campaigns took precedence. The "living wage" campaign, for instance, was estimated to be the single most important cause of industrial action in 1987 (SARS, in WM 9/4/87). Abandoning its previous argument that only people in waged labor should be considered part of the working class, COSATU (1986:6) now suggested that students and youth were natural allies of workers: they, like workers, "exploit no one." COSATU's executive committee told members:

> The problems facing us at work and in our communities are the same. Nowhere do we have control over the decisions that affect our lives: the rent we are forced to pay; high transport costs; terrible conditions in the townships .... That is why COSATU workers are leading the struggle to build street committees in

the townships. Like our unions in the workplaces,
street committees will give us the democratic organization and unity and strength to fight for all the things
we need—including control over every aspect of our
lives through our own democratic organization under
the leadership of organized workers.

Speakers from the political opposition regularly addressed union
meetings, which increasingly focused on political issues. About
1,500,000 workers stayed away from work to commemorate the
1976 students' uprising on June 16, 1986. At least as many as
stayed away the previous month on the more traditional workers'
day, May 1 (WM 6/20/86). In May 1987, a series of stayaways
marked the extent to which the labor movement now viewed itself
as a component of the political movement: in particular,
COSATU's strong support for a two-day national protest against all-
white elections underlined the shift toward joint antigovernment
campaigns.

The organizing efforts of individual unions also began to
shift, both in terms of undertaking industrial actions to make
demands against the state, and of attacking symbols of apartheid
as well as workplace issues. Workers across the country stopped
work when union organizers were detained in police swoops in
June 1986. Employers, blaming the state for strikes beyond their
control, argued that union organizers should not be considered
political activists, but failed to block detentions (WM 6/27/86).
Strikes against individual employers, often motivated by political
conflicts, increased dramatically: in 1987, mandays lost to industrial
action (excluding explicitly political stayaways) had increased
nearly thirty-four fold since 1980 (noted in the table). In 1987, for
example, the Metalworkers and Allied Workers Union carried out
repeated national work stoppages, hoping to push employers to
demand that the government release the General Secretary Moses
Mayekiso, jailed for community activities. Some unionists came to
view such strikes against the detention of organizers as providing
a measure of protection for individual activists, because the
interruption in production could push employers to protest against
detentions (interviews, East Rand, 1987).

Beyond these political protest strikes, however, industrial
actions themselves took on new patterns: individual unions began

to engage in prolonged strikes, framing workers' demands in clearly political terms and relying heavily on community support. Generally, black South African workers have not had the resources required for prolonged strikes; stoppages have generally been simply demonstrations of strength, lasting at most a few days. During a recession and in a highly polarized political atmosphere, both workers and employers seemed to resist concessions, and community support proved crucial for even minor victories. Late in 1986, a commercial workers' union engaged in a national strike against a supermarket chain patronized by black customers; an informal consumer boycott certainly strengthened their effort (Obery, 1987). Their demands were reinforced by explosions in some store branches, possibly carried out by the ANC's armed wing.

More dramatically, in early 1987, over 20,000 railway workers struck for union recognition and an end to discriminatory employment practices. The union involved was a small UDF-affiliated union; union organizers were hardly prepared for either the strikers' militancy or for the level of community support the strike received. Against the backdrop of an all-white parliamentary election campaign, this strike by unskilled migrant workers became a national symbol. The state's involvement was transparent: the state-owned company clearly discriminated against black workers, and the police and army were brought in to break the strike. Used to carry blacks from segregated black areas to city centers, the railroads are themselves symbols of apartheid. For weeks, violence against railroad property was widespread, and burning train cars became visible evidence of community support. Bombs in railway property—empty train stations, train cars and trucks—demonstrated the active support of the ANC's military wing. Community groups in Soweto, South Africa's largest black township, organized a three-day stayaway in support of the strikers. Finally—after all the strikers had spent months without work, several strikers had been killed, and scores of workers jailed—the company was forced to rehire strikers (SARHWU, 1987).

Symbols of apartheid became targets of worker action, while community support strengthened prolonged strikes. Unions increasingly focused on the apartheid system, rather than on individual employers. In mid-1987, this trend was illustrated by the National Union of Mineworkers (NUM), whose 250,000 members are unskilled migrants who face expulsion to rural bantustans if they lose their jobs. Providing approximately half the total value of South Africa's exports, the mines are the cornerstone of the national economy; previous black miners' strikes invariably ended in heavy repression and mass dismissals. The NUM announced it would challenge mining companies to build family houses instead of single-sex migrant hostels; the union moved miners' wives into hostels to underline their demand. This campaign clearly placed political goals high on the miners' agenda: to comply, employers would have had to ignore apartheid legislation (WM, 2/27/87; 4/3/87). Later the same year, at least 340,000 miners joined a legal strike for higher wages and an end to job discrimination. Despite police repression, the strike lasted three weeks, and most workers were allowed to return to work. The wages demanded, and finally accepted, by the workers were scarcely higher than those initially offered by employers, suggesting that the mine strike should be understood as an indication of deepening labor organization and militancy rather than simply as a bargaining tool against employers (Obery, et al., 1987).

The creation of a strong alliance between the labor movement and the political opposition has shaped the opposition as well as the labor movement, and seems to have reinforced an understanding of apartheid in terms of class interests, rather than simply in terms of racial domination. The ANC had long argued that the working class would play an important role in the transition to a post-apartheid society, but following the 1986 meeting between COSATU's general secretary and ANC officials, the ANC seemed to strengthen its support for workers' struggles. A widely circulated illegal ANC pamphlet (n.d.) told that:

> The job of the revolutionary fighter is to build the leading force of our struggle—the working class. The job of the revolutionary fighter is to make sure the workers' voice is loudest, that the workers' way forward is accepted inside every one of our mass organizations. And with this position, we go out, to build support from the poor [and] the middle class—and from everyone who is willing to live without oppression and exploitation.

By 1987, most political groups included support for COSATU in their campaigns. Black youth groups, probably the most energetic of the various community organizations, placed support for striking workers, organizing the unemployed, and assisting COSATU's living wage and antirepression campaigns at the top of their agenda (WM, 12/24/87). When the UDF national bulletin published a scathing attack on "workerism"—essentially defined as any attempt to keep the organized labor movement separate from the broad opposition—as a threat to a broad democratic front, the UDF National Executive Committee reminded readers that discussions of socialism should be considered democratic, rather than divisive (Isizwe 1986:13-31; UDF, 1987). Working-class leadership was clearly important within the broad front: a survey of sixty-two UDF regional executive leaders found thirty-three in "economic positions that can be defined as working class" (Swilling, 1987:27). Finally, the increasing visibility of Communist Party symbols and pamphlets at rallies inside the country—after decades in which the party kept a low profile within the underground movement—suggested that the national liberation movement wished to give new priority to articulating workers' concerns (interviews, Johannesburg, 1987).

By the mid-1980s, economic restructuring was high on the agenda of the anti-apartheid movement: a survey of urban blacks found that 77 percent preferred socialism, "in which workers have a say in the running of businesses, and share in the ownership and profits," to capitalism, "in which businesses are owned and run by private businessmen, for their own profit" (Orkin, 1986:52,73). As one observer put it, COSATU's decision to move closer to the ANC "has already made a great difference to the liberation movement," by strengthening "the left wing of liberation politics," and by "increasing the potential for developing the leadership and hegemony of the working class in the struggle as a whole and on its many fronts—youth, communities, students and political organizations" (Von Holdt, 1987:15).

By 1988, the South African government and employers no longer believed that the labor movement would restrict itself to shopfloor issues. A leading management consultant asked plaintively, "What happened to those unions that were supposed, when government gave them legal standing eight years ago, to devote themselves to worker advancement, to be an escape valve for black grievances and to stay out of politics?" (Quoted by Parks 1987). Employers saw the emphasis on political rights as a threat to a fragile system of industrial relations; they warned that individual employers, unable to respond to political demands, might refuse to bargain at all. Anonymous bombings of union offices suggested the far right would retaliate further if the trend toward "political" unionism continued. In February 1988, the government used its state of emergency regulations to restrict COSATU to "normal" union activities; six months later, despite a national three-day stayaway protesting restrictions on the labor movement, the government gazetted a new bill aimed at penalizing unions for community support. Consumer boycotts, spontaneous strikes, and any political involvement could now result in severe financial losses for unions; with apparent support from employer associations, the state seemed determined to end what it viewed as the labor movement's involvement in a "revolutionary conspiracy."[15]

Conclusion

As the nonracial labor movement developed into a national force, it was probably inevitable that unions would play an important role in South Africa's deepening political conflict. Without a severe recession or a simultaneous rise in community mobilization, however, it is possible that the unions would have followed a separate course, remaining distinct from the broad political opposition. Industrial workers, organized at the workplace, might well have retained a separate identity from community activists, and continued to work in separate national campaigns.

As argued earlier, however, from the early 1980s structural pressures on the labor movement pushed unions to change their relationship to community organizations. The combination of a severe recession and a community-based uprising forced union leaders to adopt a new approach. The labor movement redefined

---

[15]The bill was passed and gazetted quite suddenly in August 1988, as soon as employers seemed to withdraw their public support for the new bill.

its constituency to embrace workers outside the factory: it sought increasingly to appeal not only to workers, but to workers' families, to students and the unemployed, as part of a broad working-class movement mobilized against the state. From an initial shopfloor emphasis, it moved toward "social-movement unionism," rooted as much in segregated black townships as in the factories where nonracial unions first emerged.

At the same time, union participation in the popular political movement has changed the discourse within community groups, to emphasize a challenge to existing economic relations as well as the demand for a nonracial political system. As more and more activists came to express their struggle against the state in terms of working-class goals, it seemed unlikely that the class consciousness developed on the shopfloor and extended to black communities could simply be erased, either by this government or in the future.

Does this shift toward politicized unionism mean that South Africa is indeed a unique case, whose political arrangements make "normal" unionism impossible? While South Africa is, fortunately, unique in many ways, the factors that allowed this "new unionism" to emerge, and then pushed it toward increasing political involvement, certainly exist in other NICs. Industrialization strategies based on imported capital-intensive technology and semiskilled, low-paid workers are hardly unique; industrial workers, organized at the point of production, may well be able to force employers in other cases to "normalize" labor relations, as South African workers did in the 1970s. Second, rapid urbanization accompanying industrialization has created huge working-class and poor communities in most NICs, which have rarely received the benefits promised by trickle-down economic theory. Authoritarian states have tended to repress community and/or political groups; the communities in which industrial workers of most NICs live have little access to social services, and urban social movements around housing, transport or schooling tend to have a distinct class character. While racial dynamics may have strengthened the sense of identification between union members and community groups in South Africa, it seems at least plausible that union members in other NICs will be drawn into community attempts to improve conditions, and that strikes will be used to back demands for political change. Third, NICs are generally vulnerable to international recessions; while South Africa's case may have been aggravated by international outcries against apartheid, states in other NICs may prove equally incapable of carrying out reforms that require redistribution of social services to working-class communities, or of reducing unemployment. Under these conditions, far from being safety valves for workers' shopfloor frustrations, it seems possible that labor movements will join with community-based social movements to challenge existing models of economic development.

Different industrialization patterns create different conditions and opportunities for working-class mobilization, both in factories and in new urban communities. The reliance of NICs on imported capital and technology may affect workers' ability to organize within the factory, and to shape the identity between unions and working-class communities; a competitive international context—in which late industrializers stand at a definite disadvantage—means that industrial strategies will almost inevitably run into crisis that will precipitate further conflict over the distribution of the benefits of economic growth. Under different industrialization strategies, the precise nature of these struggles may differ; but it seems reasonable to expect that as labor movements emerge in other NICs, they may not look like the conservative labor aristocracies predicted by most development theory.

Chapter 11

WHAT CONSTITUTIONAL LESSONS DOES ZIMBABWE'S EXPERIENCE TEACH?

Robert B. Seidman

Introduction

S OON, INDEPENDENT Namibia and South Africa will engage the task of constitution-making.[1] If other African experience serves, they will undergo a blizzard of advice, some well-meaning, some not so well-meaning. The core of that advice—intriguingly, of both sorts—will consist of the injunction to copy the great democratic constitutions of the West, especially Britain's and the United States'. Many African constitution-making debates, for example, centered upon the relative desirability of a parliamentary-style (i.e., British) as opposed to a presidential-style (i.e., U.S.)

---

[1]During my stay in Zimbabwe, I served as consultant for various ministries; this paper therefore rests in part on participant observation. I am deeply indebted to Professors Ann Seidman, Neva Makgetla and Paul Brietzke for valued comments; mistakes are, of course, all mine.

constitution, sometimes phrased as the relative desirability of a ceremonial as opposed to an executive head of government.

Implicit in these discussions lay the acceptance of the classical perspective on constitutions: that they function mainly to draw lines between private right and public power. That perspective holds that everywhere constitutions should address the same difficulty: The tendency of power to aggrandize itself and to use the machinery of state to institutionalize its own power. A contrary perspective, the anticlassical, argues that constitutions prescribe the basic organs of government and their power relationships— and that these determine what social problems government will likely address, and what range of potential solutions it will likely consider. In that view, the African versions of both the British ("Westminster-style") and the U.S. ("independent executive") constitutions in practice served to create governments that addressed as difficulties only government's tendency to interfere in the economy, and the threat of majoritarian control over decisionmaking. To solve these two perceived difficulties, the African version of the classical constitutions made it as difficult as possible for government to interfere in the economy, and for the majority to participate in governmental decisionmaking.

Everywhere, however, Africa faces the same two overarching difficulties: poverty and vulnerability. To solve those, of course government must do what it can to improve the economy, and to empower the mass—basically, to broaden participation in decision-making. From the anticlassical perspective, the classical-style constitutions of Anglophonic African countries became, not part of the solution, but part of the problem.

Zimbabwe provides a useful case study. It had two character-istics likely to exist also in Namibia and South Africa. First, Zimbabwe entered independence with a government which, in a radical, socialist mode, proclaimed its intention to overcome Zimbabwe's black masses' poverty and vulnerability. History gave those assertions badges of sincerity. Zimbabwe had just emerged from a great war in which, led by the ruling parties (Zimbabwe African National Union, ZANU, and Zimbabwe African People's Union, ZAPU), by main force of arms and by blood Africans wrenched freedom from the white supremacists. Second, to carry out government's proclaimed intention required that it address six great issues: eradicating apartheid; transforming the economy to alleviate poverty; preventing reaction from exacerbating ethnic differences; ensuring popular participation in governmental decisionmaking; and guaranteeing legality by government officials. Those five issues required massive changes in social, political and economic institutions. Those changes sat uneasily with the sixth great issue that Zimbabwe's independent government had to confront: keeping the machine going even while it underwent fundamental transformation.

As part of the independence settlement, like all other Anglophonic African countries, Zimbabwe had entered independence with a classical-style constitution (Westminster model) that its apologists advertised as promising instant electoral democracy and accountable government. Zimbabwe constituted in effect a trial run for southern Africa. Its issues were homologous with those that will confront independent Namibia and South Africa, and its government had both radical rhetoric and the hard-won mark of truthfulness.[2] It had a Westminster-type constitution. Zimbabwe provides an intriguing case study from which to learn about constitutions and change in southern Africa.

In fact, for at least the first three years after independence the government did relatively little to transform Zimbabwean society. Many causes contributed to this inaction, among which there loomed most ominously South African intransigence. Without dismissing the power of the other social, political and economic causes of stagnation, it is useful to determine how Zimbabwe's constitution contributed to relative post-independence stagnation.

Propositions can then be formulated about what governmental structures seem necessary to address the six issues that Zimbabwe faced and that in turn Namibia and South Africa will confront. Independent Namibia and South Africa will of course

---

[2]Some try to explain Zimbabwe's seeming stagnation by the government's presumed insincerity in its radical rhetoric. (E.g., Astrow, 1983). That explanation wallows in circularity: To explain stagnation, its authors postulate insincerity; to prove insincerity, they point to stagnation. In my view (methodological circularity aside) leaders who for so long and at so great a personal cost fought a dangerous war have positioned themselves beyond doubts about personal sincerity.

require a parliament, an executive, and a judicial system. Many choices exist about what sort of a parliament and electoral system, what sort of an executive, and what sort of a judicial system will best serve these new nations. The focus, here, however, is on institutions less frequently identified as having a constitutional stature, for example, a leadership code, an ombudsman, and a planning commission. This chapter examines, first, very briefly Zimbabwe's record of change in the first three years following independence; second, offers an explanation for its relative stagnation; and finally, suggests the constitutional implications of that supposition.

Zimbabwe's Independent Years: Radical Rhetoric, Welfare State Reforms, Institutional Changes

Better schooling, better health care, higher wages and better roads and widespread state intervention do not make a socialist polity. All are characteristics of states following a basic needs strategy. (Such states are also considered welfare states or are said to be following state capitalism—Makgetla and Seidman, 1987.) All can as well be characteristics of socialist polity.

Socialism, however, requires more. It requires simultaneously a shift in class power, and therefore radical changes in the institutions of the economy, government and the armed forces. The economy must change from one in which private owners make decisions for their own selfish reasons, to one in which the mass of the population own the means of production, and, with maximum feasible participation, decide how to use it according to a plan. Socialism does not, however, suddenly appear. It results from a long, transitional process of which the earliest steps consist of nationalizing the "commanding heights" of the economy (banks, key enterprises, export-import trade), land reform, economic planning, and planned reinvestment of locally earned surpluses. The institutions of government must change so that state decisions reflect and enhance working class and peasant interests and power. The police and armed forces must support socialist rather than capitalist power.

Like all ruling classes, Rhodesia's capitalist class expressed its power through the institutions that defined the economy and the state. At independence a new government took power, populist in orientation, and articulating a socialist rhetoric. A truly revolutionary moment existed, seemingly pregnant with change. Elected by the mass of the population, claiming to represent them, and flaunting war-won credentials of its populist orientation, the government took over reins of power that nominally controlled a capitalist economy, state, and law.[3] A government elected on a socialist platform had to rule through institutions and laws that embodied and bolstered not mass power but the power of the tiny, then all-white ruling capitalist class. To a considerable extent this class was based not locally but in the boardrooms of multinational corporations in London, New York and especially Johannesburg. For its ultimate source of power, at independence, the government had to rely on an army and a police force that yesterday vigorously supported the enemy, and today existed virtually unchanged. A race ensued. Would the government find the key to change the economic, political and military institutions that bolstered capitalist class power before those institutions either overthrew the government or seduced it?

Three years after independence, how had Zimbabwe run that race? How had it dealt with the six great issues it faced at independence? First, with respect to desegregation, although it had amended many discriminatory laws, others still remained formally on the books. The government had enacted only weak anti-discrimination laws regarding housing and unemployment, neither requiring affirmative action to rectify historical injustices. (Only in the civil service did it undertake an affirmative action program). In the economy, the professions, the university, the civil service, the army and police, whites still held power in numbers and place vastly disproportionate to their numbers.

Second, with respect to poverty, Zimbabwe had undertaken a number of welfare state reforms. For example, it had expanded education three-fold to reach blacks hitherto without opportunity for schooling; it had raised the minimum wage (only to see the

---

[3]The Supreme Court Act 1981 reaffirmed the existing law as the law of Zimbabwe; the Constitution so stated as well.

gains eroded by inflation); it introduced free health care for people earning less than $150 per month. Government, however, had done very little to transform the economy. The large government corporation sector inherited from the ousted regime of Ian Smith still operated as a set of private entities, not as government agencies; government acquired an interest in some private firms—for example, a new Holiday Inn (50 percent ownership); a commercial bank (40 percent); a vegetable oil firm (40 percent); and the nation's only coal mines (majority interest). The government began three potentially important government corporations—the Minerals Marketing Corporation, a development bank, and Mining Development Corporation. The government resettled some 36,000 peasant families on land bought from commercial farmers on a willing seller-willing buyer basis (some estimates held that 600,000 families required new land). The government retained in force the old labor legislation that the Smith regime had used to control black labor. (New industrial relations legislation, scarcely less repressive than the old one, would emerge in 1984.) Otherwise, the economy Zimbabwe inherited from the ancient regime continued, structurally unchanged. Zimbabweans continued to produce huge surpluses for the white farmers and multinational corporations who owned much of Zimbabwe. The law left decisions about the uses of that surplus to its private owners. They invested precious little of that in Zimbabwe—and without continuous reinvestment of surpluses, no country's economy can grow. After a brief flirtation with a reduced sales tax (the most regressive of taxes), the government continuously increased it until it stood at 19 percent (23 percent for consumer durables). By most indices of growth, Zimbabwe's economy stagnated, reproducing the poverty and powerlessness of its black masses.

Third, far from solving problems of ethnic division, the government seemed to have only one answer to the discontent stirred up among the Ndebele people by South African trouble-making and political malcontents. It responded with force, terror, and demands that ZAPU (largely supported by the Ndebele) disappear by folding itself into ZANU (the government party, largely supported by the Shona people).

Fourth, aside from winning the vote for blacks in the Lancaster Constitution,[4] the government did nothing to extend mass participation in central-government decisionmaking. To a degree, it did improve mass participation in local government. In the former native reserves (now called communal areas), in place of government by local *gauleiter* (the district commissioner), the government substituted democratically-elected local councils. In the white commercial agricultural areas, by contrast, as under the Smith regime, only landowners (usually white) voted for local rural councils—not their black farm workers who outnumbered the landowners by huge majorities. The government also introduced a system of relatively popular courts, mainly for civil suits between Africans. On the level of central government, however, participation amounted to the right to vote for the legislators who selected a government that purported to supervise the senior civil servants who made the decisions far away in Harare, behind closed Ministerial doors, protected by an Official Secrets Act that remained unchanged in all its draconian harshness.

Fifth, the Constitution required the government to appoint an ombudsman. The legislation implementing that provision, however, gave the ombudsman little power. Elsewhere, then old forms continued: high court judges in wigs and gowns, parliament with a Mr. Speaker with his wig and gown, and knee-breeched functionaries in bizarre eighteenth-century costumes who solemnly moved the mace from the top shelf to a lower one when Parliament went into committee. Those forms had not protected legality during the Smith regime; there seemed little reason to expect them to serve better the new regime.

Finally, how well did the government keep the machine running? Roads, schools, hospitals, university, the economy: all continued to function. To meet demands of its mass constituency, however, the government borrowed heavily. Without a restructuring of economic institutions in ways likely to increase productivity, Zimbabweans experienced no increase in the gross national product (a trend exacerbated by three years of devastating drought). The IMF entered to impose its usual stringent condi-

---

[4]Not however, one person, one vote; the Constitution gave whites (about 3 percent of the population) 20 percent of the seats in Parliament.

tions. Faced by serious unrest in the southwest, the government seemed incapable of winning the allegiance of an Ndebele peasantry who had hardly received the benefits for which they had fought the independence war. Without tangible benefits, how much longer would the Shona peasantry continue its seeming unflagging support of the government?

Explanations

No one "cause" explains anything. Today, all social theory rejects monocausality. Scholars and others put forward a pride of propositions to explain why Zimbabwe maintained old institutions instead of creating new ones: the hazardous international milieu, especially the diminishing military threat along her southern border; South African destabilization; white flight; the dislocation that followed the long armed struggle; transnational corporate power; manpower shortages; insecure security forces; explicit disagreement with the socialist objective within Zimbabwe's highest ranks, even within the cabinet itself; the colonial miseducation of the leadership[5]; the difficulty of dismantling ninety years of colonial rule in a short period. Whatever the force of these interconnected causes, to what extent did the constitution contribute to the result?

Action consists of choices. Choices do not come about in mid-air. They take place in a confining world with its constraints and its limited opportunities. We explain behavior by describing the constraints and resources within which actors choose, including in those constraints and resources not only what transpires in their external environment, but also what goes on in their heads (i.e., their ideologies, domain assumptions, and interests). We can never describe the totality of those constraints and resources; a map on a one-to-one scale stretches as far as the globe itself. We disentangle reality by examining how a particular set of constraints and resources condition choice, never forgetting, however, that we describe only a slice of reality. That a map details soil types but

---

[5]Ibid.

omits road networks and political boundaries does not lessen its utility for its designed purposes, but it obviously tells only part of the story. This analysis pursues only that story's constitutional themes.

We concern ourselves with constitutions as charters of government. To explain what happened in Zimbabwe, we therefore address only issues of the state and the legal order, taking as given all the other constraints and resources affecting Zimbabwe's choices. How, in the turbulent post-war milieu, did Zimbabwe's existing state and legal order, and the constitution that defined them, constrain the government's choices in making changes to economic and political institutions that would undercut capitalist class power, enhance the power of workers and peasants, and start the transition to socialism?

Capitalist class power has no meaning apart from the institutions through which it manifests itself. One cannot even describe the economic power of that class without simultaneously describing institutions: property, contract, corporations, banking, insurance, agriculture and the like. One cannot describe the political power of that class without describing political institutions: elections, parliament, the judiciary, the ministries, and so forth. To make good the shift from capitalist to working class and peasant power that lies at socialism's heart required massive changes in Zimbabwe's economic and political institutions.

To change these institutions required the government to make choices in a context of constraints and few resources. These limitations can be described by three propositions:

1) Unless the government changes the legal order, institutional change will occur only incrementally and by happenstance;
2) Every state structure pre-forms the range of possible decisions it will make; unless restructured, the state will not produce laws or other decisions looking towards a socialist restructuring of the society; and,
3) The very conditions of rapid development constitute a seedbed for the growth of a bureaucratic bourgeoisie (Seidman, 1978).

Call the first the Law of the Reproduction of Institutions, the second the Law of Transforming the Bourgeois State, and the third the Law of the Growth of the Bureaucratic Bourgeoisie. From the anticlassical perspective, this chapter argues that the independence constitution made it difficult for the government to make the changes whose necessity these three general laws imply.

The law of reproduction of institutions

Two alternative theories purport to account for the function of law in social change. In one, right-wing theory and one strain of neo-Marxism paradoxically join. They agree that the law can only record behavioral change, but cannot bring it about. Some right-wing theorists assert that "values" determine behavior, and law cannot; others, that people act so rigidly in their self-interest that law can only affect their behavior by appealing to their self interest (Posner, 1986); some neo-Marxists believe that the economic basis so rigidly determines law, that until the basis changes, the law cannot change (Williams, 1980). These contradictory notions coalesce in a denial that law can affect behavior.

A contrary school (including more orthodox Marxists, e.g. Engels, 1967, and some non-Marxist law and society theorists, see e.g. Ellickson, 1986) holds that the legal order constitutes one among several variables that affect behavior. The legal order (including the constitution) contributes either by its commands, or by the way in which it facilitates action. Those commands and facilitative rules and their implementing institutions make up a part of those constraints and resources. In choosing what course to take, an actor takes into account those commands, threats, promises and facilitative rules, just as he takes into account economic, social, ideological and other constraints and resources in his environment. A constitutional command will never of its own force bring about conforming behavior. Behavior will conform only if to the prescription's addressees, taking all in all, conformity seems to them the right way to go (Seidman, 1978; cf. Moore, 1984).

By definition, an institution consists of repetitive patterns of behavior. For every important institution of the economy or the state, some law structures the actors' environments in order to help channel their behavior in ways that will support the institution. Property law buttresses the institution of property; contract law, the institution of contract; corporation law, the institution of corporations. The laws defining parliament support it; the laws concerning ministries buttress them; the laws concerning agricultural extension, credit and marketing boards underpin those institutions. The relative weight that different laws have in channelling behavior, of course, varies. The law that requires motorists to drive on the left side of the road probably has relatively small impact on behavior, for they must drive on the left or risk their lives at every curve. The laws that require payment of income tax have great influence on behavior, for without those laws people would not pay the tax at all.

As previously argued, class power and the institutions that embody and manifest it constitute opposite sides of a coin. One cannot discuss the one without describing the other. Similarly, one cannot adequately describe an economic or governmental institution without describing how the legal order supports it. One cannot describe a corporation without describing the law that calls it into being, and helps to channel the behavior of its officers, directors, shareholders and employees. One cannot describe the institution of property without describing property law. At the same time, no description of a law suffices that ignores the behavior that takes place under it. The legal order and the institutions to which it relates again constitute opposite sides of a single coin (*Contra:* Kelsen, 1967).

If institutions and class constitute a single but analytically divisible whole, and if institutions and the legal order also constitute a single but analytically divisible whole, then the legal order and class power also must have that same close nexus. Class power, institutions and the legal order form a trinity. One cannot conceive either of class power, institutions or the legal order without conceiving of the others.

Because of their intimate nexus, to change one of these three requires that a change in the others. Of the three, however, government has most direct control over the legal order. That does not say that it has unlimited control—the legal order is at best an ambiguous, dull and slippery tool—or that the legal order constitutes a free good in unlimited supply. In fact, it constitutes an expensive, scarce resource. It says only this, that in order to induce changed behavior, the government's tool of choice consists of the legal order. By changing the legal order, it can hope to channel behavior in new directions, thus to change institutions. By changing institutions, it can hope to change the locus of class power.

In order to induce changed behavior, however, government must begin by prescribing the new behavior desired. To do that, it must promulgate a new rule—statute, regulation, subsidiary legislation, appellate court decision, sometimes, military decree—and sometimes constitutional prescription. It must prescribe the new behavior in a way that people identify as official.

Governments have always used law to bring about changed behavior. In Zimbabwe, until the enactment of The Customary Law and Primary Courts Act, 1981, nobody held Village Courts or Community Courts. Now they dot the land. Until by law government raised the minimum wages, employers paid only $20 per month minimum wage. Now they must pay $55 per month. Until the constitution so provided (Constitution, Zimbabwe, 1980, Sched. 3, §3(1)), blacks did not vote for members of Parliament. Now they do.

Until government changes the applicable law, planned structural changes in institutions rarely come about. Three examples are instructive. First, cooperatives law: the received, colonialist-enacted cooperatives law for Africans aimed to create marketing and consumer cooperatives, not producer cooperatives. With respect to producer cooperatives, that law proves dysfunctional. A marketing cooperative serves only as a marketing corporation whose shareholders consist of the individual producing units. As in any corporation, the shareholders want centralized management, obtained through a board of directors,[6] which employs the cooperative's workers. In a producer cooperative, the members do the cooperative's work. To require that they limit their participation in management decisions to voting annually for a board of directors effectively reduces them to employees of their own cooperative, with no more control over their lives than employees in other shareholder-owned enterprise.

A second example is land tenures for resettlement schemes. From the Muzorewa regime Zimbabwe inherited a system of land

---

[6]In the Cooperatives Society Act, called the "Committee."

tenures for black settlers that gives them only permits to use the land, terminable at the whim of the minister. Accepted wisdom teaches that without long-term, stable tenures, farmers mine the soil (Parsons, 1956). Until the government restructures those land tenures, resettlement in Zimbabwe will likely not result in high settler productivity.

The shareout of profits provides a third example. Zimbabwe's property law gives to the owner of agricultural property the power to determine what crops to grow (subject only to minimum wage legislation and the market), how much to pay his workers, and (again subject only to the market), the prices of his crop. The difference between what he pays to produce the crop and the selling price constitutes his profit. That all belongs to him—never mind that his workers' efforts also contributed to produce that crop. In Zimbabwe in 1981, 76,000 tobacco workers received in wages for their combined efforts about half as much as 1,200 tobacco farmers received in profits (Seidman, A., 1983). The property law did not change, and those inequitable relationships necessarily continued.

In short, the legal order contributes to structuring behavior. When Zimbabwe became independent, the legal order then in force contributed to the behavior that constituted its capitalist economic institutions and its authoritarian political ones, and that embodied capitalist class power. That legal order constituted a major constraint on Zimbabwe's government's capacity to change those institutions. Until the legal order changes, radical changes in institutions rarely occur. That constitutes the Law of Reproduction of Institutions.

Three years into independence, Zimbabwe's leaders had barely honored the Law of Reproduction of Institutions. The actual roll call of change-oriented legislation seemed pathetically small. Without exception, the changes in institutions earlier mentioned came about through legal change. Without exception, the stagnation that occurred with respect to other institutions—especially economic ones—occurred where Zimbabwe's government introduced no new legislation. In some countries, legislation purporting to induce institutional changes frequently failed to do so—the problem of "phantom" or "symbolic" law. That problem did not yet seriously plague Zimbabwe.

A corollary of the Law of Reproduction of Institutions therefore constitutes the first lesson from Zimbabwe's experience: Unless Namibia's and South Africa's new governments change the laws affecting the relevant institutions, they will continue to operate as they have in the past, changing only incrementally. Capitalist institutions define a capitalist economy and embody capitalist class power. Unless those new governments undertake to transform them into socialist institutions, socialism will not come about. Unless they undertake a massive transformation of laws affecting the economy—property law, contract law, commercial law, insurance law, banking law, cooperatives law, company law, the law of the public productive sector, planning law and so forth—those institutions will not change in a socialist direction.

A second-order explanation then comes up for discussion: why did Zimbabwe's new governors not introduce the sorts of change-oriented law required by their proclaimed socialist ideology and the Law of Reproduction of Institutions?

The law of transforming the bourgeois state

In the struggle between Zimbabwe's socialist-oriented government and its capitalist economic and political institutions, intuitively it seemed that the governors held all the high cards. Their declared socialist goals required that they transform economic and political institutions. In the constraints and resources that made up the governors' arena of choice, the constitutional power they held gave them control over the machinery of state. If they wanted to change the laws, surely they could do so. If they did not change them, their failure must result from lack of will. That intuitive explanation, however, errs. Whatever the government's subjective desires, all the probabilities militated against changing Zimbabwe's institutions. The government's first charge required it to feed its people. At independence, no matter what injustices and inefficiencies of the economic institutions, those institutions did feed Zimbabwe's people at a level to which, over time, they had accustomed themselves. To do that, and to perform all the other myriad functions of an economic system, at the outset the government had no choice but to rely on the very economic institutions that its ideology told it must change radically.

Similarly, the government took over a state machinery that, whatever its faults, managed to perform the functions of a state: to run a school system, the police, state security, the health system and a host of other services with which the new governors had no experience and sometimes precious little knowledge.   Both economic and governmental institutions required high-level personnel who knew not only general theory, but the details of how these institutions operated in the Zimbabwean context. Again, the government had to rely on the very machinery it proposed to transform—and that machinery embodied and manifested capitalist class power.

All this conspired to tell Zimbabwe's government not to risk a breakdown in economic or governmental machinery.   One avoids risks by making only incremental changes.   The other constraints in the government's arena of choice already mentioned—South Africa's threats and destabilization, drought, dissident activity, and so forth—combined to place heavy pressure on Zimbabwe's government to make haste with no more than glacial speed.

The more slowly they changed the institutions, however, the more the institutions tended to change the governors.   That constituted Zimbabwe's dilemma. Namibia's new government will ineluctably face the same dilemma: how to change the machine while keeping it operating? How to feed and govern a population which transforming the very institutions that feed and govern it? How to avoid cooptations of government by the old, exploitative institutions?

The problem of land reform exemplifies the dilemma. At independence, 850,000 peasant families produced only slightly more than 6,000 commercial farmers. Most of what the peasants produced, they consumed themselves. To feed the 330,000 farm workers and their families, and the millions in Zimbabwe's cities, Zimbabwe relied upon the commercial farm sector. Revolutionary restructuring of that sector—seizing the farms and creating producer cooperatives and state farms—would cast Zimbabwe adrift in unknown, uncharted seas. Revolutionaries could, and did, urge the government toward rapid, radical land reform. They could not, however, guarantee the productivity of the new cooperatives and state farms. The government believed that it could not risk possible dramatic decline in agricultural production. It compromised. It insisted on a careful, slow resettlement that it hoped would ensure continued agricultural productivity. It did not, however, change the institutions of land tenure to make that possible. Instead, it continued the same permit system that the old regime had used. Three years after independence, Zimbabwe had resettled a bare handful of those needing land. The capitalist farming sector—and capitalist class power—continued unabated. The dilemma involved in changing the ongoing machine remained unresolved.

Zimbabwe's government recognized this dilemma.   It announced that 1982 would become the "year of transformation." That did not happen. The Three Year Transitional Plan stated:

> While the inherited economy, with its institutions and infrastructure, has in the past served a minority, it would be simplistic and, indeed, naive, to suggest that it should, therefore, be destroyed in order to make a fresh start. The challenge lies in building upon and developing on what was inherited, modifying, expanding and, where necessary, radically changing structures and institutions in order to maximize benefits from economic growth and development to Zimbabweans as a whole.

Despite the plan's bold words, however, by 1983 Zimbabwe had not brought about much institutional change.

The Law of Reproduction of Institutions says that changes in the legal order are a prerequisite to institutional change. Among the principal constraints that Zimbabwe's governors faced in seeking to change the laws and therefore the institutions that embodied ruling class economic and political power were the institutions of state decision making themselves. As a case study, the machinery that creates statutes and subsidiary legislation, that is, that creates the most formal of the norms included in the legal order, is enlightening.

From the earliest days the government promised a new Labor Relations Act to replace the old Industrial Conciliation Act, a relic of the old regime, that served simultaneously to maintain high wages for a minority of white workers, and to keep 92 percent of Zimbabwe's workforce—practically entirely black—unorganized, vulnerable and poor. The Ministry of Labor assigned the task of creating that legislation to a new black civil servant. He labored to produce a draft bill. The earliest draft of that bill made every effort to put state power behind the process of organizing the unorganized, and behind unions in negotiating with employers. There ultimately emerged from the ministry, however, a proposed Labor Relations Act, 1983, that would make organizing the unorganized practically impossible, that gave workers almost no right to democracy in the workplace, that gave employers weapon after weapon to use in preventing unionization, and that effectively destroyed the right to strike while replacing it with a claim—not a right—to compulsory arbitration at the discretion of various officials. How did a ministry in a government with an announced socialist perspective produce so reactionary a piece of proposed legislation?

A second example is the proposed Under-Utilized Lands Tax Act. Early in 1981, the Ministry of Lands and Resettlement proposed a heavy annual tax on under-utilized land to force farmers to "use it or lose it." [7] As a tax bill, it went to the Treasury Ministry. There it disappeared. In two successive annual speeches to parliament the President announced that the bill would appear. Nothing happened.

How did these aberrations occur in the drafting process? Why did so few legislative initiatives of whatever sort emerge from the ministries? Orthodox administrative theory perceives bureaucracy as a neutral tool operated by the political masters. When the Labor Party holds power, the civil service nationalizes industry; when the conservatives win, the same civil service denationalizes those same industries. Silent, anonymous, and above all, neutral, the civil service has no policy. It only faithfully executes the policy of the government of the day. Zimbabwe's experience falsified that theory.

A contrary theory holds that regardless of the political notions of civil servants, the state's structure and processes pre-form potential outputs. The general range of a decisionmaking

---

[7] A government party had run and won on a platform calling for a similar tax in 1926!

structure's output (its decisions) results from its input, feedback and conversion processes. (Seidman, 1978) (See Figure 1.)

This model tells us that the range of outputs of a decision-making institution—and the state consists of a gaggle of those—depends upon the range of inputs and feedbacks, and the sorts of conversion processes used. These components depend upon the repetitive patterns of behavior of the various actors who guard the gates and make decisions. Formal law defining those processes bears a systematic relationship to that behavior. In short, the way the legal order structures the state machinery determines the sorts of inputs (issues, data, theories, personnel) that will enter the system, the sorts of conversion processes that it will use, and therefore the range of potential outputs.

Over time, every state develops working rules for its decision-making machinery that limit the outputs of those institutions to decisions that will tend to further the interests of those with the most power in the society. (That both reflects and enhances their power). State institutions practically never produce decisions that threaten the existing socio-economic system from which the rich and powerful derive their power and privilege. The input, feedback and conversion processes ensure against that happening.

In Zimbabwe, to a great degree, the government relied upon the first notion of how the state works. It seemed to believe that it could lay hold of the existing state machinery, put its own people into positions of power, but not change the processes and structures within which they operated. After independence, the old machinery continued, mainly unchanged. It continued to operate by rules that limited its inputs, feedback and conversion processes to those that existed during the Smith regime. Inevitably, it continued mainly to crank out the sorts of decisions that the old regime cranked out. Those decisions ensured the continuing power and control of the existing rulers of the economy. They continued to do so. They made very difficult any change in existing laws. Not having changed the machinery of state, Zimbabwe's government had great difficulty in bringing about the legislation and other governmental decisions required to change institutions and class power (Mugomoba, 1980:49).[8]

Lenin put it better. The first task of the revolution, he said, is to smash the bourgeois state machinery. One does not smash state machinery with a sledgehammer. One smashes it by transforming its process and structure to ensure that the range of output will match the demands of the new regime, not the old one.

Failure to change existing economic and political institutions does more than merely delay the day of change. By encouraging the creation of a bureaucratic bourgeoisie it may put off that day forever.

The law of the growth of a bureaucratic bourgeoisie

At independence in Zimbabwe, a race began. Would the government change the received institutions, or would the

---

[8]"The Africans assumed control over institutions that had never been designed to serve majority interests... Thus were the ascending African elites expected to repeat the processes they had seen in operation during their period of apprenticeship at the terminal stages of colonial rule."

institutions co-opt the members of the political elite, so that the radical rhetoric would come to have no content, and in time even the rhetoric would become muted? By 1984, in Zimbabwe the race had not ended. The longer the government failed to change the institutions of the capitalist political economy that it inherited, however, the more chance existed that the left-over institutions would seize in their hot embrace ever more members of the political elite.

That members of the political elite moved into the private sector needs not be independently documented. In his Independence Day speech (April 19, 1983), Prime Minister Robert Mugabe charged members of the Cabinet with having purchased commercial firms and businesses. Doing so necessarily places in jeopardy their devotion to the socialist cause. Does anybody doubt that a minister or a secretary who owns a commercial farm with a hundred-odd workers will not feel a certain waning of the socialist flame burning in his breast?

Man's being determines his consciousness. We hold our ideas in the main because of our webs of life. A man immersed in the calculations and maneuvers required to keep and hold a large profit-making enterprise has difficulty in cleaving to an ideology that holds the very act of making money from the labor of others as immoral.

In Zimbabwe, the arenas of choice of high-ranking officials in their individual capacities included the same capitalist institutions that embodied and manifested capitalist, ruling class control of the economy that they confronted in their official capacities. Those institutions held out opportunities for people with money and credit to become capitalists.

Ministers become the owners of farms because they have the purchase price themselves, or because banks or friends or favor-seekers will lend them the money. They see their friends and relatives cashing in on the opportunities with which, for those strategically placed, every newly independent state abounds. All the while protesting their socialist purity, they justify their entry into the exploiting class by the claim that their abstaining from seizing the main chance will only give somebody else the chance to grab. Keeping their money in their sock, they argue, will not bring socialism closer. They have a whole packful of other justifications too: that as politicians they need an economic fall-back position; that the polity needs capital investment, and their investment helps meet that need; that to prohibit government people from investing will make it difficult to recruit people into government.

The only long-term solution for the problem posed by the development of the bureaucratic bourgeoisie, of course, lies in the rapid transformation of the political economy in a socialist direction. If the government owns all the land in the commercial farming sector, leasing it on very long, non-alienable leases to new settlers and producer cooperatives, it removes the ministers' opportunities to acquire commercial farms. In Tanzania, President Julius Nyerere thought it necessary to nationalize rental housing in order to effectively eliminate a favorite investment target of the new rentier class.

This suggests a third lesson for Namibia's new government, a corollary of the Law of Reproduction of Institutions: to reproduce themselves, capitalist institutions must create capitalists. In any polity, of those strategically located to become capitalists, members of a political elite have the most strategic location. That constitutes the Law of the Growth of the Bureaucratic Bourgeoisie: Unless guarded against during the transition to socialism, the inevitable existence of capitalist institutions will seduce members of the political elite into becoming capitalists (Seidman, 1978).

Zimbabwe's Constitution and Its Constraints on Change

To what extent did Zimbabwe's relative stagnation depend upon its constitution? As earlier suggested, the anticlassical perspective argues that constitutions like Zimbabwe's, drafted in response to the classical perspective, program the government to follow a laissez faire development strategy (Seidman, 1987). It holds that in general they accomplish this through three stratagems. First, they prescribe a set of Thou Shalt Nots that serve to protect the institutions of private productive property from radical change. Second, they prescribe political institutions that, in title of representative democracy, make it theoretically possible but practically difficult for an elected government to change the structure of state decisionmaking. Finally, and most important, they specify institutions apt to deal with the problems that nineteenth-century British government perceived as pressing but practically nothing concerning the great issues on Zimbabwe's agenda. The classical constitutions created institutions to deal with lawmaking (the legislature), dispute resolution (courts), and law-and-order (the executive), but no planning commissions, no Affirmative Action Commissions, no government corporate sectors, no ombudsmen, no requirements for openness in the government. Zimbabwe's constitution in general followed the classical pattern.

The constitution and the law of reproduction of institutions

In a variety of ways, the Constitution made it difficult but not impossible to change institutions, both by erecting roadblocks to change and by failing to provide institutions to facilitate change. First, the Constitution gave disproportionate representation for whites in the national assembly.[9] Had the black vote split among the three parties with candidates, the twenty white parliamentary seats might have held the balance of power. (Zimbabwe's government repeatedly pointed to those provisions to justify its inaction). In fact, however, ZANU alone won 57 percent of the parliament, and in any event the black elected representatives—80 percent of the chamber—held ranks against every white effort to split them. The government had ample legislative power to do most of the things required to transform economic institutions. Second, the Constitution contained a provision prohibiting the taking of property without compensation (Art. 16), a provision to which the government pointed to justify its relative inaction in land reform. That provision, however, contained so many loopholes that a determined government could easily have found constitutional means to carry out a thoroughgoing land reform (Seidman, 1984).[10] Third, the Constitution contained an anti-

---

[9]Whites elected 20 percent of the seats. The entire population (including whites) elected the other 80 percent. CONSTITUTION, 1980, Art. 38.

[10]It may be that foreign—read British and United States—opposition might have nevertheless had enough power to influence the government against radical land reform. The government, however, never put that to the test; it made no effort at expropriating the great white farms for the benefit of their impoverished workers or to distribute to the peasantry. (It never attempted to take by condemnation a single piece of land).

discrimination clause (Art. 23), with a provision permitting affirmative action in the public service (Art. 75(2))[11]. The anti-discrimination clause arguably made affirmative action in the private sector difficult; again, the government never put the issue to the test.

More important, however, than these potentially ineffective positive roadblocks, the Constitution did nothing to facilitate the government's path towards institutional change. It made no mention of economic planning. It made no mention of the parastatal sector. It did not create roles charged with specific developmental duties, such as to systematically examine the country's institutions for discrimination and racial and gender imbalance, to change economic institutions, or to take steps against ethnic rivalries. In the classical tradition, the Constitution so far as it could distanced the government from the levers that instituted social, political and economic change.

In principle, the government could have nevertheless seized those levers by introducing legislation creating institutional frameworks for change. Absent constitutional provisions to facilitate change, however, by and large the government found it easier to do nothing. For example, as we have seen, the Constitution explicitly provided for affirmative action in the public service. Affirmative action ensued, so that in short order even in the senior ranks blacks outnumbered whites. The Constitution did not require affirmative action in the private sector. None ensued. It made no provision for an Affirmative Action Commission, with power to root out and remedy past discrimination. The government appointed none. The Constitution provided for an ombudsman to police legality, albeit with constrained powers. In time, the government did appoint an ombudsman and enacted the requisite legislation. Constitutions make a difference, although many factors besides the constitutional norms shape the resultant behavior. Wherever it could, Zimbabwe's Constitution made

---

[11]"The president may give general directions to the Public Service Commission with the object of achieving a suitable representation of the various elements of the population in the Public Service and the Prison Service."

radical change for a determined government probably not impossible but certainly difficult.

The constitution and the law of transforming the bourgeois state

To what extent did Zimbabwe's failure to change the machinery of state result from its constitutional provisions? The Constitution prescribed an independent civil service commission, with power not only to appoint and discipline members of the public service, but also "to regulate and control the general organization of the Public Service" (Art. 75). The chairman and at least one other member of the commission had to have held a post in the public service of a grade higher than under secretary for a period of more than five years—a qualification that at independence no black had. The constitution provided that in exercising its powers, the commission would receive directions from no one (Art. 109(1)). So far as it could, the constitution took the power to transform the received state structure out of the hands of the elected government.[12]

As with respect to changing the economy, more important than its minimal roadblocks to government action to transform the state sector, the Constitution made no provisions to point the government in that direction. With respect to legality, the Constitution did provide for an ombudsman (Arts. 107, 108). She or he had, however, only a narrow constitutional function: to investigate official action where a person alleges injustice, and no remedy seems reasonably available in court.[13] She or he had no power to search out illegality, or to suggest (let alone implement) institutional changes to make it less likely. Nothing in the Constitution pointed the government towards changing the structure of bureaucracy, to make more likely change-oriented decisions. Aside from provisions for representative elections (Chapt. V), nothing in the Constitution required the government

---

[12]In practice, the government found ways to reduce the independence of the commission, finally amending the Constitution to permit a chair without the stringent qualifications originally required.

[13]The Constitution permitted Parliament to give him additional tasks, id., Art. 108(3), but it never did so.

to enhance political participation by the mass of the population. No Constitutional goad prodded the government to transform the bourgeois state. Absent that goad, the government did almost nothing to change the state structure.

The constitution and the law of the growth of the bureaucratic bourgeoisie

Experience worldwide demonstrated that strong tendencies existed in every developing country towards the creation of a bureaucratic bourgeoisie. Unlike Tanzania's and Zambia's constitutions, however, Zimbabwe's contained no provisions for a leadership code or for a commission to enforce it. No other provisions pushed the government to adopt measures to prevent the development of a bureaucratic bourgeoisie.

Unless the government does something about it, on independence the received economic institutions will roar on; the received political institutions will grind out the same sorts of decisions they ground out under the previous regime; between them, they will recreate the classes that existed under the old regime. All that spells the defeat of the revolution. What can the Constitution do about it?

Solutions: Constitutionally-Defined Institutions for Development

In order to accomplish the transition to socialism, the Law of Reproduction of Institutions requires rapid changes in Namibia's and South Africa's institutions (Mugomba, 1980:53)[14] and therefore, of their legal orders. That, in turn, imposes the imperatives suggested by the Laws of the Transformation of the Bourgeois State and of the Growth of the Bureaucratic Bourgeoisie: to develop state structures that will produce change-oriented institutions and laws, and prevent the development of a bureau-

---

[14]"In independent Africa in general, and in transitional southern Africa in particular, there is a desperate need to dismantle colonial institutions and structures in order to foster genuine political, economic and social changes."

cratic bourgeoisie. What constitutional provisions seem appropriate to that task?

Of course, that a constitution commands hardly guarantees performance. As Hotspur put it to Owen Glendower, "anybody may call up the spirits of the vastly deep, but will they come?" Constitutional prescriptions bear much the same relationship to behavior that ordinary rules of law bear to behavior. Whether addressees obey either set of norms depends upon a complex interplay between the objective and perceived constraints and resources of the addressee's position, what goes on inside the addressees head (what Alvin Gouldner calls her domain assumptions), the nature of the rule addressed to the actor and to the implementing authorities, and the actual behavior of those authorities (Seidman, 1978). Only a rare rule of law or of constitution, however, has no behavioral consequences. Repercussions are sometimes perverse, sometimes negligible, but rarely nonexistent. With respect to the issues raised by these three Laws, however, Zimbabwe's Constitution said practically nothing—and its silence served to help remove those issues from the government's ken.

As we have seen, in general, the anticlassical perspective would in part explain the post-independence behavior of Zimbabwe's government by the particular constraints of its classical-model Constitution, and by that Constitution's failure to prescribe institutions necessary to development. In those same general terms, the solution that theory prescribes becomes self-evident. First, a constitution that aims at solving the six dilemmas of development must foreswear provisions that in advance tie the government's hands, for example, with respect of the use of property, or discrimination. Second, even in the name of representative democracy, the institutions it does prescribe may not make more difficult the institutional changes required to address development's six challenges. Finally, in general, lawmakers see to it that jobs get done by identifying roles and prescribing powers and obligations appropriate to those tasks. Thus a constitution that seeks to address development's six challenges must prescribe specific institutions aimed at them, with powers and obligations sufficient to address them. Thus can a constitution institutionalize the processes of change that constitute development.

Constitutional Implications of the Law of Reproduction of Institutions

Destroying Apartheid

Since institutions reproduce themselves unless the law changes, the government must organize itself to change the apartheid-drenched, capitalism- reproducing institutions it will receive at independence. That calls for:

- A human rights provision not only guaranteeing non-discrimination on grounds of race or gender, but requiring affirmative action to rectify past injustices, and
- Avoidance of a provision that denies individuals the power to invoke the aid of the courts to declare specific discriminatory statutes unconstitutional.

Alleviating poverty

Alleviating poverty requires radical changes in the institutions of both distribution and allocation. That calls for constitutional provisions concerning property relationships and planning.

Like most African constitutions, Zimbabwe's contained a provision guaranteeing private property against expropriation without compensation. That became a bar to many sorts of distributional and allocative changes. No provisions in the Constitution required the government to make changes in the structure of production, either in the private sector, or among the many parastatal corporations (the Constitution did not even mention the latter). As a result, government felt no prick to make changes and precious few resulted.

This experience suggests that the constitutions of Namibia and South Africa should contain the following:

- Property rights provisions that make possible both distributive and allocative changes (The West German model might serve nicely [West German Constitution, Art. 15])[15];

---

[15]"Land, natural resources and means of production may for the purpose of socialization be transformed to public ownership or other

- Land reform provisions; and
- Aspirational clauses[16] concerning both the alleviation of poverty (for example, clauses creating a "right" to a job, schooling, housing, health care and social security) and the organization of the economy (for example, clauses ensuring governmental control over the parastatal sector, and enjoining the government to bring about cooperative and state ownership of productive property).

Transforming economic distribution and resource allocation implies transforming economic institutions. That only restates development's dilemma: How to change the machine while keeping it running? Planned resource allocation changes must remain fragmentary and incremental unless accompanied by a plan for institutional change. Only by planned institutional change can the government analyze and solve the problem of how to keep the machine running while changing it.

It does not suffice, however, merely to proclaim that Namibia or South Africa will institute economic planning. A government that seriously proposes to undertake the transition to a democratic, humane, egalitarian, developed society must plan institutional transformations. The constitution must require the planning agency to produce a blueprint that does so, not one that merely proposes new resource allocations. Only so can a government engage development's dilemma: to transform the machine while it continues to produce.

Alleviating ethnic tensions

Another problem Zimbabwe shares with many other African countries is that ethnic tensions arise because of the organization of electoral politics. Following the classical tradition, the Zimbabwe Constitution said almost nothing about that, perceiving

---

forms of publicly controlled economy by a law which shall provide for the nature and extent of compensation."

[16]By an "aspirational clause" I mean a human rights provision that requires the government to undertake a positive action requiring the expenditure of resources—for example, granting each citizen a right to education, or the health care, or employment.

political parties as private organizations whose right to contest elections the Constitution guaranteed. The Constitution said nothing about the control of the parties. Inevitably, ethnically-based political parties arose. Unless restrained, in Namibia and South Africa that tendency will likely produce an ethnic politics of extraordinary ugliness, with white parties contesting elections against African parties that beat the tribal drums.

Devices exist to negate that development. Following the Nigerian election law example, a constitution might require that to field candidates for a national election, a party must also field candidates in a stated minimum number of local constituencies. The constitution might also require:

- a reasonable mix of racial and ethnic representatives on a party governing council;
- constituency boundaries that prevent electoral bodies based on a single race or ethnic group; and
- constituency boundaries that reduce the size of local government units (counties, provinces) so as to splinter the power of ethnic groupings.

Constitutional Implications of the the Law of the Development of a Bureaucratic Bourgeoisie

In the long run, of course, the only sure cure for the pervasive problem of the bureaucratic bourgeoisie lies in shrinking the private sector. By definition, however, the transition to socialism implies the continuation of a substantial private sector for a long period of time. As Zimbabwe's experience demonstrates, that sector will have especial vigor at independence and in the years immediately following. Some direct controls over the development of a bureaucratic bourgeoisie seem desirable. As a first step, to prohibit members of the political elite from acquiring investments in the private sector, a leadership code seems required. Zambia's and Tanzania's constitutions require a leadership code; each has one in place. Zimbabwe's constitution did not require one. Despite good deal of hemming and hawing - and several drafts—Zimbabwe still does not have one.[17]

Idealism reaches its zenith during the euphoria of independence celebrations. It then seems easy to achieve unanimous support for a leadership code and its ancillary legislation. From the day that a minister first acquires a farm or a business, that selfless enthusiasm declines. As its first governmental act a new SWAPO or ANC government could strike no greater blow for socialism than to write a constitutional requirement for a leadership code.

Constitutional Implications of the Law of the Transformation of the Bourgeois State

All these desirable changes in social and political institutions imply radical changes in the decisionmaking structures of the state. Here we discuss in turn the changes in the state machinery required by the need to transform the economy. We then discuss changes required by the imperatives to enhance popular participation, reorganize bureaucracy, ensure legality, and reduce the

---

[17]Leadership codes require careful study to ensure adequate supporting legislation. Like any law directly prohibiting acts not universally abhorred by society (sometimes called "victimless crimes"—for example, prohibitions against drinking alcoholic liquor, having more than two children, extramarital intercourse or smoking dagga), without adequate implementing institutions they will not otherwise achieve a high rate of compliance. Tanzania seems to have had limited success with its Leadership Code, Zambia none at all, mainly for lack of implementation. I suggest three measures ancillary to a Leadership Code: A prohibition on the extension of credit to leaders without specific public permission; a prohibition on leaders acquiring real property without permission; and controls over the potential for corruption. The first two seem self-evident. Because banks are few (and, in the transition to socialism, become the very earliest targets for governmental acquisition), and transfers of real property require public recordation, control over credit and buying real estate seems relatively easy. I discuss the problem of corruption in the next section. These provisions seem better adapted, however to statutory enactment than constitutional provision.

potential for corruption. Some of these require transformations within existing institutions. Others will require the creation of a completely new institutions. Only two are suggested here—the Planning Commission and the ombudsman, the latter of which will become in effect a fourth branch of the government.

State Institutions to Transform the Economy

In Zimbabwe, the parastatal sector operated as independent economic units, not as government agencies (Makgetla and Seidman, 1987). The constitution should unambiguously declare that:

- parastatal corporations serve as the government's agent, and
- the government can give it directions that the parastatal must obey.

Planning commissions stand in uneasy relationship to both ministries and cabinet itself. In case of a conflict between ministerial or cabinet initiatives and the plan, which has precedence? The government's compartment-alism, expressed in the differentiation of ministerial portfolios, exacerbates the problem. The position and function of the planning agency—nowadays usually a ministry on a level with other ministries—constitutes a principal constitutional problem. That conflict plainly reaches constitutional dimensions, for it concerns basic allocations of governmental power. The constitutions should state:

- The Planning Commission's mode of appointment, organization and powers;
- the precise extent that governmental units have a legal obligation to conform to the Plan; and
- the form of planning required (for example, institutional transformations as well as resource allocations).

Participation in decisionmaking

The model earlier suggested argues that the range of potential decisions depends in part upon input and feedback processes. The principal device that limits inputs and feedbacks (and thus pre-forms the decisional output) consists in limits on access to the decisionmaking machinery. The critical question for every polity becomes, "who has access?"

Between informal, easy contacts with members of the elite and upper classes, the lack of organization of the poor and the built-in biases of senior civil servants (themselves members of the elite), as well as the formal rules that, in effect, frequently clothe decisionmaking in secrecy except for consultations with elite and upper class groups, only members of those groups have generally easy access to the centers of power. The poor do not. In the end, in Zimbabwe, as in other former colonial countries, at independence the elite and ruling classes dominated the formal and informal input and feedback channels.

What constitutional provisions might ensure popular participation not merely in election, but in ongoing state decisions?

- The traditional fundamental human rights ensuring a minimum level of participation (for example, rights to free speech and assembly, and to petition the government) together with aspirational clauses requiring the government to provide the material basis for their exercise;
- A general fundamental human right of maximum feasible participation might help, if only to provide a focus for protest at ministerial or bureaucratic authoritarianism;
- A guarantee of worker participation in shopfloor decisions might help towards achieving democracy in the workplace;
- A requirement that ministers adopt subsidiary legislation only after a public hearing might enable public inputs;
- A provision guaranteeing openness in the government might prevent the use of Official Secrets Acts to hide government decisions (cf. Swedish Constitution, Art. 15.[18]; Campbell, 1967);
- A change in parliamentary procedures might facilitate popular discussion of bills before the cabinet puts on them its final stamp of approval;

---

[18]Citizens to have free access to public documents "subject only to such restrictions as are demanded out of consideration for the maintenance of privacy, security of person, decency and morality."

- Provisions guaranteeing labor unions, peasants and other popular organizations the right to organize,[19] and the right of their representatives to have access to the government, might also help;
- The constitution must require a highly participatory planning organization; and
- So far as possible, the constitution must protect local autonomy in decisionmaking.

Bureaucratic structures for innovating

Authoritarian, compartmentalized bureaucracy may prove useful for tending a machine. It does not work well for changing it. If Namibia or South Africa follows the bureaucratic structures of most other governments it will fall into the same trap. It must find new ways of organizing its public service to emphasize the innovative, problem-solving role that the public service must play during the transition to socialism. The books on public administration suggest a variety of models. An adequate administrative code must prescribe ways of interacting in the public service that will produce new ideas and rapid adaptability to new situations, not the rigidity and conservatism that follows from a hierarchical, compartmented structure.

- The constitution must therefore contain a provision— probably an aspirational clause—requiring the government to institute non-hierarchical, non-compartmented administrative structures.

Many African independence constitutions contained provisions creating an independent civil service commission, usually to ensure that the civil service remained uncorrupted by what the outgoing British overlords perceived as an inherently corrupt set of African politicians. Not for that reason, but to devise ways to transform the existing bureaucracy into a development administration—that is, to implement its obligation to discover new methods of organizing the government—

---

[19]Whether the conventional human rights provision guarantees a right to labor union organization remains in doubt. An explicit provision would protect the right.

- Constitutions for Namibia and South Africa should contain provisions charging an appropriate agency (perhaps the ombudsman?) with that duty.

Ensuring official obedience to the law: The rule of law and socialist legality

Properly understood, socialist legality and the rule of law agree on their central tenet: officials must obey the law. That core tenet of legality constitutes not the wraith-like vagaries of a dreamer, but a concrete injunction that we disobey at our peril. The rule of law evolved in response to demands for political freedoms. In time, these came to represent demands on the legal system made by bourgeois ideologies—their very rhetoric in terms of individual rights reveals their origins. These idealistic "individual" rights, however, have a substantial material social basis. Unless officials obey the law, all hope for planned change under the leadership of the state—that is, everything for which SWAPO and ANC fought so long—vanishes. Corruption more than any other single factor undermines legality.

In sum, therefore, the constitution must create institutions likely to ensure the legality. That calls for

- Basic human rights provisions making it relatively difficult for the government to make decisions without hearings and procedural regularity (for example, rights to fair hearing, representation, open and speedy trials, habeas corpus, and so forth) together with aspirational clauses requiring the government to provide the material basis for their exercise (for example, a constitutional provision requiring a legal aid system [Cf. Constitution, Zambia]);
- Basic human rights provisions making it relatively difficult for the government to invade citizen privacy;
- Basic human rights making it difficult for the government to shut off feedback channels from citizens to the government (for example, provisions ensuring freedom of expression); and
- Provisions requiring the government to structure official discretion.

Controlling corruption

Every government program must be designed with a wary eye to the potential for corruption. That calls for constitutional provisions requiring

- Narrow grants of discretion;
- Adequate financial accounting practices; and
- Publicity for every transaction in which the potential for corruption lurks (foreign exchange allocations, import licenses, government contracts of all sorts constitute the principal categories).

Building capacity to change laws

The central lessons from Zimbabwe's history consist of the laws of The Reproduction of Institutions, Transforming the Bourgeois State, and the Growth of the Bureaucratic Bourgeoisie. These require massive changes in the received legal order, and, to ensure that it can make and implement the necessary changes, in the structure of the public service. "Ought" implies "can" or the word becomes empty. All the proposals made here suppose necessary capacity in the public service. In 1982, Zimbabwe's Cabinet Office informed ministers that in drafting a complicated bill, staff shortages required a delay of as much as one year—and, as we have seen, Zimbabwe did not exactly burn up the roadways that head toward legal change. That requires an institutional structure to avoid the blockages that developed in Zimbabwe's lawmaking at the ministry level.

Without a unit whose role requires it specifically to originate legislation for the transition to socialism, Zimbabwe's experience teaches that legislation will emerge, if at all, with distressing slowness. South African and Namibian constitutions ought to include provisions for

- Creating a developmental research and drafting unit designed to produce the sorts of change-oriented legislation the countries will require (probably as part of the ombudsman or procurator general organization, perhaps as a separate institution).

The Ombudsman (or Procurator General)

All this suggests the need for a major institution to serve as what amounts to a fourth branch of government, charged with ensuring that the government carries out its developmental tasks. That institution—embodied in the ombudsman—searches the statutory texts to find instances of discrimination remaining, examines particular institutions to root out discriminatory practices and to institute affirmative action programs, drafts and implements a leadership code, redesigns the bureaucracy, protects against ethnic rivalries, polices governmental institutions to ensure that they encourage participation in every way, pushes ministries to reorganize in developmental ways, guards against administrative, parastatal or other official irregularity or illegality (with special emphasis on corruption), and ensures the consistent and whole-hearted governmental application of constitutional guarantees. That demands not only a constitutional place for the ombudsman, but legislation ensuring his or her easy availability to citizen complaint, and prescribing a whole corps of local officials to carry out these tasks at every level.

Governments ensure that their programs become more than dreams by creating specific roles, and charging their occupants with certain tasks, and providing some means for monitoring their performance. Many of the tasks required for development governments in nondevelopmental circumstances do not require, and historical experience hardly comprehends them. The traditional tripartite division of government into legislative, executive and judicial does not adequately comprehend these developmental functions. In the socialist countries, the procurator general has the potential for playing some of these roles. The ombudsman proposed here could do so, and thus become that fourth branch of government.

- The new constitutions should therefore define the institution of the ombudsman, and outline its powers, duties, appointment and organization.

To accomplish these radical changes required Zimbabwe's governors to make choices in favor of change and therefore usually—and increasingly—against their own immediate self-interest. Existing institutions clothed the governors with power and privilege. Those institutions' seductive song began even as the colonial flag fluttered to the ground. That song had a refrain: go slow, don't rock the boat, make change slowly, slowly, slowly. Zimbabwe's governors paid strict heed.

How to counter that seductive song? That required three things, all from the perspective, and representing the interests, of the mass: decisionmaking inputs of issues and data; theories explaining the world and proposing general solutions (that is, ideological leadership); and monitoring of the government's stewardship of the change processes.

In the broadest sense, the only sure guarantors of the revolution are those who will benefit from the revolution. Only the classes that stand to benefit from the transformation to a socialist society can readily ignore the seductions of power and privilege. Only for them does self-interest serve as a goad to transformation. Unlike the political elite, for the masses the existing capitalist institutions hold no allures.

As elite theory correctly holds, however, the undifferentiated mass cannot readily goad anything. They lack organization and perspective. No organization generally representing Zimbabwe's disinherited exists, and precious few representing specific sectors of them. Until Zimbabwe has an organization to represent the interests of the mass in the same persistent, ideologically clear way that ruling-class organizations represent the ruling class, no revolution has much hope for success.

That requires a highly organized, ideologically clear, vanguard party whose nerve-ends reach deep into the masses of the population. Only such a party can fulfill the three-fold task required of it. Only such a party can criticize government itself. To do that requires a certain space between them. Government and party cannot coalesce.

That does not necessarily require a one-party state. In South Africa's and Namibia's historical position, it seems unlikely that either ANC or SWAPO could push through a open-party constitution even if desirable. Probably the prescriptions mentioned here concerning the party's obligation must, therefore, remain outside the constitutional purview. The party's importance, however, should warn us that however important, constitutional prescriptions will likely not induce wholehearted governmental conformity unless someplace in society a dynamizing institution exists. Within the government, to the extent that these function have a techno-cratic aspect (for example, drafting, for examining laws for remnants of apartheid), the ombudsman may serve. But, as Cicero said, who will guard the guardians?

Conclusion

At independence, Zimbabwe had a government which gave every external evidence of desiring rapid, deep-seated social change in the direction of socialism. It ruled a state and a society organized in capitalist institutions that embodied the power of the capitalist ruling class. The government's task lay in transforming those institutions into ones that embodied and manifested working class and peasant power. To do that it had to embark on a massive program of legislation, designed to change all the institutions that make up Zimbabwe's existing formula for capitalist economic power, mass poverty and upper-class luxury. The Law of Reproduction of Institutions taught that unless the government did so, those institutions would continue. To bring about the necessary changes the government had to respect the Law of Transforming the Bourgeois State. Every state institution required re-examination, to ensure that its input, feedback and conversion processes guaranteed working class and peasant control, and therefore that its outputs would likely forward the transition to socialism. Finally, the Law of the Growth of the Bureaucratic Bourgeoisie called on the government to build walls between ongoing capitalist economic institutions and the political elite. Zimbabwe's government did not make massive changes in socio-economic institutions or in the state structure, nor did it build those walls.

From this emerge a variety of recommendations for the new constitutions of Namibia and South Africa, most of them non-intuitive. In particular, the makers of those new constitutions ought to consider including prescriptions for a planning commis-sion and for an ombudsman (or procurator general), both with wide and (for English-speaking countries) novel powers. It will not do for ANC's and SWAPO's constitutional lawyers to copy their predecessors in drafting African constitutions, that is, mainly to stare bemusedly at the great democratic constitutions of the West, and dream that there they can find inspiration from which to draft constitutions suited for their newly independent countries.

In Zimbabwe the comrades in the bush fought the long, dreadful fight in order to seize state power from the colonialist, white, economic ruling class. ZANU-Patriotic Front took control of state power for the benefit of the mass of impoverished Zimbabweans, almost entirely black, whom the received legal order deprived of access to either economic resources or state decision-making. As of 1990, Zimbabwe's government has not yet found the key to unlock state power to use it to undertake the arduous, long, step-by-step transition to socialism. In the meantime, the existing capitalist institutions, like the sirens of old, continuously seduced new paramours from officialdom.

In Zimbabwe's case, three years seems much too short a time for those sirens to have accomplished their task, although no doubt every day that passes without changes in the state machinery made victory over them more difficult. It is never too late to make those changes. For Zimbabwe the game had by no means come to an end.

For Namibia and South Africa, the shoe fits the other foot. SWAPO and ANC, like the Patriotic Front did in Zimbabwe, today fight to take state power. Once achieving that end, what will they do with it? For Zimbabwe it is never too late. For Namibia and South Africa it is never too early.

REFERENCES

Adler, T. 1986. "Social Welfare and the Democratisation of the Economy," in W. Thomas (ed.) *Post-Apartheid South Africa's Economic System,* Johannesburg: *South Africa International* (special issue) XVII.2.

Adulis, Journal of the Eritrean People's Liberation Front.

ANC (African National Congress). n.d. "Communique of Meeting Between Congress of South African Trade Unions, COSATU, South African Congress of Trade Unions, SACTU, and African National Congress (ANC-South Africa)," New York: mimeo.

——. n.d. "The Workers' Way Forward is the Strongest Way Forward," South Africa: mimeo.

Ajayi, S.I., and O.O. Ojo. 1981. *Money and Banking: Analysis and Policy in the Nigerian Context.* London: George Allen and Unwin.

Amin, S. 1986a. "Les conditions d'une autonomie dans la région méditerranéenne," in S. Mappa, et al. (eds.) *Pour une définition de nouveaux rapports Nord-Sud.* Publisud.

————. 1986b. "Etat, nation, ethnie et minorités dans la crise: quelques aspects de la critique de l'idéologie de la nation et de l'ethnie," *Bulletin du FTM* No. 6.

————. 1987. "Introduction," in Amin, S., Chitala, D., and I. Mandaza (eds.) *SADCC: Prospects for Disengagement and Development in Southern Africa.* London: Zed Press.

————. 1988a. "Déconnexion, révolution nationale populaire et rôle de l'intelligentsia," (originally published in Arabic).

————. 1988b. "L'eurocentrisme et la politique," *IFDA Bulletin* No. 65, Geneva.

Anonymous. 1984. "Contract Workers Perceptions of Return Migration: A South African Case Study." Unpublished Manuscript.

Astrow, A. 1983. *Zimbabwe: A Revolution that Lost its Way.* London: Zed.

Baran, P. 1957. *The Political Economy of Growth.* New York: Monthly Review.

Bardill, J. and J. Cobbe. 1985. *Lesotho: Dilemmas of Dependence in Southern Africa.* Boulder: Westview Press.

Barrell, H. 1984. "The United Democratic Front and National Forum: Their Emergence, Composition and Trends," *South African Review II.* Johannesburg: Ravan Press, pp.6-21.

Baskin, J. 1982. "Growth of a New Worker Organ: the Germiston Shop Stewards Council," *South African Labour Bulletin* VII(8):42-53.

Baxter, P.T. 1978. "Ethiopia's Unacknowledged Problem: the Oromo," *African Affairs* 77(308-July).

Bell, T. and V. Padayachee. 1984. "Unemployment in South Africa: Trends, Causes and Cures." Cape Town: Second Carnegie Inquiry into Poverty in South Africa, No. 119.

Berg, E. 1982. *Accelerated Development in Sub-Saharan Africa.* Washington, D.C.: World Bank.

Bhatia, R.J., and D.R. Khatkhate. 1975. "Financial Intermediation, Savings Mobilization and Entrepreneurial Development: The African Experience," *IMF Staff Papers*, 22(1):132-158.

Black, A. and J. Stanwix. 1986. "Crisis and Restructuring in the South African Manufacturing Sector." Cape Town: paper presented to the Workshop on Macroeconomic Policy and Poverty in South Africa.

Botswana, Republic of. 1981. *External Trade Statistics.* Gaborone.

Bromberger, N. 1974. "Economic Growth and Political Change in South Africa," in A. Leftwich (ed.) *South Africa: Economic Growth and Political Change.* New York: St. Martin's.

———. 1984. "How Much Work Do the African Unemployed Do?" Cape Town: Second Carnegie Inquiry into Poverty in South Africa, No. 271.

BI (Business International). 1982. *A Fresh Look at South Africa.* New York.

Campbell, E. 1967. "Public Access to Government Documents," *Australian Law Journal* 41:73-97.

Carrim, Y. 1987. "COSATU: Towards Disciplined Alliances," *Work in Progress* 49:11-8.

Clapham, C. 1968. *Haile Selassie's Government.* London.

Clark, W.E. 1978. *Socialist Development and Public Investment in Tanzania, 1964-73.* Toronto, University of Toronto Press.

Cobbe, J.H. 1980. "Integration Among Unequals: The Southern African Customs Union and Development," *World Development* 8(4):329-36.

————. 1982a. "Emigration and Development in Southern Africa, with Special Reference to Lesotho." Faculty of Social Sciences. Roma: National University of Lesotho. Staff Seminar 27.

————. 1982b. "Migrant Labour and Lesotho: Problems, Policies and Difficulties and Constraints with Respect to Them." Maseru: The Institute of Labour Studies.

————. 1982c. "The Education System, Wage Salary Structures and Income Distribution: Lesotho as a Case Study." Faculty of Social Sciences. Roma: National University of Lesotho. Staff Seminar 29.

Cooper, C. 1982. *Strikes 1982, Jan.-June* and *Strikes 1982, July-Dec.* Johannesburg: South African Institute of Race Relations.

COSAS (Congress of South African Students). n.d. "Workers, Workers, Build Support for the Students' Struggle in the Schools." Johannesburg: mimeo.

COSATU (Congress of South African Trade Unions). Private archives. Johannesburg.

COSATU (Congress of South African Trade Unions) Executive Committee. 1986 "A Message to All Members of COSATU: 1987 - The Year of Consolidation and Action," Johannesburg: COSATU.

————. 1987a. "A Message to All Members of COSATU," reprinted in *South African Labour Bulletin* XII.2.

————. 1987b. "The Way Forward: Establishing Tasks and Priorities," Johannesburg: COSATU.

Davidson, B., Cliffe, L. and B. Habte-Selassie (eds.) 1980. *Behind the War in Eritrea.* Nottingham: Barber Press.

Davies, R. 1987. "Nationalisation, Socialisation and the Freedom Charter," *South African Labour Bulletin* XII.1.

Diamond, W. 1957. *Development Banks.* London: Johns Hopkins Press.

Dickman, A. 1986. "Foreign Capital and the Environment for Sustainable Growth," in W. Thomas (ed.) *Post-Apartheid South Africa's Economic International,* Johannesburg: *South Africa International* (special issue) XVII.2.

DPSC (Detainees' Parents' Support Committee). 1987. "Survey of Detentions, 1987." Johannesburg: mimeo.

Eckert, J. and R. Wykstra. 1980. "South African Mine Wages in the Seventies and Their Effects on Lesotho's Economy." Maseru: Ministry of Agriculture. Lesotho Agricultural Sector Analysis Report 7.

Edlin, J. 1983. "Key to Southern Africa's Economic Independence," *Africa Report* 28(3):43-6.

Ehrensaft, P. 1985. "Phases in the Development of South African Capitalism," in P. Gutkind and I. Wallerstein (eds.) *Political Economy of Contemporary Africa,* second edition. Beverly Hills: Sage, pp.64-93.

EIU (Economist Intelligence Unit). 1987. *Country Portfolio: South Africa 1986-87.* London: Economist Publications.

Ellickson, R. 1986. "Of Case, Cattle and Cooperation: Dispute Resolution among Neighbors in Shasta County," *Stanford Law Review* 38:623-687.

Engels, F. 1970. "Letter to Konrad Schmidt October 27, 1890," in K. Marx and F. Engels *Selected Works*. New York: International Publishers, 3:49-52.

Erwin, A. 1985. "The Question of Unity in the Struggle," *South African Labour Bulletin* XI(1):51-70.

Farer, T.J. 1979. *War Clouds on the Horn of Africa*. New York: Carnegie.

FCWU (Food and Canning Workers Union). 1982. "Search for a Workable Relationship," *South African Labour Bulletin* VII(8):54-8.

Firebrace, J. with S. Holland. 1984. *Never Kneel Down: Drought, Development and Liberation in Eritrea*. Nottingham: Spokesman.

FOSATU (Federation of South African Trade Unions). Organization archives. Johannesburg.

FOSATU Worker News, Federation of South African Trade Unions, Johannesburg.

Foster, J. 1982. "The Workers' Struggle: Where Does FOSATU Stand?" keynote address at FOSATU Congress, April 1982; reprinted in *South African Labour Bulletin* VII(8).

Friedman, S. 1987a. *Building Tomorrow Today: African Workers in Trade Unions, 1970-1984*. Johannesburg: Ravan Press.

————. 1987b. "The Struggle Within the Struggle," *Transformation* 3.

Friedman, M. 1953. "The Methodology of Positive Economics," in M. Friedman, *Essays in Positive Economics*. Chicago: University of Chicago Press.

Gelb, S. 1985. "Employment and Disinvestment," *South African Labour Bulletin* X(8):54-66.

Gordon, E. 1981. "An Analysis of the Impact of Labour Migration on the Lives of Women in Lesotho," *Journal of Development Studies* 17(3):59-76.

Greenberg, S. 1980. *Race, State and Capitalist Development.* New Haven: Yale University Press.

Habte-Selassie, B. 1980. *Conflict and Intervention in the Horn of Africa.* New York: Monthly Review Press.

Halliday, F. and M. Molyneux. 1981. *The Ethiopian Revolution.* London: Schocken.

Hassan, J. 1986. "Agricultural Development and Pricing Policy." Lusaka: University of Zambia, M.A. thesis.

Hill, C. 1974. "South Africa: The Future of the Liberal Spirit," in A. Leftwich (ed.) *South Africa: Economic Growth and Political Change.* New York: St. Martin's.

Hindson, D. 1984. "Union Unity," in *South Africa Review II.* Johannesburg: Raven Press, pp.90-107.

Hiwet, A. 1975. *Ethiopia from Autocracy to Revolution.* London.

Hofmeyr, W. and M. Nicol. 1987. "Deregulation: A Challenge for the Labour Movement," *South African Labour Bulletin* XII.4.

Holden, M. 1985. "Exchange Rate Policy for a Small Open Economy in a World of Floating Exchange Rates: The Case of South Africa." Durban: Economics Research Unit, University of Natal, Occasional Paper 17.

Horwitz, R. 1967. *The Political Economy of South Africa.* New York: Praeger.

Houghton, D.H. 1980. *The South African Economy.* Third Edition. Cape Town: Oxford University Press.

Hudson, D. 1981. "Botswana's Membership in the Southern African Customs Union," in C. Harvey (ed.) *Papers on the Political Economy of Botswana.* London: Heinemann.

IBRD (International Bank for Reconstruction and Development). 1987. *World Development Report, 1987.* Oxford: Oxford University Press.

IIE (Institute for Industrial Education). 1974. *The Durban Strikes 1973.* Durban: Ravan Press.

IMF (International Monetary Fund). 1985. "Impact of External Environment and Domestic Policies on Economic Performance in Developing Countries," in IMF, *World Economic Outlook, April 1985.* Oxford: Oxford University Press.

Isizwe, United Democratic Front, Johannesburg.

Jaber, T.A. 1971. "The Relevance of Traditional Integration Theory to Less Developed Countries," *Journal of Common Market Studies* IX(3):254-67.

Jack, A. 1987. "Towards a 'Living Wage': Workers' Demands Over Sixty Years," *South African Labour Bulletin* XII.3.

Jaffee, G. and K. Jochelson. 1986. "The Fight to Save Jobs: Union Initiatives on Retrenchment and Unemployment," *South African Review III.* Johannesburg: Ravan Press, pp.51-67.

JASPA (Jobs and Skills Programme for Africa) Employment Advisory Mission. 1979. *Options For a Dependent Economy: Development, Employment and Equity Problems in Lesotho.* Addis Ababa: Saint George Printing Press.

Jochelson, K. 1985. "'You name it, we got it,'" *Work in Progress* 37:27-9.

Jones, S. 1986. "The History of Black Involvement in the South African Economy," in R. Smollan (ed.) *Black Advancement in the South African Economy.* New York: St. Martin's Press, pp.1-30.

Kane, J.A.   1975.   *Development Banking.*   Lexington, MA: D.C. Heath.

Kantor, B.   1982a.   "South African Monetary Policy," in B. Kantor and D. Rees (eds.) *South African Economic Issues.* Cape Town: Juta.

———. and H. Kenney.   1982b.   "Sources of Economic Growth," in B. Kantor and D. Rees (eds.) *South African Economic Issues.* Cape Town: Juta.

———. and D. Rees.   1982c.   "Introduction," in B. Kantor and D. Rees (eds.) *South African Economic Issues.* Cape Town: Juta.

———. and D. Rees.   1982d.   "Racial Income Differentials and the South African Labour Market," in B. Kantor and D. Rees (eds.) *South African Economic Issues.* Cape Town: Juta.

Keenan, J. and M. Sarak.   1987.   "Black Poverty in South Africa," *South African Labour Bulletin* XII.4.

Keenan, J.   1981.   "Migrants Awake: The 1980 Johannesburg Municipality Strike," *South African Labour Bulletin* VI(7):4-60.

———.   1985.   "The Recession and Its Effects on the African Working Class," *South African Review II.* Johannesburg: Ravan Press, pp.133-44.

Kelsen, H.   1967.   *The Pure Theory of Law* (2nd revised and enlarged edition); trans. by M. Knight. Berkeley: University of California Press.

Kitchen, L.R.   1986.   *Finance for the Developing Countries.* Chichester: John Wiley and Sons.

Lambert, R. and L. Lambert. 1983. "State Reform and Working Class Resistance, 1982," in *South African Review I.* Johannesburg: Ravan Press, pp.218-50.

Landel-Mills, P.M. 1971. "The 1969 Southern African Customs Union Agreement," *Journal of Modern African Studies* 9(2):263-81.

Leatt, J., Kneifel, T. and K. Nürnberger (eds.) 1986. *Contending Ideologies in South Africa.* Grand Rapids: W.B. Eerdmans.

Legum, C. and B. Lee. 1979. *The Horn of Africa in Continuing Crisis.* New York: Africana Publishing.

Leipziger, D.M. (ed.) 1981. *Basic Needs and Development.* Cambridge, MA: Oelgeschlager, Gunn and Hain.

Levy, A. and Associates. 1986. *Industrial Action Monitor: An Analysis of Strike Action in South Africa, 1979-1986.* Johannesburg: A. Levy and Associates.

———. 1987. *Annual Report on Labour Relations in South Africa, 1986-1987.* Johannesburg: A. Levy and Associates.

Levy, B. 1981. "Industrialisation and Inequality in South Africa." Cape Town: SALDRU Working Paper No. 36.

Levy, N. and F. Mbali. 1987. "Profile of Black Skills: Manpower Distribution, Education and Skills in Southern Africa." Lusaka: International Labour Office.

Lewis, I.M. (ed.) 1983. *Nationalism and Self Determination in the Horn of Africa.* London: Ithaca Press.

Lewis, J. and E. Randall. 1985. "The State of the Unions," *South African Labour Bulletin* XI(2):60-88.

Lewis, J. 1984. *Industrialization and Trade Union Organization in South Africa, 1925-1955.* Cambridge: Cambridge University Press.

Lipton, M. 1986. *Capitalism and Apartheid, South Africa 1910-1986.* Cape Town: David Philip.

Lipton, M. 1985. *Capitalism and Apartheid.* New Jersey: Rowman and Allanheld.

LMG (Labour Monitoring Group). 1985. "Report: The November Stay-Away," *South African Labour Bulletin:*74-10

———. 1986. "Report: The March Stay-Aways in Port Elizabeth and Uitenhage," *South African Labour Bulletin:*87-120.

Lombard, J.A. 1979. "On Economic Liberalism in South Africa." Pretoria: Bureau for Economic Policy and Analysis, University of Pretoria.

LRS (Labor Research Service). 1987a. "Economic Notes for Trade Unions," in *South African Labour Bulletin* XII.3.

———. 1987b. "Economic Notes for Trade Unions," *South African Labour Bulletin* XII.4.

Luckhardt, K. and B. Wall. 1980. *Organize or Starve! An Official History of the South African Congress of Trade Unions.* London: Lawrence and Wishart.

MacShane, D., Plaut, M. and D. Ward. 1984. *Power! Black Workers, Their Unions and the Struggle for Freedom in South Africa.* Boston: South End Press.

Makgetla, N. Seidman. 1987. "Development Economics and Perspectives on the South African Economy," *Journal of Law and Religion* 5(2):367-419.

Makgetla, N. and R.B. Seidman. 1987. "Legislative Drafting and the Defeat of Development Policy: The Experience of Anglophonic Southern Africa," *Journal of Law and Religion* 5(2):421-72.

————. 1989. "The Applicability of Law and Economics to the Third World," *Journal of Economic Issues* 23(1):35-78.

Mann, M. 1988. "The Giant Stirs: South African Business in the Age of Reform," in Frankel, P., Pines, N. and M. Swilling (eds.), *State, Resistance and Change in South Africa*. London: Croon Helm, pp.52-86.

Maree, J. 1982. "SAAWU in the East London Area, 1979-1981," *South African Labour Bulletin* VII(4-5):34-49.

Markakis, J. 1987. *National and Class Conflict in the Horn of Africa*. Cambridge: Cambridge University Press.

Marks, S. and R. Rathbone. 1982. *Industrialisation and Social Change in South Africa: African Class Formation, Culture and Consciousness 1930-1970*. London: Longmans.

Marx, K. (1867) 1967. *Capital*. (Trans. by S. Moore and E. Aveling). New York: International Publishers.

————. (1875) 1978a. "Economic and Philosophic Manuscripts of 1844," in R.C. Tucker (ed.) *The Marx-Engels Reader*. Second Edition (trans. by M. Milligan). New York: Norton.

————. (1875) 1978b. "Critique of the Gotha Program," in R.C. Tucker (ed.) *The Marx-Engels Reader*. Second Edition, (trans. by M. Milligan). New York: Norton.

Mbelle, A.V.Y. 1988. "Are Public Firms Less Efficient than Private Ones? Evidence from the Textile Industry in Tanzania." Paper presented at the *workshop on Public Enterprises; Recent Experience, Problems and Prospects* 22nd-23rd August, 1988. Dar es Salaam.

McCloskey, R. 1985. *The Rhetoric of Economics*. Madison: University of Wisconsin.

McConnell, C. 1978. *Economics: Principles, Problems, and Policies*. New York: McGraw-Hill Inc.

McGrath, M.D. 1982. *Distribution of Personal Wealth in South Africa*. Durban: Economics Research Unit, University of Natal.

Meier, G.M. 1984. *Emerging from Poverty: The Economics that Really Matters*. New York: Oxford University Press.

MGWU (Municipal and General Workers Union). n.d. "Our Response to the Situation," Johannesburg: mimeo.

Moore, B.J. and B.W. Smit. 1986. "Wages, Money and Inflation," *South African Journal of Economics* LIV.1.

Moore, S.F. 1984. *Law as Process: An Anthropological Approach*. New York: Methuen.

Mosley, P. 1978. "The Southern African Customs Union: A Reappraisal," *World Development* 6(1):31-43.

Motlatsi, J. 1987. "1987 - The Year the Mineworkers Take Control," speech to the 1987 NUM Congress, reprinted in *South African Labour Bulletin* XII.3.

Moyle, D. 1981. "Mass Resistance to Pensions Bill," *South African Labour Bulletin* VII(3):4-7.

Muad, R. 1974. "The Myth of White Meliorism in South Africa," in A. Leftwich (ed.) *South Africa: Economic Growth and Political Change*. New York: St. Martin's.

Mufamadi, S. 1984. "Interview," *Work in Progress* 32:19-22.

Mugomba, A.T. 1980. "African Mind Processing: Colonial Miseducation and Elite Psychological Decolonization," in

A.T. Mugomba and M. Nyaggah (eds.) *Independence without Freedom: The Political Economy of Colonial Education in Southern Africa.* Santa Barbara: ABC-Clio, pp. 40-58.

Murray, C. 1981. *Families Divided: The Impact of Migrant Labour in Lesotho.* Johannesburg: Ravan Press.

––––––. 1980. "From Granary to Labour Reserve: An Economic History of Lesotho," *South African Labour Bulletin* 6:4.

Naidoo, J. 1986. "The Significance of COSATU," speech at the University of Natal, Pietermaritzburg, March 19, 1986. Reprinted in *South African Labour Bulletin* :April-May.

––––––. 1987. "Address on Health and Safety Day," 28 March 1987, reprinted in *South African Labour Bulletin* XII.4.

Nassim, B. 1984. "Education and Poverty: Some Perspectives." Cape Town: Second Carnegie Inquiry into Poverty in South Africa, No. 94.

Nattrass, J. 1981. *The South African Economy: Its Growth and Change.* Cape Town: Oxford University Press.

––––––. 1987. "Politics and Liberal Economics in the South African Context," *South African International* XVII.4.

Ndaba, N. 1984. "Malnutrition in Children in South Africa." Cape Town: Second Carnegie Inquiry into Poverty in South Africa, No. 278.

Nellis, J.R. 1986. "Public Enterprises in Sub-Saharan Africa." *World Bank Discussion Paper.* Washington. The World Bank.

New Nation, Johannesburg.

Njakelana, S. 1984. "Unions and the UDF," *Work in Progress* 32:31-4.

NPI (National Productivity Institute). 1987. "South African Strike Statistics," *Productivity South Africa,* 13(1):10-3.

NUM (National Union of Mineworkers) Congress. 1987. "Political Resolution," *South African Labour Bulletin* XII.3.

Obery, I. 1987. "OK Workers in Class War: Anti-Apartheid Bosses Are Not Our Friends," *Work in Progress* 46:3-6.

——. Singh, S. and D. Niddrie. 1987. "Disciplined Miners' Strike a Test of Strength," *Work in Progress* 49:34-7.

——. and M. Swilling. 1984. "MAWU and UMMAWSA Fight for the Factories," *Work in Progress* 33:4-12.

O'Dowd, M. 1974. "South Africa in the Light of the Stages of Economic Growth," in A. Leftwich (ed.) *South Africa: Economic Growth and Political Change.* New York: St. Martin's.

Orkin, M. 1986. *Disinvestment, The Struggle and the Future: What Black South Africans Really Think.* Johannesburg: Ravan Press.

Parks, M. 1987. "SA Black Unions Lead Fight Against Apartheid," *Los Angeles Times* Sept 9.

Parsons, K.H. 1956. "Land Reform and Agricultural Development," in Parsons, K.H., Penn, R.J., and P.M. Raup (eds.) *Land Tenure.* Madison, WI: University of Wisconsin Press, pp. 3-22.

Plaut, M. 1987. "The Political Significance of COSATU," *Transformation* 2:62-72.

Posner, R. 1986. *The Economic Analysis of Law.* (2nd edition) Boston: Little, Brown.

Prekel, T. 1986. "The Role of Black Women in the Economy," in R. Smollan (ed.) *Black Advancement in the South African Economy.* New York: St. Martin's Press, pp.31-51.

Race Relations Survey, South African Institute of Race Relations, Johannesburg.

Randall, P. (ed.) 1972. *Power, Privilege and Poverty: Report of the Economics Commission of the Study Project on Christianity in Apartheid Society.* Johannesburg: Spro-Cas Publishers.

Rees, D. 1982. "Agricultural Policy in South Africa–An Evaluation," in B. Kantor and D. Rees (eds.) *South African Economic Issues.* Cape Town: Juta.

Reitsma, H.A. 1983-84. "Dependency with Development: The Case of Lesotho," *Drumlin* 27.

Reyneri, E. and C. Mughini. 1984. "Return Migration and Sending Areas: From the Myth of Development to the Reality of Stagnation," in D. Kubat (ed.) *Politics of Return: International Return Migration in Europe.* New York: Center for Migration Studies.

Robson, P. 1978. "Reappraising the Southern African Customs Union: A Comment," *World Development* 6(4):461-6.

Rupert, A. 1981. *Strength Through Diversity.* Cape Town: Tafelberg.

Seidman, A. 1974. *Planning for Development in Sub-Saharan Africa.* Dar es Salaam: Tanzania Publishing House.

——. 1980. *An Economics Textbook for Africa.* Third Edition. London: Heinemann.

——. 1983. "A Comparative Study of Three Tobacco-Exporting Countries: Kenya, Thailand, and Zimbabwe," prepared for the U.N. Centre On Transnational Corporations. Harare: University of Zimbabwe.

——. 1985. *Roots of Crisis in Southern Africa.* Boston: Africa World Press.

Seidman, R.B. 1978. *The State, Law and Development.* London: Croom-Helm.

——. 1984. "Law and the State in Independent Namibia: Lessons from Zimbabwe's First Three Years," paper presented at United Nations Seminar on Administrative Structures for Independent Namibia, Lusaka, December.

——. 1987. "Perspectives and Constitution-making: Independent Constitutions for Namibia and South Africa," *Lesotho Law Journal* 3:45-91.

Semboja, J.J. 1985. *The Role of the Public Sector in Economic Development- Tanzania (Phase Two).* Dar es Salaam. University of Dar es Salaam.

——. 1987. *The Parastatal Study: Analysis of the Qualitative and SCOPO Data.* Dar es Salaam, University of Dar es Salaam.

——. Rugumisa, S.H.M. and L.A. Msambichaka. 1986. *The Role of the Public Sector in the Development (Phase Three): The Sisal Sector in Tanzania.* Dar es Salaam, University of Dar es Salaam.

Setai, B. 1982. "The Potential for Resources-Based Industrial Development in the Least Developed Countries: Lesotho." Prepared for UNIDO.

——. 1988a. "Little Lesotho in the Shadow of the Apartheid Giant," Burlington, VT: Report on Non-alignment and the Developing Countries.

——. 1988b. "The Migrant Labour Dependency Link," *International Forum at Yale* 8(1).

Sherman, R. 1980. *Eritrea: The Unfinished Revolution.* New York: Praeger.

Sideris, T. 1983. "MAWU Enters the Industrial Council," *Work in Progress* 27:10-3.

Simkins, C. 1984. "Public Expenditure and the Poor: Political and Economic Constraints on Policy Choices Up to the Year 2000." Cape Town: Second Carnegie Inquiry into Poverty in South Africa, No. 253.

————. 1986. "How Much Socialism Will be Needed To End Poverty in South Africa." Paper presented at Conference on the South African Economy after Apartheid, York University.

Simons, J. and R. Simons. 1983. *Class and Colour in South Africa.* London: International Defence and Aid Fund.

Sitas, A. 1983. *African Worker Responses on the East Rand to Changes in the Metal Industry*, Ph.D. thesis, University of the Witwatersrand, Johannesburg.

Sitas, A. and E. Webster. n.d. "Stoppages in the East Rand Metal Industry." Johannesburg: mimeo.

SAFCI (South African Federated Chamber of Industries). n.d. "Guidelines for Industrial Relations in the 1980s," Johannesburg: mimeo.

SARHWU (South African Railway and Harbours Union). 1987. *The History of the City Deep Dispute.* Johannesburg: COSATU.

South African Institute of Race Relations. Organization archives. Johannesburg.

South African Labour Bulletin, Johannesburg.

Spiegel, A.D. 1980. "Rural Differentiation and the Diffusion of Migrant Labour Remittances in Lesotho," in P. Mayer (ed.) *Black Villagers in an Industrial Society: Anthropological Perspectives on Labour Migration in South Africa.* Cape Town: Oxford University Press, pp.109-69.

Stadler, J.J., van den Heerer, J.P. and L. Kritzinger-van Niekerk. 1986. *The Debt Standstill and Beyond.* Johannesburg: Mercabank.

Suttner, R. 1984. "The Freedom Charter: The People's Charter in the 1980s," T.B. Davies Memorial Lecture, University of Cape Town.

Swartz, T., Bonello, F.J. and A.F. Kozak (eds.) 1983. *The Supply Side: Debating Current Economic Policies.* Guilford: Dushkin.

Swilling, M. 1984. "Workers Divided: A Critical Assessment of the Split in MAWU on the East Rand," *South African Labour Bulletin* X(1):99-123.

———. 1987. "The United Democratic Front and Township Revolt," *Work in Progress* 49:26-33.

Szentes, T. 1971. *Theories of Underdevelopment.* Budapest: Akademiai Kiado.

Tanzania, United Republic of. Bureau of Statistics (BOS).

———. *Analysis of Accounts of Parastatal Enterprises* (various issues).

———. *Economic Survey* (various issues).

———. *Statistical Abstract* (various issues).

Thomas, W. 1986a. "Towards a 'Socialist Market Economy,'" in W. Thomas (ed.) *Post-Apartheid South Africa's Economic System.* Johannesburg: *South Africa International* (special issue) XVII.2.

———. 1986b. *Post-Apartheid South Africa's Economic System* (ed.) Johannesburg: *South Africa International* (special issue) XVII.2.

Tollman, S.   1984. "Thoughts on Planning for Basic Needs in South Africa." Cape Town: Second Carnegie Inquiry into Poverty in South Africa into Poverty in South Africa, No. 9.

Tostensen, A.   1982.   *Dependence and Collective Self-Reliance in Southern Africa: The Case of the Southern African Development Coordination Conference.* Research Report No. 62. Uppsala: Scandanavian Institute of African Studies.

Toussaint.   1983.   "A Trade Union is Not a Political Party: A Critique of the Speech 'Where FOSATU Stands'," *African Communist* 93:35-46.

Trevaskis, G.   1960.   *Eritrea: A Colony in Transition.*   Oxford: Greenwood.

Truu, M.L.   1986.   "Economics and Politics in South Africa Today," *South African Journal of Economics* LIV.1.

Turrell, R.   1982.   "Kimberly Labour Compounds," in S. Marks and R. Rathbone (eds.) *Industrialisation and Social Change in South Africa: African Class Formation.* London: Longman.

UDF (United Democratic Front). 1983. "Resolution on Workers," First National Conference, Aug. 20, Mitchell's Plain.

———.   National Executive Committee.   1987. "Notes on the Present Situation," *Isizwe* 1(4):3-19.

UNDP (United Nations Development Programme). n.d. "UNDP Approach to Private Sector in Developing Countries." New York.

van Zyl, J.C.   1986.   "The Industrial Challenge," in W. Thomas (ed.) *Post-Apartheid South Africa's Economic System,* Johannesburg: *South Africa International* (special issue) XVII.2.

Von Holdt, K. 1986. "The Economy: Achilles Heel in the New Deal," *South Africa Review III.* Johannesburg: Ravan Press, pp.303-19.

———. 1987. "The Political Significance of COSATU: a Response," Johannesburg: mimeo.

Wallis, M. 1977. *Bureaucracy and Labour Migration: The Lesotho Case.* Lesotho: National University of Lesotho.

Webster, E. (ed.) 1978. *Essays in Southern African Labor History.* Johannesburg: Ravan Press.

———. 1979. "A Profile of Unregistered Union Members in Durban," *South African Labour Bulletin* IV(8):43-75.

———. 1981. "'Stay-aways' and the Black Working Class: Evaluating a Strategy," *Labour, Capital and Society* 14(1):10-38.

———. 1983. "MAWU and the Industrial Council: a Comment," *South African Labour Bulletin* VII(5):14-8.

———. 1985. "New Force on the Shop Floor," *South Africa Review II.* Johannesburg: Ravan Press, pp.79-89.

———. 1988. "The Rise of Social-Movement Unionism: The Two Faces of the Black Trade Union Movement in South Africa," in Frankel, P., Pines, N. and M. Swilling (eds.), *State, Resistance and Change in South Africa,* New York: Croom Helm, pp.174-96.

Weekly Mail, Johannesburg.

Welsh, D. 1974. "Political Economy of Afrikaner Nationalism," in A. Leftwich (ed.) *South Africa: Economic Growth and Political Change.* New York: St. Martin's.

Whitsun Foundation. 1981. *Money and Finance in Zimbabwe.* Harare.

318   *Breaking the Links*

Wilkinson, R.C. 1983. "Migration in Lesotho: Some Comparative Aspects, with Particular Reference to the Role of Women," *Geography* 68(3):208-24.

WIP (Work in Progress). 1981. "The Support Alliance: Trade Unions and Community," *Work in Progress* 19:6-12.

Work in Progress, Johannesburg.

World Bank. 1984. *Tanzania: An Agenda for Industrial Recovery.* Vol. 1. Washington.

———. 1987. *Parastatals in Tanzania: Towards a Reform Program.* Washington.

Wykstra, R.A. 1978. "Farm Labor in Lesotho: Scarcity or Surplus?" Maseru: Ministry of Agriculture. Agricultural Sector Analysis, Report 5.

Zimbabwe, Government Printer

———. Growth With Equity, Policy Statement, 1981.

———. Transitional National Development Plan (1982/83 - 1984/85).

———. AFC Annual Reports, 1984 - 1987.

———. SEDCO Annual Reports, 1985 - 1987.

———. ZDB Annual Reports, 1985/86 - 1986/87.

———. Annual Economic Review of Zimbabwe, 1986.

EDITOR

Robert E. Mazur is Assistant Professor of Sociology at Iowa State University, Ames, Iowa.

CONTRIBUTORS

Samir Amin works on the African Regional Perspectives project at the United Nations University in Dakar, Senegal.

Basil Davidson is author of works on pre-colonial African history and on subsequent anticolonial struggles, particularly in former Portuguese colonies and the Horn of Africa. He is based in the U.K.

Neva Seidman Makgetla is Assistant Professor of Economics at University of Redlands, Redlands, California.

William G. Martin teaches Sociology and African Studies at the University of Illinois at Urbana-Champaign, Illinois.

Renosi Mokate is Assistant Professor of Business and Economics at Lincoln University, Lincoln, Pennsylvania.

Theresa Moyo is Lecturer in Economics at the University of Zimbabwe, Harare, Zimbabwe.

Lucian A. Msambichaka is Associate Research Professor at the Economic Research Bureau, University of Dar es Salaam, Tanzania.

Sibusiso Nkomo is Assistant Professor of Public Affairs and Political Science at Lincoln University, Lincoln, Pennsylvania.

Gay W. Seidman is Assistant Professor of Sociology at the University of Wisconsin, Madison, Wisconsin.

Robert B. Seidman is Professor of Law and Political Science at Boston University, Boston, Massachussetts.

Joseph J. Semboja is Senior Research Fellow at the Economic Research Bureau, University of Dar es Salaam, Tanzania.

Tamas Szentes is Professor of International Economics, Department of World Economy, Karl Marx University of Economics, in Budapest, Hungary.

Immanuel Wallerstein is Distinguished Professor of Sociology and Director of the Fernand Braudel Center at SUNY-Binghamton, New York.

INDEX